The Perfect 10

THE PERFECT 10

Football's Dreamers, Schemers, Playmakers
and Playboys

Richard Williams

faber and faber

First published in 2006
by Faber and Faber Limited
3 Queen Square London WC1N 3AU

Typeset by Faber and Faber Limited
Printed in England by Mackays of Chatham, plc

A CIP record for this book
is available from the British Library

ISBN 978-0-571-21635-2
ISBN 0-571-21635-8

10 9 8 7 6 5 4 3 2 1

For George Taylor and David York,
in memory of the good season

'A great player is one who makes his team win. Anything else is just talk.'

ARSÈNE WENGER

Contents

Introduction

A boy, eight years old, is taken to his first football match. Afterwards he remembers – he will never forget – the sheer mass of the crowd and the volume of noise created by the cheering and the orchestra of wooden rattles, which more than make up for the absence of visual colour. In this austere post-war setting, in an unfashionable city on a mid-winter Saturday afternoon, at a run-of-the-mill fixture in one of the lower divisions, among spectators huddled in overcoats and flat caps on concrete terraces under old grandstands, the dominant tones are brown and grey. But what could seem a drab uniformity provides an effective backcloth for the drama occurring on the pitch, where players wearing black and white striped shirts are confronted by opponents in royal blue and white quarters.

Eventually the boy's excited senses begin to sort out the jumble of his early impressions and to classify and give a shape to the movements of the players, so different in their method and deliberation from the hectic scramble of his own schoolyard games. Television has not yet turned the professional game into a familiar series of gestures and responses. What he remembers of the match itself is the role played by the home team's inside left, a dark-haired man of medium height and unremarkable build. In almost every move of consequence, the ball passes through his careful stewardship. He finds positions in which to accept a pass, he controls the ball easily and transfers it to a teammate with what seems to be an inherent sense of the game's fluid geometry.

Other players are concentrating on their allotted roles, as prescribed by the old but still universally popular WM – or 3–4–3 – formation. The little left-winger scuttles down the touchline, taunting his marker with speed and nimbleness. The muscular centre-half bars the way to goal, using his forehead to thump the heavy dark brown leather ball away from the danger area. The wing halves tackle and forage with more industry than style. High up the field, the centre forward awaits his moment of glory.

One man alone appears to view the play from some more elevated plane, spotting and shaping its emerging patterns. And on his back, sewn on to the black and white striped shirt, is the number 10.

This book is about football's No. 10s, and Ron Wylie of Notts County was my first, the first of many. Even now, so many years after Wylie made such a mark on an impressionable young mind, the No. 10 is the player I look for first in any team and in whom I tend to invest my principal hopes for the entertainment to come. They are an exotic species, rendered more precious through the constant suggestion that they may be endangered by the game's steady evolution. By embodying much of what makes football worthwhile as a game of the mind as well as the limbs, they contribute more than their share to the spectacle. And when we talk of such men as Ferenc Puskás, Pelé, Gianni Rivera, Michel Platini, Diego Maradona and Zinédine Zidane, we are talking of the players who have commanded the centre of the game's stage over the past half-century. With all due respect to the many great players who have fulfilled other roles with grace and distinction, nothing in the game presents quite as inspiring and satisfying a sight as that of a great No. 10 giving the fullest rein to his abilities as he directs the course of a match. Through this translation of the individual to the collective, the game of football seems to reach its highest form of expression, a level at which it most obviously approximates the condition of art.

In England, they often go by the name 'playmaker'. Italian football has numerous names for the shades and nuances that define different sub-species of the No. 10: *fantasista, regista, trequartista, interno*. Sometimes definitions fail, emotions take over, and such terms as *genio* (genius) or *pibe d'oro* (golden child) are the only recourse when the greatness of individuals such as Dejan Savicevic or Diego Maradona demands a special sobriquet. A great No. 10 is the focal point, the metronome as well as the tuning fork, the man who sets the tempo and the pitch of the play. When his timing or intonation are off, the whole ensemble suffers.

One of the things that all No. 10s do is pass the ball well. A good one will be the best passer in the team. A great one will pass the ball in such a way as to suggest that, however limited his verbal articulacy, his head is full of fluid three-dimensional geometry that would earn him a Nobel prize if it could ever be transferred to graph paper or a computer screen. He sees a space before it appears and has a superior feeling for the timing and trajectory that will enable his pass to reach it.

For this reason alone it was fitting that Ron Wylie should have been the first No. 10 I saw. Wylie was a Scot, born in Glasgow, and it was in Scotland that the concept of passing a football was born, some time in the middle of the nineteenth century. Before that profound development took hold, the game had resembled a schoolyard kickabout in which a player would take possession of the ball and hold on to it, dribbling towards the opposition's goal until someone either took it away from him or he managed to get in a shot.

Ten of the game's greatest No. 10s are the subject of individual essays in these pages. All played the game within my lifetime, which allows me to sidestep the problem of having to take reputations on trust. The earliest of them, Ferenc Puskás, was a central figure of Hungary's shattering victory at Wembley in 1953, the first home defeat against Continental opponents in England's history, and then of the 1960 European Cup final, a match in which he, Alfredo di Stéfano, Francisco Gento and their Real Madrid teammates showed an astonished thirteen-year-old, sitting in front of a black-and-white television set, just what poetic extravagance the game could encompass. The remaining nine (well, ten, actually, since two of them share a single chapter) also made their mark at the game's highest levels.

No position both encourages talent to flower and invites the blight of envy and distrust more than that of the No. 10. Creativity is a blessing and a burden, often bestowed upon those least well equipped to cope with the scrutiny, the adoration and the expectation it brings. In that sense, footballers of a certain type are no different from painters or poets. The very gift of invention requires such a player to outdo himself time and again. He has no recourse, on a bad day, to mere professionalism; something more is required of him. He cannot simply fulfil his duty by making the tackles and filling the spaces while others get on with establishing the tempo and trajectory of the match. He has to be at the centre of events, demonstrating that his gifts are above and beyond those of his colleagues, who look to him for direction and inspiration. When – for whatever reason, professional or personal – he chooses to spend a day hiding his gifts, the absence is obvious. He is who he is because no one else can do the job. She is who she is, too, as the eighteen-year-old Marta proved when she inspired Brazil to the silver medal in the women's football tournament at the 2004 Olympic Games, taking the much more experienced United States team to extra time before going down 2–1; her passing, her vision and her touch set her apart from every other player in the tournament, amply demonstrating that the art of the No. 10 is not gender-specific.

Some players cope with these demands better than others; not all great painters could deal with them, either. Among the most celebrated No. 10s there have been model professionals, such as Trevor Brooking or Osvaldo Ardiles, more conscious of their duties and responsibilities than of the aura surrounding them. Just as often, given the nature of their gift and the response it generates in those who merely sit and watch, they are wilful, temperamental dreamers who somehow manage to translate their fantasies into the physical reality of a pass or a shot, but have trouble with the more mundane business of life. Sometimes their talent is cherished by a coach or manager who, during his own playing career, may have dreamed of becoming that kind of a player himself, but discovered his own limitations and settled for operating within them. More frequently they have to earn their manager's trust week after week, since the highly individual nature of their contribution appears to contravene the basic ethic of a team game. All but the most successful managers live or die by the next result; when the pressure is on, consistency is an attribute more generally prized than inspiration.

Nonetheless, if you are anything like me, these are the players you pay to see and in whom you place an emotional investment. Their moments of unorthodox brilliance can enlighten the dullest afternoon; their presence can transform a perennially negative team into something worth seeing. Their wanderings from club to club and country to country are followed with a special interest that transcends the fan's normal loyalties. Their departure from the game is a cause of a particular sadness. We give them our trust; whether they know it or not, whether they want it or not, they carry within them our hope for, and belief in, a better game, one filled with truth and beauty.

Making the choice was both a pleasure and an ordeal. Perhaps the best way to demonstrate the difficulty of the task is to name some of those who failed to make this cruellest and most exigent of cuts, in no particular order: Zico (of the desperately unlucky 1982 Brazilians), Dejan Savicevic, Pablo Aimar, Liam Brady, Carlos Valderrama, Manuel Rui Costa, Jay Jay Okocha, Trevor Brooking, Jari Litmanen, Zvonimir Boban, Ariel Ortega, Luis Suárez, Marcello Gallardo, John Giles,

Glenn Hoddle, George Eastham, Amarildo, Osvaldo Ardiles, Gheorghe Hagi, Giancarlo Antognoni, Rai, Enzo Scifo, Jim Baxter (a wing half who became a No. 10 in his later years), Omar Sívori, Jim Smith of Newcastle United, Alex Young (known as 'the Golden Vision') of Everton, Ivor Allchurch of Wales, Paul Gascoigne, Giuseppe Giannini, Wim van Hanegem, Bernd Schuster, Roberto Mancini, Andrea Pirlo, Alessandro Del Piero, Zinho, Kazimierz Deyna, Neil Young (the forgotten man of Joe Mercer's fine Manchester City side), Alvaro Recoba, Rivaldo, Ronaldinho and Teófilo Cubillas, the Peruvian pearl. Many of those – although not all – are personal favourites whose fortunes I followed as they travelled from youth to maturity to retirement, not always on a happy or an unobstructed path. The veteran Eastham's appearance for Stoke City in the 1972 League Cup final was the excuse for a visit to Wembley, and his winning goal a cause for celebration among his admirers, whether supporters of his club or not. Neil Young, a lean, dark presence with a wonderful shot, more or less disappeared from the scene after the arrival of Rodney Marsh at Maine Road, removing my personal reason for checking that team's progress. The chance to see Francescoli lead Uruguay in a friendly at Wembley was too good to miss. Litmanen's brief period at Anfield made me take a livelier interest in Liverpool's fortunes and mourn his loss when Gérard Houllier mysteriously decided that the Finn had no future there. Okocha's time at Bolton, under Sam Allardyce, invested the Wanderers with an occasional and otherwise uncharacteristic sparkle. With Recoba, known in Italy as the Chinaman, in the team, Internazionale were usually worth watching; without him they were the same old bunch of dour, squabbling underachievers.

And as they fade, one by one, into history, others arrive to take their place. Even when the game was in many ways at its least entertaining, which is to say in the years following the spread of the influence of two essentially defence-minded coaches, Helenio Herrera of Internazionale and Alf Ramsey of Ipswich Town and England, it was still possible to see a few proper No. 10s going about their task. In that era, however, their special qualities sometimes went to waste. In England, what might Stan Bowles and Tony Currie have achieved had they been born twenty-five years later, at a time when creativity was more highly valued? Not that success would be guaranteed, since the special appeal of a No. 10 often resides in his own unpredictability, in his refusal to act as though his talent could necessarily be turned on or off by the wave of a cheque book or the urging of a half-time team talk. Yet new ones are always popping up in Brazil or France or Nigeria or Uruguay; the latest of them is Ricardo Izecson Do Santos Leite, better known as Kakà, a young Brazilian who promises to provide a reason to maintain an interest in football for the next ten years or so.

From Puskás to Kakà, they span a great variety of styles and approaches to the game. Where Ardiles was a little busybody and Sívori a mosquito, Baxter was large and languid. Physical stature has nothing to do with being a good No. 10. The spindly Eastham and the barrel-shaped Van Hanegem could hardly bring themselves to run at all, but the Englishman, relegated to the supporting cast during the 1966 World Cup finals, had an awareness of the tempo of a game and an understanding of angles that would later inform the play of Dennis Bergkamp, his ultimate successor at Highbury, while the Dutch international, operating in the shadow of Johan Cruyff, possessed a left foot that could pick locks. But there is certainly a preponderance of tall, willowy players who treat the ball as their own, who stroke it with a velvet touch, who disdain hurry and scurry and seem to be gazing over the heads of their teammates and opponents alike, searching the horizon for some golden opportunity invisible to other men. Rai, Hoddle, Antognoni and Brooking would certainly be among them.

As a type, the No. 10 emerged gradually. He was the inside

left in the WM formation, which was invented by Herbert Chapman for his great Arsenal team of the inter-war years and persisted as the game's tactical foundation in most parts of the world and at most levels until the early 1960s. When Bill Nicholson's Tottenham Hotspur won the English league and cup double in 1960–61, the two inside forwards were still the architects of the play, while the three defenders, the two wingers and the centre forward went about their clearly defined business. While the two wing halves dug the foundations and carried the bricks, it was the inside right and inside left who created the structure for victory, feeding their fellow forwards in the search for goals. On the ability of such inside lefts as Alex James of Chapman's Arsenal side, Juan Schiaffino of Uruguay's 1950 World Cup winners and Johnny Haynes of Fulham and England – men who could find the gaps between the opposition's defenders and the spaces outside them – depended their team's ability to formulate varied and effective attacks.

During the 1950s more progressive influences were brought to bear. Two far-sighted Hungarian coaches, Márton Bukovi of MTK and Gusztáv Sebes with the national team, pioneered the concept of the deep-lying centre forward, whose wanderings flummoxed centre halves accustomed to coping with the predictable habits of conventional No. 9s. One wing half dropped back to play closer to the centre half, concentrating on defence. This formula was borrowed in Brazil, where it was imported by another Hungarian coach, Béla Guttmann. Brazil's World Cup-winning team of 1958, under Vicente Feola, deployed four defenders in a line behind two midfield men and four forwards – the system that was christened 4–2–4.

Football was shifting its internal balance, inverting its priorities under the influence of a sort of gravitational pull. When Scotland and England had met in Glasgow in 1872 in the first international fixture ever played, the two teams fielded fourteen designated forwards between them (Scotland six, England a remarkable eight). Realism gradually overcame romance and optimism, however, and less than a century later, when managers such as Herrera and Ramsey came to the fore, bringing success to their teams through a new emphasis on pragmatism, the shape of the basic formation was altered to suit the change of philosophy. The wing halves and inside forwards were consolidated into a four-man midfield. In the hands of Hungary and Brazil, the four-man defensive line had provided a springboard for attack; others, including Ramsey with England and Herrera with his European Cup-winning Inter side, saw it differently and used the flat back four as an impregnable barrier.

Gradually the mutated inside left, still with the No. 10 on his back, emerged in a special role. While wingers were now ordered to track back and tackle their opposite numbers, eventually becoming known as 'wide midfielders', and the inside right fell back into an all-purpose role that would ultimately lead to the invention of the 'holding midfield player', the burden of creativity was focused more heavily on one man. 'Us left-footed players are easier on the eye,' Diego Maradona once said, and there is truth in that, but left-footed No. 10s also see the game from a different angle, psychologically as well as geometrically. In a predominantly right-footed world, they work across the grain of the play, exploiting angles of incursion that no one else has spotted. By no means all No. 10s are left-footed, however. Pelé favoured his right, although his father's instruction ensured that his left was more than useful. And to return to the example of Ron Wylie, my first idol, a player with a stronger right foot could turn it into an asset when trying, from the inside-left position, to curl the ball into the path of an outside left or when cutting inside at an angle to search for an opportunity to shoot. Stan Bowles was just such a player, attacking defences from an unfamiliar angle, forcing right-sided defenders to use their weaker foot; this must have been what Brian Clough saw in December 1979 when, planning Nottingham Forest's defence of the European Cup, he paid Queen's Park Rangers a quarter of a million pounds in the hope of rescuing Bowles from the betting shops and dog tracks, only to find the player going absent without leave on the eve of the 1980 final against Hamburg – another occasional occupational hazard of those charged with the task of harnessing the talent of the more wilful type of No. 10.

Embedded within the description of the lives and careers of the players in this book is the story of how, over half a century, the professional game went from being the pastime of the common man to being an all-round family-entertainment business run along the lines of the giant multinational corporations, with an increasing concern for profit at all levels and a need for marketable icons to feed the balance sheet. As a simple game becomes an omnivorous monster, we see how hard it can be for someone who began his footballing life as a child kicking a home-made ball in an unmade street to handle the exigencies of commerce and celebrity. And sometimes these No. 10s, burdened with the responsibility of bringing our fantasies to life, seem to be not just the obvious beneficiaries but also the biggest victims.

The story of Puskás illustrates the advantages and the difficulties experienced by athletes whose lives were structured by the communist system in the years immediately following the Second World War, when sporting achievement was deemed necessary to boost the pride of the state in a battle between competing ideologies. Pelé, by contrast, was nurtured by, and remained loyal to, one of the world's most chaotic nations, demonstrating how glory on the track or the pitch can give a sense of identity to a people who have little else, apart from a friendly climate, to comfort them. When we come to Zinédine Zidane, we find a player whose ethnic origin enabled him, willingly or otherwise, to embody the tensions and potential of an old nation experiencing the phenomenon of expansion through the arrival of immigrants from former colonies. With large-scale transmigration becoming one of Europe's dominant and most troublesome phenomena at the turn of the twenty-first century, it was seen as a significant moment when the wall of a high-rise block in Marseille, the city of Zidane's birth, was covered during the 1998 World Cup with a portrait of this son of north African immigrants, a member of a team affectionately described (with a nod to Duke Ellington's celebratory suite, *Black, Brown and Beige*), as *blacks, blancs et beurs*.

There are also tales of naked exploitation here, although it's possible to imagine that in any era and no matter what the particular circumstances the life of Diego Armando Maradona would not have been a simple affair. The need to maximize the dividend from his talent as early as possible, however, led others to take decisions on his behalf that were not always in the best interests either of Maradona the player or Maradona the man; in the end those choices conspired to limit his tangible achievements, which might have been even greater had he not fallen victim to the sort of temptations from which it can be difficult to turn aside.

Today it is harder than ever to be a No. 10, for one reason above all. The problem was outlined not long ago by Sócrates, the midfield orchestrator of Brazil's 1982 and 1986 World Cup teams, when he said: 'A football player of the 1970s ran an average distance in each game of four kilometres. Today this has almost tripled. Which means that the spaces between the players are relatively smaller. This causes a lot more physical contact, and makes it a lot more difficult for the player to create moves. Today, if you can't play with one touch you have little chance of playing at the top level. As a result, football has become uglier.'

One doesn't necessarily have to agree with Sócrates' conclusion – the AC Milan of Kakà and Andrei Shevchenko and the Arsenal of Thierry Henry and Dennis Bergkamp regularly disprove it, and in any case there was plenty of ugly football in his time – to accept the accuracy of his basic diagnosis. New formations can change the way the game is played (the emergence of the second centre back diminished the effectiveness of Johnny Haynes's passing even more effectively than the mid-career road accident that took the edge off the ability of one of England's few truly distinguished No. 10s), but a far more profound alteration has come with the increased emphasis on physical fitness. To a coach such as Arsène Wenger, a high level of technique is no use if it does not come on winged heels. In Wenger's Arsenal, or Carlo Ancelotti's Milan, every outfield player needs to be able to cover the ground at speed in order to maintain the kind of continuous movement that is the side's most powerful weapon. Looking, more than four decades later, at a video of the sublime 1960 European Cup final between Real Madrid and Eintracht Frankfurt, it is impossible not to remark on the gentle gait of the players and the vast acreage of unoccupied pitch into which they can direct their passes and make their runs. But with the increased pace of the game and the reduced amount of space available for self-expression has come a premium on the sort of instant skill and appreciation of angles and distances that is available only to the greatest players in any generation. And currently, as usual, a disproportionate number of those who succeed are wearing the No. 10 shirt, although some of them, such as Joe Cole when he left West Ham for Chelsea, discover that a sublime gift for the game is no longer enough by itself in a world where every scrap of possession must be defended and contested as though it were the last.

All the men in my selection spent most of their careers with the No. 10 on their backs. In terms of players who have exerted a gigantic creative influence on the game, strong cases could be made for the inclusion of Alfredo di Stéfano of Real Madrid, Argentina and Spain, who spent the 1950s directing the flow of great teams, or for Johan Cruyff, who exerted a similar influence on Ajax and Holland during the golden era of

Dutch football a generation later, or for Ruud Gullit. Each would make it into any serious judge's list of the ten greatest players of all time, challenging Pelé and Maradona for the very top spot. None of them, however, quite fits my criteria for inclusion. Di Stéfano and Cruyff were nominally centre forwards who turned themselves into players *sui generis*, granting themselves the licence to take up virtually any position on the field that took their fancy. In any case, to raise a more frivolous objection, Don Alfredo wore the No. 9, while Cruyff became permanently associated with the No. 14. (To those anxious to point out that Zinédine Zidane wears the No. 5 shirt at Real Madrid, where Luis Figo had possession of the No. 10 when the Frenchman arrived, it should be mentioned that two times five is ten, and Zidane was at least twice as good as any other No. 10 of his generation.) Gullit wore the No. 10 but turned out to be even less susceptible to role-definition.

What is absolutely certain is that no reader will approve of the selection in its totality, and perhaps even my definition of a true No. 10 will be disputed. That's fine. Argue away, as Ferruccio Valcareggi must have argued with himself when trying to fit Gianni Rivera and Sandro Mazzola into the same Italy team in the 1970 World Cup finals, and failing. For as long as football is played and watched, the topic will prompt argument. These are men worth arguing over.

Numerology: A Note

Where would we be without it? Ten out of ten. The ten commandments. The Top 10. Decimal currency. The decimal point. There she goes, a perfect 10. The 10 o'clock news. On a scale of one to ten. Ten minutes between halves (until television decided it preferred a quarter of an hour, to give more time for ads). Ten outfield players, plus a goalkeeper.

Once man had begun to do his sums, the arrangement of his fingers and toes must have had a great deal to do with the significance of the number 10. Three and a half millennia before the birth of Christ, the Egyptians had special symbols for it in their hieratic and hieroglyphic script, as, later, did the Sumerians and the Cretans. Decimal systems sprang up among nomadic herders counting their cattle on the plains of Africa, Australia and China.

To Pythagoras and his secret society of mathematicians living in the southern Italian town of Crotone, then a part of the Greek empire, in the sixth century BC, the number 10 was 'the number of the universe'. They called it the Sacred Tetractys. 'Both the Greeks and Hebrews held 10 to be the perfect number,' the historian Alfred G. Hefner wrote. 'Pythagoras considered that 10 comprehends all arithmetic and harmonic proportions, and, like God, is tireless. All nations calculated with it because when they arrive at 10, they return to 1, the number of creation. Pythagoreans believed the heavenly bodies were divided into 10 orders. According to the Kabbalah, there are ten emanations of numbers out of Nothing. The emanations form the 10 sephiroth of the Tree of Life, which contains all knowledge and shows the path back to God.'

Inspired by Thales, a rich merchant who travelled widely,

helped to advance thought on astronomy and philosophy and brought Egyptian arithmetic to Greece, Pythagoras and his followers lived according to a strict but progressive and only mildly eccentric code. The Pythagoreans' *modus vivendi* included an acceptance of gender equality and commonality of property, an insistence on picking up anything that had been dropped, a vegetarian diet strictly excluding beans, and a prohibition on stoking fires with iron implements or touching white cockerels. In Pythagoras' view, 'The world is built upon the power of numbers.' Numerology could explain everything in the universe, including the music of the spheres. According to Aristotle, writing more than a century later, the Pythagoreans 'saw that the ratios of musical scales were expressible in numbers [and that] all things seemed to be modelled on numbers, and numbers seemed to be the first things in the whole of nature. They supposed the elements of numbers to be the elements of all things, and the whole heaven to be a music scale and a number.'

Numbers 1 to 4 were of particular significance, and the Pythagoreans were impressed by the realization that if you added up those numbers, 1 + 2 + 3 + 4, it equalled 10. Therefore, they reasoned, 10 contained everything within the universe, itself a thing which came in fours: the seasons, the ages of man, the faculties (reason, knowledge, opinion, sensation), types of society (individual, village, city, nation), and even the parts of a living being (the body plus the three parts of the soul). And their most binding oath centred on the number 10: they swore 'by him that gave to our generation the Tetractys, which contains the fount and root of eternal nature'.

At that stage they had no written numerals. For each number they made a series of dots, arranging them in rows as the numbers became bigger. When they got to 10, the arrangement looked like this:

So we can say that as well as putting his name to a formula (actually devised by Euclid) enabling schoolboys to confirm that the square of the hypotenuse of a right-angled triangle equals the sum of the square of the other two sides, Pythagoras was also some 2,500 years ahead of Tottenham Hotspur and Terry Venables in the development of the 'Christmas tree' formation, with its four defenders, three midfield men, two secondary forwards and a lone striker. Including, of course, a 'No. 10', whatever the number on his shirt.

An Apology

At this point it probably needs to be made clear that all foot-ballers who wear the No. 10 on their shirts are not necessarily true No. 10s within the definition of this book. In some cases the distinction is a subtle one; elsewhere it is blindingly obvi-ous. Denis Law, for instance, wore Manchester United's No. 10 on his back with such distinction that most judges would grant him an automatic place in an XI drawn from the club's entire history. But Law's role was that of a finisher, a scorer of goals from inside the penalty area, using his phenomenal instinct, reflexes and athleticism. It was not his job to create the opportunities in the first place. He was, if you like, more of a second No. 9, playing alongside a bigger man, such as David Sadler or Brian Kidd.

Geoff Hurst, the only man to score a hat-trick in a World Cup final, would be another example of a No. 10 whose sole job was not to provide a match with its creative flow but to give a point to that flow by scoring goals. Likewise one of his England successors, Gary Lineker, who played off the shoulder of the last defender, constantly searching for a weakness in the offside trap, looking for his speed to give him the half a yard that was all he needed in which to do his work, while also rely-ing on the strength of his striking partner to keep the defence stretched. Michael Owen is his spiritual successor: an out-and-out striker, a scorer of goals often more beautiful in execution than Lineker's, and another who happens to wear the 10.

In a different register comes Luis Figo, the great Portuguese forward who took the No. 10 shirt when he made his contro-versial transfer from Barcelona to Real Madrid, thus appear-ing to set himself up as the successor to Ferenc Puskás. But

Figo was a winger, albeit of a highly unorthodox variety, and during his long international career he wore Portugal's No. 7 shirt, the team's No. 10 going to his old friend Manuel Rui Costa, an authentic playmaker. When Figo arrived at the Estadio Bernabéu, however, the No. 7 was already worn, misleadingly, by Raúl González, a pure striker and the local idol. Figo's decision to take the vacant 10 shirt meant that when Zinédine Zidane arrived from Juventus a year later the great Frenchman had to make do with the No. 5, normally allocated to a centre back but not in use at the time.

Many great true No. 10s, Zidane among them, have also been prolific goalscorers, but that is never their primary function. They are there to play a major part in 'inventing the game'. Their imagination and vision are of higher value to the team than their name on the scoresheet. Dennis Bergkamp used a Dutch term when he described himself to me as a 'shadow striker' – and he scored some of the finest goals ever seen by a player in an Arsenal shirt – but his time at Highbury was notable more for the manner in which he established the tempo of the side, the angles of attack and the fluency of the collective movement.

When Rafael Benítez left Valencia for the manager's job at Liverpool in the summer of 2004, the first thing he noted on arrival at Anfield was that his new squad did not possess a player of the type of Pablo Aimar, the curly-haired little Argentinian who had worn the No. 10 shirt with such distinction in his championship-winning team at the Mestalla stadium the previous season. He gave the shirt to one of his first signings: Luis García, a winger who liked to come inside and strike for goal. In midfield were Didi Hamann, a defensive specialist; Xabi Alonso, a deep-lying expert in the long pass; and Steven Gerrard, an old-fashioned right half whose game is built on strength and speed. Without a real No. 10, Liverpool would have to find a different way to win the 2005 European Cup final against Milan, a team with at least three players answering that description – Rui Costa, Kakà and Andrea Pirlo – in their ranks. Benítez proved it could be done, albeit at the expense of aesthetic purity, as Liverpool recovered from a 3–0 deficit and held their nerve in a penalty shoot-out to win the cup for the fifth time. It was a price that his team and its supporters were happy to pay, and it was a great victory for a certain kind of English wholeheartedness, even though there were only a couple of English players in the team, but a neutral would probably not want it to happen all the time. The fondness in England for giving the No. 10 jersey to other kinds of players appears to make a very clear statement about the way the game is supposed to be played in the country where it was born, and where there remains a reluctance to accept fundamental change.

1 Ferenc Puskás

Halfway through his film *Notre musique*, Jean-Luc Godard is giving a seminar in Sarajevo when he suddenly starts to talk about the match at Wembley in 1953 in which Hungary beat England by six goals to three, inflicting on the home team a defeat whose faint reverberations would still be heard more than half a century later. Real communism, the actor-director remarks, existed only for two halves of forty-five minutes each: on the day when Hungary beat England. 'The English played as individuals,' Godard says. 'The Hungarians played together.'

There is nothing in the film, made in 2004, or its credits to tell us whether Godard is portraying himself or a fictional French director who happens to share his interest in the history of cinema, his sardonic humour and his talent for opaque aphorisms, as well as his straggly grey hair, black-rimmed spectacles, red scarf, big cigar and love of football. His interest in the Hungarians of 1953, however, comes directly from his own experience. He was twenty-two years old when the members of Hungary's 'golden team' left Budapest on a journey that would conclude with their historic triumph in London. Born in Paris, the son of a doctor and a banker's daughter, Godard had been educated in Switzerland before enrolling at the Sorbonne, where he planned to study ethnology. Movies soon had him in a stronger grip, however, and by 1953 he was skipping classes and selling his mother's first editions in order to spend as much time as possible at Henri Langlois's Cinémathèque, where he became involved with a group of young enthusiasts that included François Truffaut, Eric Rohmer, Jacques Rivette and Claude Chabrol, and began contributing impassioned, iconoclastic articles to *Cahiers du cinéma.* His first short film was still two years away and not until 1960 would he astonish the cinema world with *À bout de souffle,* his first feature, which would become one of the signature works of the French New Wave.

For all his devotion to the films of Howard Hawks, Fritz Lang and Nicholas Ray, however, and his immersion in the intellectual activity of the Left Bank in general, Godard retained an interest in sport: tennis, motor racing, and football in particular. In 2001, for example, he gave an interview to *L'Équipe,* France's daily sports paper, in which, while discussing the problems of putting sport on the screen, he criticized the 'depersonalization' of football and footballers. His point was illustrated with a reference to Nicolas Anelka, the controversial young French forward whose career offers a paradigm of the way that vast amounts of money have gradually driven considerations of loyalty out of the heads of contemporary players. 'They're just like film stars,' Godard said. 'They want to withdraw inside their shells and live in a closed world. If I were the boss of Paris Saint-Germain, I would have it put in Anelka's contract that he had to be filmed at home, eating his lunch and talking to his girlfriend. Show it on television and watch it get a two per cent rating. Then nobody would care any more and he'd be left in peace.'

The Hungarians of 1953 were the biggest celebrities of their time in international football. Artists and innovators of the first order, they filled the gap between the Italians of the pre-war years, winners of the World Cups of 1934 and 1938, and the Brazil of 1958 and 1962. That Hungary failed to win their own World Cup final, in 1954, added a layer of poignancy to their legend. All sorts of people, all around the world, were touched by their magic. In his novel *Budapest,* written in 2003, Chico Buarque, the celebrated Brazilian singer, composer, author and occasional football critic, creates characters called Kocsis, Grosics and Puskás. And it is for them that Jean-Luc Godard's mind reaches when his thoughts turn to football. In an interview with an English journalist to promote *Notre musique* he seemed happier to expand on the reference to the 6–3 match at Wembley than to analyze the film's use of Sarajevo as a setting or its many allusions to the Arab–Israeli conflict.

'Apart from the goalkeeper, I remember them all,' he said, sifting his memory of the Hungarians and listing first the inside left Puskás ('the galloping major'), followed by the right half Bozsik ('the deputy') and the inside right Kocsis ('the golden head'). They were, he said, 'a discovery, like modern painting'. And he reached for a comparison to another contemporary art form when he went on to say that the only side that approached the level of the Hungarians in subsequent generations were the Ajax of Johan Cruyff, the creators of Total Football. 'Everybody played in defence and attack,' Godard said. 'It was like free jazz.' But even ensembles devoted to free jazz need players who can shape the music; for the Hungarians of 1953, the conquerors of the team whose ancestors had invented the game, that player was Ferenc Puskás.

When the move began, midway through the first period, he was dropping back over the halfway line. László Budai, the right-winger, flicked the ball away from George Robb, England's left-winger, on the touchline and knocked it back to Jeno Buzansky, one of Hungary's two centre backs. Buzansky took a touch before transferring it across the pitch to Puskás, who was now fifteen yards inside his own half, just beyond the centre circle. Puskás sprinted quickly forward, the ball at his feet, before initiating a series of passes up the middle of the field: he pushed it to Sándor Kocsis, who slid it first time to Zoltán Czibor, who moved it on to Nándor Hidegkuti, who turned it back to Budai, still on the right and now moving up inside the England half. Sensing a momentary weakness in the home defence, Budai found Czibor running into the space wider on the right, where England's left back, Bill Eckersley of Blackburn Rovers, should have been. Czibor was able to make ground before turning towards goal and pulling the ball square into the penalty area, where Puskás, having made fifty yards since the start of the move, met it with his back to the near post.

Behind him, on the corner of the six-yard box, stood Billy Wright, the faithful captain of Wolverhampton Wanderers and England, an archetype of the honest diligence of the English game. Having first touched the ball towards the byline, Puskás immediately dragged it back with the sole of his left boot, turning with bewildering speed to put Wright off balance and leave him scything at thin air. With his head bent over the ball – a craftsman at his lathe – and with Wright on the seat of his pants, Puskás used his low centre of gravity to send a powerful, rising left-foot shot past the left glove of Gil Merrick, England's goalkeeper. As the ball passed inside the near post and hit the netting, it appeared to have been fired from a catapult.

In the twenty-two seconds that elapsed between Robb's failure to retain possession and Merrick's vain attempt to keep out Puskás's shot, eight passes had been made. It was like watching a team of red-shirted jugglers. And suddenly, having conceded the first goal inside the opening minute of play, England were down by three goals to one and on the way to their first home defeat by a Continental team in their history. In a place where they had imagined themselves to be impregnable, the spectators were now puffing out their cheeks in astonishment and asking each other, 'Did you see *that*?'

Puskás was then twenty-six years old and already a hero in his home country. He had been born in Kispest, a village just outside Budapest, in April 1927, to a family whose German origins were obscured when the family name was changed from 'Purczeld' in the 1930s, apparently in line with nationalist sentiments at a time when the country was run by a right-wing military government. Next to the row of apartments in which they lived was the ground of Kispest Football Club. Puskás's father, a centre half, played first for Vasas and then for Kispest as a semi-professional while working initially as a railway mechanic and later as a book-keeper in a local slaughterhouse.

Hungary had taken to football with great enthusiasm in the final years of the nineteenth century. Three of the big Budapest clubs, Ujpest Dozsa, MTK and Ferencváros, were founded in 1885, 1888 and 1899, respectively. In 1901 a visit from Southampton, the first English professional club to tour abroad, stirred considerable interest, even though the English side thrashed a Budapest selection 8–0 and 13–0 in their two meetings. The Hungarian league went professional in 1926, and a couple of years later its members began a brief domination of the Mitropa Cup, a forerunner of the European and UEFA Cups, contested between the wars by clubs from Italy, Austria, Hungary, Czechoslovakia, Switzerland and Romania. Jimmy Hogan, a native of Lancashire, arrived from England, via Holland and Austria, to take charge of MTK, inspiring a generation of Hungarian coaches. In 1934 the national team travelled to Italy to compete in the World Cup finals for the first time; they succeeded in reaching the quarter-finals, only to be beaten 2–1 in Bologna by Austria's '*Wunderteam*', managed by the innovative Hugo Meisl, in a match defaced by a level of violence which surprised those anticipating a feast of cultured middle-European football.

Puskás, whose nickname of 'Ocsi' (little brother) would later be taken up by the entire nation, grew up listening to the cheers from the Kispest stadium. He played football in the streets and on vacant lots, often with a ball made of rags, with a group of boys including his best friend, Jozsef Bozsik, whose family lived in the next apartment. If the proximity of the Kispest club gave inspiration to the young footballers, even more so did Hungary's performance in the 1938 World Cup, where they thrashed Sweden 5–1 to reach the final in Paris before going down 4–2 to Italy, the defending champions, a well-balanced team who exploited the defensive inadequacies of the Hungarians. Football-mad, the young Puskás and

7

Bozsik joined Kispest that same year, although Ferenc, at eleven, was a year too young and lied about his age, giving a false name to get around the national regulations.

By that time his father had stopped playing and was coaching Kispest's junior, reserve and first teams. A local cobbler made Ferenc his first pair of boots, and the boy, who was small for his age, responded to the encouraging environment by working hard to strengthen his physique and increase his speed. War broke out when he was twelve, and as more and more men were called up to join the army before being sent to fight alongside the Nazis on the Russian front, gradually the ranks of professional players began to thin out. Bozsik was given his first-team début in the spring of 1943, with the sixteen-year-old Puskás joining him in the side that December, although his father was no longer the coach. Puskás's first league goal came in his third match, a 2–2 draw at home to Kolozsvár (now the Romanian city of Cluj); three months later he scored two goals against the mighty Ferencváros in front of a crowd of 12,000 in Budapest while the Germans were resisting the Red Army and warplanes flew overhead. Allied bombing and the destruction of the bridges over the Danube by the retreating Germans put an end to organized football for a while, but in February 1945 Puskás and his friends came out of the cellars, headed straight for a football pitch and played an informal game against some Russian soldiers who had just liberated the city. In May the local clubs began to play each other again, although Puskás did not enjoy an auspicious return: he was sent off as Kispest fell by 7–0 to Ferencváros before losing 8–0 to Ujpest.

Nevertheless, with Budapest in ruins, he made his international début that same year, in the second of two victories against Austria in matches held on consecutive days in the Ferencváros stadium before capacity crowds. A young team, short of physical fitness and without having had much of an opportunity to train together, they won the second match 5–2 against similarly ill-prepared opponents, with Puskás, now eighteen, scoring his first international goal. In 1946, when full-scale league football resumed in Hungary, he became the captain of Kispest, with his father restored as coach and Bozsik by his side in a team that was suddenly on the rise and heading for fourth place in the championship and the runner-up position a year later. Against Luxembourg the following season he registered his first hat-trick for the national team, in a 7–2 away win.

A year after the end of the war Hungary declared itself a republic and began a programme of nationalization and land redistribution. Within two years it would be a satellite of the Soviet Union, run by a regime favouring the use of secret police and show trials. Now sport was seen as a way to gain national prestige. In May 1947 the Hungarian team travelled to Turin, where they were beaten 3–2 by Italy, the reigning world champions (the war had led to the cancellation of the 1942 and 1946 tournaments). Puskás scored from the penalty spot and made such an impression that he was approached by representatives of Juventus, who offered him the enormous sum of $100,000 to join the Fiat-backed club. However, the possibility that his family's German ancestry would make them vulnerable to post-war reprisals in Hungary led him to decline the invitation and he returned to Kispest, knowing that his continued presence would be enough to protect them. And within months the government was making it clear that the country's talented young footballers would not be allowed to take advantage of the riches with which they were being tempted by agents of foreign clubs.

In 1948–49, in imitation of the USSR's policy towards its major sports clubs, Kispest were renamed Honved, 'defenders of the motherland', and nominated as the official representatives of the Hungarian army. Ferencváros, a much bigger club, had been considered but were rejected because of their historic links with right-wing nationalism. Now the Hungarian game fell under the visionary influence of the newly appointed national coach, Gusztáv Sebes, one of Jimmy Hogan's many disciples. An active communist who had lived before the war in Paris, where he helped organize a workers' strike at the Renault car factory, he was now also the chairman of Hungary's National Olympic Committee and the country's deputy sports minister. Sebes's plan was to concentrate as many of the nation's best footballers as possible at a minimum number of clubs, a project in which he was greatly aided by his ability to conscript players and transfer them at will. Honved were the chief beneficiaries, and before long Puskás and Bozsik had been joined by Gyula Grosics, the country's best goalkeeper. Also on the way were Kocsis, the striker, and the two wingers, Czibor and Budai, all members of Ferencváros's title-winning side before being called up for military service and offered the choice of being sent to guard a border post or being drafted into the Honved squad.

On their talents Sebes brought to bear a study of the work of Vittorio Pozzo, the coach of Italy's pre-war world champions, and Hugo Meisl, Austria's coach, as well as that of Hogan. In a radical modification of the WM formation devised by Herbert Chapman, the great Arsenal manager, who deployed two full backs, one defensive centre half, two wing halves and five forwards in a relatively rigid structure, Sebes adopted the concept of the deep-lying centre forward, creating a pattern which over the next few years would become known throughout the world as the 4–2–4 formation. Instead of acting as a conventional spearpoint, the No. 9 would drop back into midfield, throwing his direct opponent into confusion. If the centre half followed him towards the halfway line, a hole would be left in attack; if the defender stayed where he was, Hungary would make the most of their numerical advantage in midfield. For his No. 9 Sebes chose Nándor Hidegkuti, from MTK, whose coach, Márton Bukovi, had already been experimenting with a similar formation which offered the opportunity for forwards to develop a more fluid, spontaneous game. It would only work, however, if the players were intelligent enough to exploit its potential; as with the teams selected by Rinus Michels in Holland in the 1970s, Sebes's Hungary consisted of footballers who were capable of thinking for themselves while adhering to a basic formula. They also had to be eager to undertake the sort of hard work that makes improvisation seem effortless, and at Honved and in their national training sessions – sometimes with the veteran Hogan in attendance at Sebes's invitation – the players endlessly rehearsed the moves that would, over the next five or six years, dismantle so many defences.

After a 5–3 defeat at the hands of Austria in Vienna in the spring of 1950, their great run began. Between that fixture and the 1954 World Cup final they would play thirty-one matches without experiencing defeat, drawing only four times, scoring 139 goals and conceding thirty-three. That sequence included victory in the 1952 Olympic tournament in Helsinki: four years after being excluded from the first post-war Games in London, they were allowed to compete in Finland after the Hungarian government changed their status from professional footballers to amateurs employed by the government as members of the armed forces. It was during the preparations for the tournament that Sebes first replaced Peter Palotas, his regular No. 9, with Hidegkuti and watched the thirty-year-old newcomer, formerly an inside right, blossom in the withdrawn role. With each success, such as a 6–0 walloping of Sweden in the semi-final, new levels of understanding and interplay were reached by Puskás, Bozsik, Kocsis and Hidegkuti. In the final, the biggest test yet faced by the Hungarian team, Sebes's players overcame their anxiety to beat Yugoslavia 2–0 with goals from Czibor and Puskás, who also missed a penalty. Back in Budapest, 100,000 ecstatic fans thronged the streets to welcome them home.

After the semi-final they had been approached by Stanley

Rous, the secretary of the English Football Association. It was time, he suggested, for the two countries to meet again; coming from the representative of the nation that invented football, one that still held a unique position within the game, the invitation was warmly received. Rous, who did not suffer from the insularity that afflicted most English football administrators, would have been under no illusion about the nature of the challenge facing his own men. By the time Sebes and his squad set off for England on 18 November 1953, they were unquestionably the dominant force in Europe and the object of great interest among those who believed them to represent a significant development in the way the game was played.

A film crew recorded their journey in the carriages of the Compagnie Internationale des Wagons-Lits et des Grands Express as they passed through alpine scenery and arrived in Paris, where they saw the sights – the Eiffel Tower, Arc de Triomphe, Notre Dame – and warmed up for their match against England by playing the factory team of the Renault motor company, thanks to Sebes's old contacts. Eighteen goals were blasted past the amateurs.

At Wembley on the afternoon of 25 November there was consternation when they led the home side by four goals to two at half-time, making a line-up including Stanley Matthews, Nat Lofthouse, Stan Mortensen, Jackie Sewell and Alf Ramsey look like a factory team. A full house of close to 100,000 spectators had been anticipating a chance to see their representatives assert the natural order of things; now, on a dank day, the air was electric with discussion of Puskás's remarkable goal and the deftness of his teammates who, in their lightweight cutaway boots and abbreviated shorts, appeared to have landed from a different planet. Soon after the start of the second half the Hungarians forestalled any hope of an English revival by scoring a fifth, through Bozsik, before finishing the game off with an even more extraordinary collective move that gave them a sixth goal. There were ten passes in this sequence, a tidal wave lasting twenty-one seconds which reached its climax when Puskás sent a perfect lob from the left high over the entire England defence on to the right boot of Hidegkuti, whose instant volley crashed past Merrick.

Hungary had thirty-five attempts on goal during the match, to England's five. 'They shot with the speed and accuracy of archers,' Geoffrey Green reported in *The Times* the next morning. 'It was Agincourt in reverse.' After the match was over, Gyorgy Szepesi, a Hungarian radio commentator, walked across to the spot where Puskás had dragged the ball away from Wright. 'I was thinking that after an historic battle they usually erect a memorial,' he said. 'They should place one here, where Puskás scored the goal that beat England for the first time.' Even in their dismay, however, the English took defeat well. The *Star*, one of London's evening papers, carried its report beneath the headline: 'Our Team Outclassed and the Unbeaten Record Shattered'. Other national paper headlines included 'Puskás (Mr Football Himself) Leads the Rout of England' and 'Wonderful Hungary Smash That Record'.

There had been a warning two years earlier, when Austria came to Wembley and left with a 2–2 draw after doing more than enough to earn a victory. Now it had happened. 'To those who had seen the shadows of the recent years creeping closer and closer there was perhaps no real surprise,' Green wrote. 'England at last were beaten by the foreign invader on solid English soil. So history was made. England were beaten at all points, on the ground, in the air, and tactically.' The moment Puskás wrong-footed Wright, leaving England's captain helpless and bewildered, summed up the message of this profoundly significant defeat.

In *The Football Man*, a classic study, Arthur Hopcraft meditated on the match's crushing effect on the assumed superiority of the English. 'The fifties relentlessly exposed the lie we had been cherishing as noble truth for so long,' he wrote. 'We could not play football better than any other country, after all.

Far from knowing all there was to be known about the game we found that we had been left years behind by it. We even looked old. Our shorts were longer, thicker, flappier than anyone else's, so that our players looked like Scoutmasters struggling to keep pace with the troop. We lost dignity in our disorder, blatantly shoving with our hands at nimbler players as they went past. The dull training routines, aimed at deep chests and stamina and doggedness, had done exactly what they were intended to do. Hungary, with a marvellous constellation of players grouped around Puskás and Hidegkuti, crushed us 6–3 on a November afternoon at Wembley in 1953, and in the following year stamped us into the ground with a 7–1 win in Budapest. We have always been aware of our capacity for laughing at ourselves, but the degree of self-derision in which we were now invited to indulge was beyond us.'

'They destroyed us, mocked us, annihilated us,' John Moynihan wrote in *The Soccer Syndrome*, and it was Hungary's No. 10 who took the honours as tormentor-in-chief. Others were vital to the collective effort, but somehow Puskás's glittering skills and deadly shooting enabled him to rise even higher. His army rank, meaningless in real terms since it required nothing other than a willingness to put on a uniform for ceremonial occasions, had given this stocky figure the headline-friendly nickname of 'the galloping major', building on the impact of an extrovert personality that had already automatically conferred upon him the role of leader – whether or not he was officially the captain – in every side in which he had played since childhood. For all his independent spirit, however, he was the most team-conscious of players and rose naturally to the challenge of Sebes's theories; today we can only look at his impressive statistics and imagine how many more goals he might have scored had he not chosen, time and again, to pass to colleagues in marginally better positions. It was, after all, Hidegkuti who scored the hat-trick at Wembley.

Sebes, it turned out, had left nothing to chance in his preparations for a match that he knew would set the seal on his team's reputation. He had visited Wembley a few weeks earlier to see England play the Rest of the World, noting the unusual width of the pitch and the lushness of the turf, its lack of bounce a strong contrast to the harder pitches found on the Continent. He had asked Rous for an example of the heavier English ball, and the gentlemanly Rous sent three, all of them used to familiarize the Hungarian players with the ball's properties. However, on the squad's arrival in England on the Golden Arrow express from Paris, Sebes's request to be allowed to train at Wembley was refused; they were invited to use Fulham's Craven Cottage ground, while England were given Stamford Bridge, Chelsea's headquarters, barely a mile away. Back in Hungary, shops and factories closed early so that the entire population could listen to the radio broadcast from London, and loudspeakers were set up in streets and squares. Afterwards Jimmy Hogan, who had attended the match, told Sebes: 'That was the kind of football I dreamed Hungarians might one day be able to play.'

As they began their return journey they were cheered off by a large crowd at Victoria station, leading Puskás to remark: 'We will never forget the way everyone we met in England greeted our victory without resentment.' They were mobbed, too, on a second stopover in Paris, and again when their train passed through Vienna. On their arrival back at Kaleti station, from which they had set out, their fans climbed lamp-posts and stood on rooftops to catch a glimpse of the heroes who had reasserted the identity of a nation of ten million people.

Six months later, on 23 May 1954, the two sides met again in the return fixture, this time at the Népstadion. Some Englishmen believed that this was an opportunity for their players to undo what had been merely an aberration. They were mistaken. Puskás again scored twice as the Hungarians' superiority was driven home by a 7–1 margin, on their own pitch and with their own ball, in front of 100,000 of their own delighted fans, representing one in ten of those who had applied for tickets. Sebes's players were surprised to discover that, although Tom Finney had returned from injury to replace George Robb, England's tactics had not changed at all. The lessons had clearly not been learnt.

To Puskás and his colleagues, the second match was the final part of their preparations for the 1954 World Cup finals in Switzerland, a competition they were expected to dominate. Three weeks later they smashed South Korea 9–0 in Zurich, completing the group stage by demolishing a weakened West Germany, who fielded seven reserves, 8–3 in Basel. Puskás beat four men to score the second goal before Werner Liebrich, brought in for this match by the German coach, Sepp Herberger, kicked him on the knee so badly that the No. 10 missed the next two matches. Nothing in the quarter-final or semi-final, however, suggested that their progress would be interrupted, even without Puskás, who could only watch as his teammates went through their routines at the squad's training camp. In the quarter-final against Brazil, in front of a crowd of 50,000, they went 2–0 up inside seven minutes and maintained their advantage to win 4–2 in an increasingly bad-tempered match between two wonderfully skilful teams. The English referee, Arthur Ellis, dismissed Bozsik, who had taken over the captaincy from Puskás, and Nilton Santos for fighting midway through the second half and then sent off Humberto Tozzi for jumping on Kocsis. There could have been more expulsions during the course of a match that became known as the Battle of Berne, and hostilities were continued when several Brazilians made their way to the Hungarian dressing room, where light bulbs and bottles were smashed and doctors were called to attend to the injured.

Having defeated the beaten finalists of 1950, now Hungary went to Zurich to face the reigning champions. And whatever had gone awry against Brazil, Hungary versus Uruguay turned out to be a classic, marred only by the absence of Puskás and the South American team's captain, the great attacking centre half Obdulio Varela. It was Czibor who put Hungary ahead in the first half, and Hidegkuti increased the lead soon after the interval, but the holders fought back, inspired by their clever forward Juan Schiaffino and with two goals from their naturalized Argentinian attacker Juan Eduardo Hohberg. The same player hit a post in extra time, but two headers from Kocsis – only five feet nine inches tall but a marvel in the air – were enough to remove the trophy from Uruguay's grasp.

Puskás returned for the final against West Germany, shaking the hand of Jules Rimet, FIFA's honorary president, before the kick-off on a rainy day in Berne and putting his team ahead in the sixth minute with a close-range shot after Czibor's effort had been deflected. Although the Hungarian squad's sleep had been disturbed by the finals of the Swiss national brass band competition outside their hotel on the night before the match, Czibor was alert enough to score another two minutes later. But the Germans struck back quickly through Max Morlock and Helmut Rahn, paving the way for seventy minutes of intense effort in increasingly muddy conditions. There had been rumours that Puskás was only half fit, or worse, and as Hungary laid siege to the German goal he was certainly not the most prominent of their attackers. When the ball came loose after Toni Turek dived at the feet of Mihály Tóth, Hidegkuti hit the post. A header from Kocsis ran tantalizingly along the top of the crossbar. Then, with three minutes left, Rahn controlled a poor clearance on the edge of the area, shifted the ball from right foot to left and sent a precise shot through a thicket of defenders into the left-hand corner of the net. But even in the worsening conditions Puskás retained enough strength to run on to Tóth's pass and slip a shot under Turek. The Hungarians were already celebrating their escape when the linesman's flag was brought to their attention. The surviving footage of the moment is inconclusive, and perhaps it is the heart rather than the head which carries the conviction that the goal should have been allowed to stand, thus enabling Hungary to make one last effort to win the trophy that would have secured, beyond dispute and for all time, their place in history. Once again they had overwhelmed the opposition in terms of shots on goal, with twenty-five to Germany's eight. Yet although this marked the end of their run of thirty-one matches without defeat, a streak lasting four years, one month and two weeks, it was, in a sense, the beginning of their legend.

For the squad, the return to Budapest was as bitter as the welcome after the Olympics had been sweet. The dashing of expectations provoked all sorts of questions. Had the team become complacent, too comfortable in their long sequence of victories? Had their privileges, including the knowledge that customs officers would overlook their habit of smuggling goods back home after away trips, made them soft? Had Puskás really been fit to play in the final? Had he been allowed to accumulate too much influence on selection and tactics? Had he let his weight get out of control? And why had Sebes's tactics failed at the last?

Suddenly the coach had become the object of widespread criticism, and even Puskás, formerly the nation's untouchable hero, was forced to listen to jeers at Honved's away games. Hungary's own inner turmoil began to exert a direct effect a few months after the final when Grosics, the goalkeeper, was arrested on charges of anti-government activities. Told he would never play for Hungary again and banned from any level of football for fifteen months, eventually he was sent to play for a miners' club, where he languished for the remaining seven years of his career, although he would eventually be allowed back into the national team.

The statistics suggest that Hungary recovered quickly from the defeat in Berne, putting together another unbeaten run, this time of fifteen wins and three draws, with 112 goals scored and twenty-five conceded before Turkey ended the run in

Istanbul in February 1956. But the figures mask a swift disintegration, not least of Sebes's carefully assembled squad of
coaches, dispersed to various parts of the world by the
Hungarian sports ministry, which had come to the conclusion
that power over the team should not be vested in one man and
began to dismantle the structure he had put in place. In March
1956, after the team had lost three games out of four, Sebes
was demoted to a lesser position in the sports ministry and
replaced by a committee of selectors and coaches. That
September, with Puskás still in the team, they went to Moscow
and, in a match with powerful political undercurrents, beat the
Soviet Union by the only goal of the match.

A month later Hungary's process of de-Stalinization came to
a shattering end when the secret police and Red Army troops
put down demonstrations that had been intended to topple the
old Politburo and bring a new democratic socialist government
into power. Five days of street fighting, pitting the tanks of a
professional army against an informal coalition of students
and factory workers, appeared to have died down when the
troops withdrew and the formation of a new Hungarian
Socialist Workers' Party was announced. Six days later, however, the Russians were back and fighting took place throughout the country until, a week later, the uprising had been
crushed, leaving hundreds dead. The final symbolic gesture
came when Russian tanks ringed the Népstadion, denying
entry to those who had planned to meet for an assembly of the
Central Workers' Council.

When the uprising began, on 23 October, the players had
been at their training headquarters, preparing for a match
against Sweden. Grosics took part in a demonstration, while
Puskás heard shooting in the distance when he returned to his
home in Budapest a few days later. Even after the fighting was
over, it seemed a good idea for the top players to spend as
much time as possible out of the country, and when Honved
travelled to Bilbao, where they lost their first European Cup

match by 3–2 against Athletic, they played several friendly fixtures in Spain as a way of delaying their return. At a charity match in Madrid, playing against a team selected from players of the Spanish capital's two major clubs, Puskás met Santiago Bernabéu, the president of Real Madrid, and Alfredo di Stéfano, the great Argentinian centre forward who had already led the club to victory in the inaugural European Cup.

The problems in Hungary meant that Honved played the 'home' leg of their tie against Athletic Bilbao in Brussels, where they could only draw 3–3, so putting them out of the competition. Their next journey was to South America, where the president of Flamengo, the Rio de Janeiro club, had offered them a series of seven friendly matches for an appearance fee of $10,000 a match plus travelling expenses. Although the Hungarian FA, fearing defections, refused to give permission, the tour went ahead, organized by the club's financial secretary, Emil Österreicher. When the team returned to its temporary base in Vienna, a deputation from the Hungarian authorities arrived to instruct them to return home to face punishment, which included an eighteen-month ban for their captain.

Puskás, whose wife and daughter were with him in Vienna, knew that his future did not lie at home. Czibor had decided to take up an offer to play in Italy, and Kocsis had fled to Switzerland. Both would eventually find themselves in Barcelona's colours. At thirty years of age, however, Puskás attracted few offers for his services, and when it became apparent that he intended to remain abroad, the Hungarian FA persuaded FIFA to ban him from playing anywhere for two years. Eventually he travelled to Italy, where he trained with Internazionale and pleaded with FIFA for leniency. By the time they agreed to reduce the suspension to fifteen months, a possible deal with Inter had broken down. As the months ticked away to the end of his ban, in July 1958, he began to lose hope. He was training with a local amateur club in San Remo when he received an offer from Real Madrid, where Österreicher, who had also defected, was now employed by Santiago Bernabéu. Surprised that the Spanish champions would want to employ a player of his age and expanding waistline, Puskás was nevertheless delighted to put his signature to a four-year contract which guaranteed him $100,000. He took his family to Madrid, where he lost 18 kg in six weeks and began to learn a new language in preparation for the final chapter of his playing career.

Perhaps it says something about the way Puskás approached the game of football that he appeared on the winning side in two of the most famous matches in the history of the game, and in both of them his team conceded three goals. Six and a half years after the historic destruction of England at Wembley, he returned to Britain in the guise of Di Stéfano's co-conspirator, the pair of them inspiring Real Madrid's 7–3 victory over Eintracht Frankfurt in the European Cup final of 1960, believed by many to have been the most captivating football match ever played.

If the humbling of England had come too early to catch the eye of the generation born just after the end of the war, the 1960 European Cup final was perfectly timed to reshape the ideas of countless schoolboys who were still at the stage of giving their first pair of boots pride of place in their bedrooms and in whose households the television set was a newly invited guest. In England, the BBC transmitted the whole of the 1960 final live from Hampden Park, Glasgow's great temple of the game. When it came to the European Cup, invented by the French journalist Gabriel Hanot and first contested in the 1955–56 season, Scotland had been quicker on the uptake than England, whose 1955 league champions, Chelsea, were withdrawn from the first round. Hibernian had reached the semi-final of that inaugural tournament, losing to Reims, who went down to Real Madrid in the final. After the English FA finally abandoned their isolationist stance, Manchester United reached the semi-finals two years in a row, followed by Wolverhampton Wanderers, who made the quarter-finals in 1959–60. Yet if the idea of European competition was becoming familiar, the sight of foreign players certainly was not.

In Hampden Park, a crowd of around 135,000 assembled on the night of 18 May 1960. Out of curiosity and a love of the game they had paid between five shillings (25p) and £2.10s (£2.50) for admission to the biggest club match yet played in the British Isles. The vast majority of them were Scots, devoted admirers of a species of gifted individualists known locally as 'tanner ball players' whose skills had been developed in the alleys and yards separating Glasgow's tenement slums before illuminating the Scottish and English leagues. They had seen nothing like this, however, and the rough sound of the surviving BBC broadcast preserves their collective astonishment as they witness Di Stéfano's back-heels, Puskás's shooting and the sprints of Francisco Gento on the left wing. There are no chants or songs. There are bursts of applause as the Madrid players link the play in little sequences distinguished by high skill and well-developed understanding. There is the sound of 135,000 people gasping in unison. Even when a move breaks down, the knowledgeable spectators cheer the cunning intention behind the pass that was just too long for its intended recipient.

To watch it then, through the eyes of childhood, on a small black-and-white television set in a living room a few hundred miles from the action was to see a revelation of the game's possibilities. Here was a kind of football in which almost every player in the white shirt and shorts of Madrid easily matched the rarefied standards of a Stanley Matthews or a Tom Finney. There were no carthorse centre forwards or dogged full backs. There was only a symphony of space and time, an ease and a grace with the ball and, above everything, a sense of imagination at play. What Di Stéfano and Puskás did seemed to spring from some kind of artistic impulse: when they scored goals – and they scored all seven of Madrid's that night – it was important that each one carried some kind of flourish. Of them all, the one with which Di Stéfano completed his hat-trick was the most extraordinary: straight from a restart there are six passes and a wonderfully smooth acceleration up the middle of the field before the balding No. 9 guides a low shot into the right-hand corner of the net. It takes thirteen seconds from start to finish. But it was Puskás who claimed the majority of the goals: two brutal left-foot shots from inside the area, a left-footed penalty kick and a header from Gento's cross, which the winger delivered at the end of a blinding run.

On his arrival in Madrid, Puskás had found the game faster and more competitive than he had been used to in Hungary. Nor was there the same kind of fraternal relationship he had enjoyed in Budapest among players with whom he had grown up. Di Stéfano commanded the stature he had enjoyed at Honved, and Puskás was old enough and wise enough not to attempt to fight him for it. Instead he encouraged Di Stéfano, who already played as a deep-lying centre forward, to develop the role in the way Hidegkuti had done, adding his own greater gifts of technique, vision and leadership. Proud and demanding, Don Alfredo was always the boss, and in Puskás he acquired a *consigliere di lusso*, a lieutenant and adviser whose standards and experience matched his own. For a friend, Puskás found Gento, the small, dark winger from Santander, with whom he shared a room on away trips throughout his time with Madrid. But his relationship with the club's manager, Luis Carniglia, made for a difficult start at the club. The Argentinian showed little interest in Puskás and dropped him, at the last minute, from the team to play the 1959 European Cup final, against Stade de Reims, depriving the Hungarian of his first chance of a winners' medal in the continent's leading club competition, even though his goal had won them the semi-final. To make things worse, Carniglia invented a non-existent injury as his pretext for dropping the Hungarian. That summer the coach was invited to leave, to be replaced first by Fleitas Solich of Uruguay and then by Miguel Muñoz, a former wing half with the club. There were to be no more problems with coaches for Puskás.

To watch him and Di Stéfano and their teammates in action at Hampden Park on that magical night in 1960 now is to be immersed in a lost purity. There are no close-ups in the telecast and therefore no concentration on facial expressions at the expense of the action; no gesticulations, remonstrations or other acts of pettiness. There is just the simplicity of medium and long shots, with hardly any editing (except around the four minutes missing from the first half, which were lost to a power cut). Nothing distorts the game. The emotion comes entirely from the fluid geometry of the play itself, the sense of personality from the cross-rhythms of Madrid's work and from the explosive climaxes. And today its effect is just as intoxicating.

Puskás remained with the club until 1967. There was another hat-trick in a European Cup final in 1962, when he scored all the goals against Benfica, but on that occasion the Portuguese, under the direction of Béla Guttmann, another gifted Hungarian coach, scored five. He, Di Stéfano and Gento were still in the side in 1964, when they lost 3–1 to Internazionale in Vienna. But when Real Madrid recaptured the trophy in 1966, beating Partizan Belgrade 2–1 in Brussels, he was not selected. The following year, at the age of forty, he retired. Two years later 80,000 fans attended his testimonial match at the Estadio Bernabéu.

He opened a restaurant in Madrid, before giving it up to coach a Canadian club in the short-lived North American Soccer League. He moved on to Greece, taking Panathinaikos to the 1971 European Cup final at Wembley, where they lost a drab match 2–0 to Ajax of Amsterdam. There were then spells in Chile, Saudia Arabia and Egypt, where Hidegkuti was in charge of a rival club, Spain again, Greece, with AEK Athens this time, Paraguay and finally Australia, coaching Hellas of Melbourne. In 1981 he returned to Hungary for the first time since 1956, accepting an invitation to celebrate the twenty-fifth anniversary of the end of the run of six years with only one defeat. He was mobbed on his arrival, gave an interview for a commemorative film, took part in a Budapest vs The Rest match and visited his parents' grave. Thereafter he paid regular visits to his homeland, and in 1992 he made a permanent return to Budapest, where he coached the national team for a few months before accepting the Hungarian FA's offer of a post involving ceremonial duties and managing the youth teams. Over the years his waistline had expanded and eventually he was no longer able to take part in games celebrating this or that anniversary. But in the minds of those who, like Jean-Luc Godard, watched the newsreel footage of the match at Wembley in 1953, or of those who, as young boys, had sat at home in front of a primitive television set and watched his deeds at Hampden Park in 1960, Ferenc Puskás remained that sturdy figure, his dark hair slicked back, whose left foot kicked open the door into a new world.

2 Pelé

He was standing on the steps of a hotel lobby in Chicago, half a mile or so from Soldier Field, where, in a couple of hours' time, Germany and Bolivia were scheduled to play the opening match of the 1994 World Cup, after a bizarre ceremony in which he would help Diana Ross, the singer, in her attempt to score a ceremonial goal from the penalty spot while wearing high-heeled shoes. But now he was alone, a middle-aged man of medium height, an unobtrusive figure in a blazer and tie, waiting for a courtesy car. There was no one around until two fans wearing Germany scarves appeared and, after whispering together for a moment, approached him to ask for autographs and a photograph. He smiled at them, signed their pieces of paper, and then took charge of arranging the photographs so that each one would have a picture with his arm around them. They thanked him and walked off towards the stadium, leaving him to wait for his transportation. Then another man approached him, asking for an autograph for his small son. 'To Jack,' he wrote in a looping and meticulous hand. 'Good luck for football. Pelé.'

These small gestures of courtesy from the world's most famous retired footballer, far away from the spotlights, said a great deal about what had made Edson Arantes do Nascimento not only famous but also so greatly loved by all fans of the game, irrespective of nationality. Pelé always stood for the better side of the game: the sportsmanship, the fellowship, the beauty. While we think of his moments of extraordinary skill – dummying the goalkeeper, attempting to score from the halfway line, flipping the ball over a defender's head before volleying it into the net – we also remember the indelible image of Pelé embracing Bobby Moore, the opposing captain, at the conclusion of a marvellous game between the two sides during the 1970 World Cup in Mexico, a moment encapsulating all the things we would like sport to be and to which we long ago accepted that it can seldom aspire.

In 1994, however, he was in Chicago on business. Twenty years earlier his gifts of warmth and generosity had made him the perfect choice to lead the game's assault on the United States. The North American Soccer League had been set up in the 1960s but received its boost when Pelé and Franz Beckenbauer, Germany's captain, joined up in the 1970s. The Ertegün brothers, Nesuhi and Ahmet, jazz-loving sons of a Turkish diplomat, had lived in the US since the late 1930s and had made their fortunes from Atlantic Records, a New York-based label on which they released music by the Drifters, Ray Charles, Aretha Franklin, John Coltrane and many others. But their immersion in American culture never eroded their love of football, and when Warner Communications bought their company, retaining the Erteguns as executives of the new conglomerate, they saw the opportunity to invest some of the corporation's resources in a new team, the New York Cosmos. With the support of an enthusiastic chairman, Steve Ross, they offered the world's most famous footballer a sum not far off $7 million – more than he had earned in his eighteen years with Santos, for whom he made 1,114 appearances and scored 1,088 goals – to end his career as a missionary for the game.

The arrival of Pelé in 1975, followed two years later by that of Beckenbauer, took soccer in the US to a new level. The Cosmos immediately became a kind of all-star team, a version of Santiago Bernabéu's Real Madrid, attracting crowds so large that eventually they were forced to move from the ill-favoured Downing Stadium, underneath the Triborough Bridge, to Giants Stadium in New Jersey. Other new clubs were franchised around the country, in cities such as Miami and Atlanta, some of which were able to draw on a base of immigrant fans – particularly Mexicans and Italians – still yearning for the game of the old country and now delighted by the arrival of fading stars from the international game to bolster the efforts of the willing but inexperienced local players. For a while things looked good. The Cosmos attracted huge amounts of publicity and sizeable crowds, and Pelé and Beckenbauer became honorary New Yorkers. But somehow the roots of the game failed to take hold in US soil. When Pelé finally retired at the end of his contract in 1977, some of the lustre dimmed. Network television walked away, crowds dropped, gradually the franchises began to fold, and in 1984 the league shut up shop. The next ten years were spent trying to re-establish the game, principally by mounting, with the help of Nesuhi Ertegün's contacts and Warner Communications' resources, a successful campaign to host the 1994 World Cup as a launch pad for a new organization, the Major Soccer League. Through all this Pelé's name continued to be, as it would remain, synonymous with the game.

He was born on 23 October 1940 in Três Corações, a small town in the mountainous province of Minas Gerais, about a hundred miles from the coast and virtually equidistant from Rio de Janeiro and São Paulo. His father was a footballer, a centre forward, known as Dondinho; his mother's name was Celeste. Dondinho's career took the family to Bauru, a city two hundred miles to the west, before a knee injury brought a premature end to his time as a player. He stayed on at Clube Atlético Bauru as an assistant coach, however, and was there to watch his son's first matches in the club's junior side. Brazilians love nicknames, and Dondinho and Celeste called their son 'Dico'. The boy's teammates, however, knew him by a different name. It was one that he never understood or particularly enjoyed, but it would become as famous around the world as a brand name. One day in 1950 Dondinho and his nine-year-old son listened to the deciding match of the first post-war World Cup on the radio, and the boy saw his father cry as Brazil went down to an unexpected defeat by Uruguay. 'I didn't really understand what was happening,' Pelé would say, 'but I told my father, "Don't worry. One day I'll win it."'

Many years later, Pelé recollected that Dondinho had taught him not only to kick the ball with both feet but to head it with his eyes open. The father had, after all, once scored five times with his head in a single game. Another lesson was how to control the ball on his chest: if you breathe in when the ball is in the air and breathe out just before it hits you, the softened chest will provide a more effective cushion and the ball will fall at your feet instead of rebounding away. These things became part of his vocabulary and syntax in a language that he mastered more effectively than any man before him.

At Bauru he also benefited from the presence of Waldemar de Brito, the chief coach, who had missed a penalty for Brazil in the 1934 World Cup finals when they lost 3–1 and suffered elimination at the hands of Spain in their only match. By the time De Brito's young protégé reached his teens it was apparent that he had marvellous finesse to go with his abundant creative imagination. But what really marked him out was the unremitting physicality of his approach to the game. Pelé was a supreme athlete whose gifts were deployed, first and foremost, to enable him to keep possession of the ball until he was close enough to do whatever damage he had in mind. Watching film clips from his heyday, it is impossible not to wonder at the sheer zest with which he went about his business. This was a man who could clear six feet in the high jump and run a hundred metres in eleven seconds. When he carried the ball past an opponent it was not in the manner of a winger, with feints and sidesteps, but with a muscular dash and an instinct that allowed him to take half-blocks and deflections in his stride, to hurdle attempted fouls and to come out with the ball still firmly in his ownership. He could stop on a sixpence, paralyzing an opponent before leaving him for dead with his blistering acceleration on a curving sprint into the penalty area. His eye was always on the ball and his mind had made its decisions far in advance, so he hurled himself towards goal with a commitment that must have petrified those charged with the task of stopping him. And after growing up playing football on rough, uneven pitches, with hardly a tuft of grass to be seen, and usually without the benefit of boots or even shoes, he was used to compensating for an unexpected bounce or a sudden sideways skip. His unearthly balance allowed him to absorb them all.

Against the wishes of his mother he became a footballer, and at fifteen, having been watched by most of Brazil's big clubs, he signed his first professional contract. Santos was a coffee port on the coast, with a population of around one million, whose club competed in the São Paulo state championship alongside Corinthians, Palmeiras and São Paulo FC itself. This was De Brito's old club, which may have had something to do with the move. In 1955 they had won the state title for the first time in twenty years, and they won it again the following year, when Pelé finished as the club's top scorer with thirty-two goals. He had scored on his league début, after coming on as a substitute in a 7–1 victory over Corinthians in September 1956, and he scored again on his international début for Brazil in a 2–1 defeat at the hands of Argentina in the Roca Cup in Rio's Maracanã stadium on 7 July 1957. Three days later Brazil beat the same opponents 2–0 in São Paulo, and Pelé scored again, the second goal going to the nineteen-year-old José Altafini, then known in his home country as 'Mazzola', after a famous Italian footballer, and destined for greater things under his baptismal name after a move to Milan.

Already Pelé was the sensation of South American football, and eleven months later, still only seventeen years old, he landed in Sweden with the rest of the Brazil squad for the 1958 World Cup finals. Great preparations had been made, including detailed reconnaissance to select a suitable training camp and the use of a psychologist, Dr Hilton Gosling, to assess the squad's state of mind. Yet Pelé was carrying a knee injury when they arrived, suffered during Brazil's last warm-up match against Corinthians, causing him to miss Brazil's opening games, the 3–0 win over Austria in Uddevalla, in which Altafini scored twice, and the unlovely goalless draw with England in Gothenburg's futuristic Ullevi stadium. After the setback against the English, several senior players approached the coach, Vicente Feola, to insist that he make changes before the final group match against the Soviet Union. As a result Garrincha, Botafogo's right-winger, came back in and ran Boris Kuznetsov, the left back, to distraction, while Zito improved the service from midfield. Pelé hit a post but other-wise had a quiet game, overshadowed by the established stars of the forward line as Brazil won 2–0, Vavá scoring both goals.

It was a different story in the quarter-final, however, when he scored the goal that divided Brazil and Wales, who were without their all-purpose hero, John Charles. There were seventeen minutes left in the Ullevi stadium when Pelé used the technique his father had taught him to cushion the ball on his chest inside the penalty area before flipping it up to deceive a defender and prodding it home from eight yards out, a deflection off the leg of the right back, Stuart Williams, making little difference. It was the decisive goal, it propelled Brazil into the last four of the tournament, and it was the one with which Pelé announced himself as a player of international consequence, as well as making him, at seventeen years and 239 days, the youngest man to score a goal in the World Cup finals.

In Stockholm five days later he was to do even better as Brazil beat France 5–2, a scoreline which did little justice to the losers. Although Vavá scored first, with a ferocious volley, France were able to manufacture a quick reply, forcing their opponents to concede their first goal in the finals when Just Fontaine ran on to a cunning pass from Raymond Kopa, soon to be named Europe's footballer of the year, before taking the ball round Gylmar. After twenty-six minutes, however, Bob

Jonquet, France's captain and right half, went down under a foul from Vavá and, with no substitutes permitted, limped out on the wing for the remainder of the match. Didi was the first to take advantage of France's reduced state, sending Brazil in at half-time with a 2–1 lead. But it was the seventeen-year-old who ignited the northern lights in the second half with a hat-trick of goals in the fifty-second, sixty-fourth and seventy-fifth minutes. 'This was the match that exposed me to a wider public,' Pelé would say. His first was a tap-in after France's goal-keeper, Claude Abbes, dropped the ball; for the second, he put away a rebound from close range with the outside of his right foot; only the third gave unmistakable evidence of his virtuosity as he met Didi's pass on the edge of the area, knocked it up with his thigh and volleyed it home. He was, and remains, the youngest player to achieve the feat in the World Cup finals. Roger Piantoni scored a final consolation goal for France to complete the scoring.

Sweden were Brazil's opponents in a final which saw Pelé setting yet another record by virtue of his age. Managed by an Englishman, George Raynor, the hosts took the lead after four minutes through Nils Liedholm, their captain and playmaker, but two goals by Vavá, both from Garrincha's crosses, gave Brazil a half-time lead. Between his strikes, Pelé had hit the bar from the edge of the area with a shot of sudden violence. But it was after the interval that the teenager unleashed his full reper-toire, first increasing the advantage after fifty-four minutes when he beat his marker to a diagonal ball from the left, chested it down, lifted it over a second defender's head and met the dropping ball with a right-foot volley past the goalkeeper from ten yards out. Mario Zagallo added a fourth and Agne Simonsson replied for Sweden before Pelé sealed the match 5–2 in the final minute. After back-heeling the ball out to Zagallo he ran in to meet the cross with a lobbed header that arced over Karl Svensson, the helpless goalkeeper, and passed just inside the far post. It was a goal of cool audacity and technical originality, and it burned a lasting image into the minds of all who saw it. 'I was seventeen,' he said, 'it was my first World Cup and I was just a member of the squad, without any particular responsibility or pressure. I felt like I was living in a dream.' Brazil had won the World Cup for the first time, erasing the disappointment of 1950, and a great individual talent had arrived.

They flew home from Sweden via Recife, where the first of many victory parades took place. Then it was on to Rio, where jet fighters accompanied their plane, streaming ceremonial smoke trails. A fire engine carried them to a reception at the presidential palace, where they were promised houses and jobs for life. For Pelé there was another flight, to São Paulo, and then the final leg of the journey to Bauru, where the celebrations would last another four days. A street had been named after him and the municipality presented him with a car, a Romisetta, a 247cc three-wheeled 'bubble car' with a door that opened at the front, manufactured in Brazil under licence from BMW; unfortunately, he was not yet old enough to take the wheel. Even though many promises were never kept, in the weeks to come the members of the squad would drown in gifts: clothes, washing machines, refrigerators, televisions. They became the target of offers to endorse products of all kinds.

Demonstrating the common-sense approach to his business life that would stand him in good stead when his playing career was over, Pelé got himself an agent. Pepe Gordo, a Spaniard, negotiated a revised contract with Santos, bringing his client about $500 a month, to be reviewed at the end of the season. Others who went to the directors of their clubs with similar expectations but without professional help, notably Garrincha, fared much less well. The big European clubs were sniffing around the squad, Didi leaving Botafogo for Real Madrid and Altafini accepting AC Milan's offer. There was a great deal of interest in Pelé, but somehow Santos would manage to find the money to pay the prodigy enough to enable him to repel the advances not just of Santiago Bernabéu but of Gianni Agnelli, who put the resources of Fiat, his family firm, behind his repeated attempts to persuade the player to swap the black and white of Santos for the magpie shirt of Juventus. With a capacity of 20,000 at Vila Belmiro, the stadium in which most of their home matches were staged, Santos needed to undertake an apparently endless round of exhibition matches in Europe and Asia in order to amass the necessary funds. As a result Pelé found himself playing more than a hundred matches a year and was expected to produce his characteristic miracles in each one. On tour in Europe in the spring of 1959, for example, the squad visited seven countries to play twenty-two games in the space of forty-four days. For their star player to miss one of those fixtures would be as unthinkable as the Rat Pack taking the stage in Las Vegas without Frank Sinatra. The star kept his side of the bargain, to the extent of scoring six goals in two matches against Milan and Barcelona, with only a day's rest in between.

He played in four World Cups, and no single image is more closely associated with the competition than that of him leaping into Jairzinho's arms in the 1970 final, punching the air after heading in Roberto Rivelino's cross to give Brazil the lead against Italy, just one of the many moments of magic studding their performances that year. Before that, however, the tournaments of 1962 and 1966 had brought the kind of painful disappointments that might have ended the career of a lesser man.

He was twenty-one and hiding a groin injury when the squad arrived in Viña del Mar, a town on the Chilean coast where they would be based for the 1962 finals. Under a new coach, Aymoré Moreira, they had flown from Rio on the same airliner and with the same pilot that they had used in 1958, but to begin with it seemed that luck had not travelled with them. A poor first half in their opening match against Mexico was forgotten after the interval, when Pelé beat two men and crossed for Zagallo to head the first goal, and then scored himself with his left foot after carrying the ball through what seemed like the entire defence. Against Czechoslovakia, three days later, he hit a post with a shot after twenty-five minutes but, as he stretched for the rebound, felt something give in his groin and lay on the ground, screaming for help. No amount of treatment with ice packs during the interval could bring him back to full effectiveness. With no substitutes allowed, he was forced to remain on the field, limping out on the left wing and grateful for the refusal of the Czechoslovakian defenders to tackle him with full force as the game petered out into a goalless draw. 'One of those things that I shall always remember with emotion, and one of the finest things that happened in my entire career,' he would say. Four days of intensive work by the squad's medical staff were to no avail and Amarildo took his place against Spain, scoring both goals in a 2–1 win. Pelé offered to take injections that would allow him to play, bur Dr Gosling ignored his entreaties and pressure from elsewhere, wisely refusing to jeopardize the player's physical integrity. Without Pelé, they went on to wins by 3–1 over England in the quarter-final (with a show-stopping performance from Garrincha) and by 4–2 over Chile, the hosts, in the semi-final. Pelé was still begging to play in the hours before the final, against Czechoslovakia, but again they managed without him, winning 3–1 with goals from Amarildo, Zito and Vavá, after conceding an early lead in Santiago's Estadio Nacional, with 68,000 present. It was Pelé's second world championship, but it bore no comparison to the first.

There had been immediate solace for missing the final rounds when he scored all five goals as Santos thrashed Benfica, the champions of Portugal and Europe, in the 1962 World Club Championship, a title they won again the following year. With Santos he had already won the São Paulo state championship five times, and he would go on to capture it on another four occasions. In 1964 he scored eight goals in a single match. In 1965 the Brazilian government declared him a 'national treasure'. Yet his readiness to accept the cortisone injections that would have enabled him to play in the 1962 final had its origins in Santos's touring schedule, when his presence on the pitch had been required even while he was suffering from one injury or another in order to justify the club's appearance money and keep their appeal alive. And by the time he arrived in England for the 1966 World Cup, aged twenty-five and theoretically in his prime, he had a lot of miles on the clock and a lot of repairs in the service record.

'We arrived thinking the group matches wouldn't be a problem,' he said, but there was a hint of what he could expect during Brazil's opening match against Bulgaria at Goodison Park, where a banner reading AVANTE BRASIL hung from the grandstand in which 5,000 of their fans were clustered. Brought down just outside the area by Dimitar Yakimov as he moved on to a pass from Jairzinho, the powerful young winger, Pelé smashed a low free kick through the defensive wall to give his team the lead after thirteen minutes. But the savage treatment continued, most of it handed out by his marker, Dobromir Zhechev. 'My legs ached from Zhechev's constant tripping and kicking,' he said later. He was not the only one to take revenge for the Bulgarians' tactics. Midway through the second half the ageing Garrincha arose from the spot where Ivan Kolev's foul had deposited him, again just outside the area, and crashed another free kick high into the net, adding swerve to the ball through his unique combination of the outside of his right boot and a right leg that appeared to bend inwards at the knee, towards its opposite number rather than away from it, a deformity that some said explained his gift.

Vicente Feola, who had returned to manage the side, withheld the battered Pelé from the second match, against Hungary, thus depriving him of the chance to participate in a match that turned out to be a classic. With Flórián Albert, the

Hidegkuti of the next generation, elegantly pulling the strings from midfield, the nippy Ferenc Bene laying waste to the left side of Brazil's defence and János Farkas lying in wait to strike, Hungary evoked memories of the Golden Squad of the 1950s as they took the double champions apart. The second goal, involving five players and ending with Farkas's volley, was the most sumptuous of the entire tournament and Brazil had lost, for the first time in fourteen World Cup matches, to the nation that had inflicted their last defeat in the quarter-final of 1954.

They were not out of the competition, however, and Pelé returned to the side for the third group match, one of nine changes as Feola sent out an unbalanced side to face Portugal, who had already won both their games. Inspired by Eusebio, their Mozambique-born forward who had been attracting comparisons with Brazil's great star, and captained from midfield by the redoubtable Mario Coluna, Portugal had scored three times against both Hungary and Bulgaria, demonstrating their ability to play fast and fluent football and to create goals of the highest quality. Now they did it again, and Brazil were eliminated, although on this occasion beauty had little to do with it. George McCabe, the English referee, was unaccountably lenient as the Portuguese defenders went to work on the only survivor of the 1958 World Cup-winning side in Brazil's XI. Within minutes Pelé was rolling on the grass in agony after a defender had scythed at his knees. Then João Morais, the right back, hacked him down on the edge of the area and, as Pelé tried to get back on to his feet, cut him down again. As Dr Gosling and Américo, the squad's famous shaven-headed masseur, carried him off the pitch, the team's hopes went with him. Eusebio, already crowned Europe's footballer of the year, scored Portugal's second before wrapping up the match with a searing volley that might have maimed Manga, Brazil's goalkeeper, had he got anywhere near it. Portugal went on to recover from going three goals down to North Korea in front of 40,000 astonished spectators at

Goodison before losing to England, the eventual champions, in their semi-final at Wembley. A bitter Pelé went home vowing that he had played his last World Cup match.

Over the next four years there were more state championships with Santos, more tours of Europe, the Far East, Africa – wherever someone would meet Santos's fee – and more goals, including, in 1969, his thousandth, a penalty taken at the Maracanã stadium in Rio; he rolled the ball past the goalkeeper in his usual manner, with the inside of his right boot, before the crowd poured on to the pitch and engulfed him in adoration. And in 1970 came the decision that, at twenty-nine, he had one more World Cup left in him.

For this one, to be held in Mexico, Brazil's meticulous preparations were almost derailed at the last moment. João Saldanha, a prominent journalist and the successful coach of Botafogo, had been so persistent in his criticism of the squad that the Brazilian football association, the CBD, put him in charge. Rising to the challenge, Saldanha carefully rebuilt the team around players from Pelé's club and watched them breeze through the qualifying competition. In the weeks before the finals, however, he began to make a series of bizarre decisions. Worried by the memory of what had happened in 1966, he started filling his defence with bigger, heavier, more powerful players in order to confront, as he saw it, the physical challenge offered by the top European nations. At one point he even made public his intention to drop Pelé, perhaps after hearing that the player had been critical of his tactics during a dressing-room discussion. His hot temper started to get the better of him when these decisions were challenged, and with barely two months to go he was called to a meeting at the CBD and replaced by Mario Zagallo, the shrewd little winger from the 1958 side. Zagallo inherited a squad with a wonderfully inventive midfield, featuring the cerebral, chain-smoking Gérson de Oliveira and the dynamic Rivelino, both left-footed,

plus the swift nineteen-year-old Clodoaldo and two contrasting attackers in the deft little Tostão, only recently recovered
from an operation for a detached retina, and the electrifying
Jairzinho, both of whom had made brief appearances in
England four years earlier. Linking them all would be Pelé, not
yet thirty but the unquestioned *patron* of the team, who
formed a three-man players' council with Gérson and Carlos
Alberto Torres, the right back and captain.

This was the first World Cup to be televised in colour, and
how greedily the cameras fed on Brazil's gold shirts and pale
blue shorts. In the heat and clear air of Guadalajara, where they
played all their matches up to the final, they positively shim-
mered. As did the football, which took the Brazilian method to
a new level. Pelé himself would always say that although the
1970 team was superior in a collective sense, the 1958 team
had better individuals. He would list them: 'Garrincha, Didi,
Vavá, Nilton Santos, Djalma Santos, Zito . . .' No one, of
course, was ever in a better position to judge, but there would
still be plenty of people prepared to give him an argument on
behalf of the class of '70, who filled hearts and minds around
the world with a vision of what football could be, if it obeyed
all its best instincts. Under Saldanha and then Zagallo, they
developed a strategy that involved using the lightweight Tostão
as the pivot of their attacks, inviting him to receive the ball with
his back to goal and to lay it off to his colleagues with subtly
angled and carefully weighted flicks. The most unlikely of target men, he used wit and imagination to flummox his markers,
and close skills to drag them out of position.

Brazil began, against Czechoslovakia, with a display of
sheer impudence. Over in Europe, television audiences saw the
way they would loiter in midfield, transferring the ball
between themselves with apparent nonchalance before suddenly exploding into the sort of activity that panicked
defences. Rivelino turned Karol Dolnas, the right back, inside
out in the opening minutes. Pelé tried to lob Ivo Viktor from

five yards inside his own half, only just missing the target; it had been a prepared move, and later he only regretted not having saved it up for use against more formidable opponents. When the Czechoslovakians unexpectedly took the lead, Rivelino replied by bending a low free kick around the defensive wall, and the world knew that a dead-ball successor to Garrincha had arrived. Then Gérson began to lob his long-range passes into the opposing area, the first of them controlled by the chest of Pelé, who let it drop before volleying the second goal. The next lob found Jairzinho, who lifted the ball over Viktor, ran round the stranded goalkeeper and slid it into the net. To Jairzinho, too, went the fourth and final goal for Brazil, the product of a dribble that left four defenders in a state of utter discombobulation.

Without Gérson, rested by Zagallo after suffering a knock on his thigh, Brazil faced England in a group match that quickly acquired the status of a classic, at least in England, even though the result – a 1–0 win for Brazil – had no real effect on the fortunes of either team. Gordon Banks's save from Pelé was the game's signature moment, an extraordinary plunge and scoop after Jairzinho's right-wing cross, made on the run and at the stretch from the byline, was met at the far post with a wonderful leap and a powerful downward header. Pelé was supposed to have been screaming '*Goooooollll!*' at the moment Banks made contact and diverted the ball to safety. Brazil's approach indicated the seriousness of the contest: they played without frills or tricks, pure concentration replacing the extravagance displayed against other opponents. Against the defending champions, the team who had taken their title, it was all business. The winning goal itself, in the sixty-second minute, was the product of Tostão's persistence in twice winning the ball back, first after his shot from the edge of the penalty area had been blocked by Brian Labone and then when the ball rebounded off Bobby Moore's shins. Having then beaten Tommy Wright, he swivelled on the left-hand side of the area and, with his back to the goal, clipped over a little cross that landed at the feet of Pelé, whose feint threw two defenders off balance before, in a single movement and without looking, he prodded the ball to his right, where Jairzinho was running round the flank of the defence to meet the ball with a drive that, from a range of seven yards, sent it past Banks in a blur. England had two good chances, Alan Ball hitting the bar and Jeff Astle missing the target with his left foot, but the result was a fair one. Even deprived of the inspired passing of Gérson, Brazil had reasserted their supremacy over the world game; it remained only for them to win the tournament.

The next step was a more flamboyant performance against Romania in the final group match, for which Rivelino joined Gérson on the sidelines. Pelé opened the scoring with another free kick blasted through a flimsy wall and Jairzinho touched in Paulo César's cross to increase the lead before Romania scored the first of their two goals. When Pelé prodded in a loose ball to make it 3–1, Brazil's opponents were left with too much to do.

Peru, coached by Didi, Pelé's teammate in 1958 and 1962, had already been beaten 3–1 by West Germany in the group phase and could offer little more than deft touches in their quarter-final against Brazil. Gérson and Rivelino returned, but this was a mini-festival of slipshod defending, finishing 4–2, with goals from Rivelino and Jairzinho, and two from Tostão. The better of Peru's goals was scored by Teófilo Cubillas, their gifted No. 10, who would go on to play with success in the North American Soccer League.

A dreadful goalkeeping misjudgement by Félix allowed Uruguay to take the lead in the semi-final, but not until a minute before half-time, when Clodoaldo played a give-and-go with Tostão and smashed the return pass into the net, did Brazil show anything like the expected form. A spirited lecture from Zagallo during the interval sent them out in the mood to complete the job, and Pelé had a hand in goals by Jairzinho and Rivelino. But the moment for which the match is remembered had nothing to do with its 3–1 scoreline. It came close to the end, when Tostão played an angled through ball for Pelé, whose dummy utterly fooled the goalkeeper. Ladislao Mazurkiewicz let the ball run through as Pelé hared past him to hit a cross-shot that only narrowly missed the far post. It was an outrageous move which, although unsuccessful, seemed to symbolize the extravagant imagination that these Brazilians, led by Pelé, brought to bear on a game seen by others only in terms of sweat and blood.

A contrast of styles was expected in the final, where Brazil met Italy, the apostles of defensive football. Four days earlier, however, Italy had beaten the formidable West Germany by four goals to three in a match that, in front of a crowd of 102,000 in the Azteca stadium in Mexico City, overturned every available stereotype. The anticipated struggle between the armies of cynicism and the forces of pragmatism turned out to be an unimaginably enthralling affair played according to Brazil's code of football: if you score three, then I'll score four. The world hoped that Italy had finally found a way of unlocking the vast potential of their midfield and attack, and that the dramatic setting of the Azteca would again inspire them to give Brazil a match worthy of the climax to a World Cup.

In front of an even bigger crowd, it was indeed a memorable final. Italy, however, had little to do with it. Pelé outjumped Tarcisio Burgnich to head in Rivelino's looping cross to open the scoring after eighteen minutes, giving Brazil its hundredth World Cup goal in the process. Roberto Boninsegna then made the most of a defensive error to send the teams in at half-time on level terms. Perhaps drained by the effort needed to win the semi-final, however, Italy had little to offer but dogged resistance as Brazil knocked in three goals without reply after the interval, in the process consolidating their reputation as the most admired international team of all time. First the balding

Gérson, the sixty-a-day man, nicked the ball away from Giacinto Facchetti, Italy's captain and left back, dropped his shoulder as he slipped between two defenders and guided a wonderful left-footed shot from twenty yards past Enrico Albertosi. Then came another magical combination as Gérson's quarter-back pass to the far post found Pelé, who headed it down for Jairzinho to become the first and, so far, only man to score in every round of the finals. Brazil finished off with a ten-pass move, originated in the left-back position by Tostão and including significant contributions from Clodoaldo and Jairzinho before Pelé once more found himself in position to play a no-look square pass, again touching the ball to his right, where Carlos Alberto thundered in to strike the goal that set the seal not just on the tournament as a whole but on the team's ascent to football's Valhalla. The scorer once told a friend of mine, the football journalist Patrick Barclay, that shooting was definitely the weak point of his otherwise complete game, and yet it is the very thing for which he will always be remembered, thanks to Pelé's freakish vision and impeccable timing. After the presentations, fans flooded on to the pitch and Pelé was lifted high on their shoulders as he raised the little Jules Rimet trophy, which, since they had won it three times, was now Brazil's to keep. Around the world, something like 600 million switched off their televisions and counted their blessings for having been able to witness such a spectacle, a moment when aspiration and achievement became one.

On 21 July 1970 Pelé attained a status that can never be challenged. The World Cup winner's medals put his pre-eminence beyond question, just as winning the world heavyweight championship on three occasions helped raise Muhammad Ali to a level above that of any other boxer. Yet vision and timing were not always evident in Pelé's life away from football. One reason Santos managed to hang on to him, despite the constant entreaties coming from the direction of Madrid and Turin, was the club's repeated willingness to bail him out of the problems created by a series of unsuccessful business ventures. When he was twenty-five, a property company collapsed and his contract was extended for three years after Santos had agreed to meet his liabilities. Over the next few years he gradually rebuilt his business portfolio, which included an import–export business, a radio station, a dairy farm and a transport company, but the failure of one of them appeared to affect the buoyancy of the rest and would lead a general decline in his commercial fortunes.

He played five more games for Brazil after the World Cup final, saying his farewell after a 2–2 draw with Yugoslavia at the Maracanã on 18 July 1971, fourteen years to the month since his début. And in 1974 he announced his complete retirement from the game, marking his farewell to Santos with a grand exhibition match. He had led them to six championships and had broken every available record along the way. A few months later there was astonishment when the news of his agreement with the New York Cosmos became public. For $7 million he would spend three years as a player with the club, followed by three years as a 'goodwill ambassador' for the game in the US. His business worries, at least, were at an end.

In New York he bathed in the admiration of a new set of admirers, but he gave full value for his stipend. He took the Cosmos to the NASL championship in 1977, scoring thirty-seven goals in sixty-four appearances in his three seasons and registering thirty assists – a new concept in the game, but one through which he might have broken even more records, had such a statistic been kept in Brazil. And when the last chapter of his playing career came to an end, it was marked by an exhibition match between his two old clubs, in which he played one half in the Cosmos' shirt and the other in the white and black of Santos. He had played 1,324 games as a professional footballer, scoring 1,282 goals at an extraordinary average of 0.968 per game.

After football, goodwill became his stock-in-trade. In a game often defaced by the bitterness of its rivalries, he made sure that everyone would always be pleased to see Pelé. This was an occupation in itself, requiring an endless supply of good humour and an ability to say the right thing, or at least not the wrong thing, at all times. At a time when football was beginning to celebrate its history, no significant anniversary would be complete without his presence. Not surprisingly, he held the vice-presidency of Santos. Although belonging to no political party, for a while in the 1990s he was installed as the Minister for Sport in the government of President Fernando Cardoso. Awards for his contribution to 'international peace' rained down upon him, along with citations as the greatest sportsman of the twentieth century. He endorsed a variety of products, from Pepsi-Cola to Viagra, managing to retain his dignity in the process. But perhaps his most significant allegiance, after Santos and Brazil – and perhaps the Cosmos – was to a credit-card company that sent him round the world to give press conferences, launch initiatives and make approving noises about the latest footballing prodigy produced by whichever country he happened to be in at the time. And so, decades after his retirement, he continued to enjoy among fans of the world's most popular game the special status conferred in basketball on Michael Jordan, in motor racing on Juan Manuel Fangio and in the ring upon Ali: not merely the greatest, which is always arguable, but the finest, and the embodiment of our dreams.

3 Gianni Rivera and Sandro Mazzola

The ticket cost ten shillings; today it sits on my desk, in a small wooden frame. It came from a fellow member of my local cricket team. He and his son were fans of Manchester United, and they had applied for tickets to the second leg of the semifinal of the European Cup against AC Milan, at Old Trafford. A friend, another United fan, pulled out of the eighty-mile trip at the last minute, and I got lucky. But I wasn't going with the thought of seeing Manchester United, even though this was the spring of 1969 and Matt Busby's team were the holders of the trophy, with the great line-up that included George Best, Bobby Charlton, Denis Law and Pat Crerand. They were wonderful, but I could see them any year. This night, I was going to see Gianni Rivera.

In the 1960s Italy meant Vespas and Martinis, Fellini and Mastroianni, Antonioni and Vitti, coffee bars and slender suits in lightweight fabrics, and a certain highly desirable air of studied detachment. Throw in football, too, and you got Gianni Rivera. Seen from an English perspective, he represented the desirable elements of Mediterranean style as much as Alain Delon in *L'Eclisse* or that Positano boy who carried Julie Christie off on a scooter in *Darling*. With his fine, sensitive face and his carefully sculpted hair, Rivera exuded youthful cool. He could have been Albert Camus's existential stranger, palely loitering on the fringe of life. He had that pre-Beatle sense of style, the look that provided the basis for the whole mod thing, when a handful of English kids suddenly decided to get *that* suit and *that* shirt and *that* narrow tie and *that* haircut to go with it. And maybe, one day, the Vespa or

Lambretta, too. He even had the name: was it Rivera or Riviera? The fact that he played football, and played it like a god, made him all the more amazing.

Before Rivera, footballers had enjoyed only the most tenuous connection with matters of style. In England their mode was that of the working men among whom they grew up and still lived, and they looked, even the youngest of them, like grown-ups. Occasionally there would be one, such as the Sheffield Wednesday and Manchester United forward Albert Quixall, who wore his hair in an approximation of the sort of greased quiff popularized by Elvis Presley and Eddie Cochran. Foreign stars, such as Alfredo di Stéfano and Ferenc Puskás of Real Madrid, possessed greater sophistication; unlike their ball skills, however, that sophisticated air was nothing the new generation of teenagers would aspire to emulate.

But Rivera looked like something from the pages of *Salut les copains* or *Town* magazine. He could have been modelling Jaeger suits or Ben Sherman shirts. You could have stuck him in the window of the Ivy shop in Richmond upon Thames or one of John Stephen's Carnaby Street boutiques and he would have looked perfectly at home. To see him in the mid-1960s, if you were of the right age and inclination, was to experience one of those moments when worlds collide, when obsessions that you had believed to be mutually exclusive suddenly acquire interesting relationships. Without warning, the world seems a bigger and more promising place.

Rivera looked as if he knew all this. Perhaps he really was the only member of the AC Milan team with a copy of *Kind of Blue* parked next to the radiogram in an apartment filled with Swedish modern furniture and abstract expressionist prints. Perhaps he even felt some kinship with the young London boys, such as Mark Feld (later Marc Bolan) and Pete Townshend, who were turning the Continental formula into the mod look. But it seems unlikely. He was the son of a railway worker and he ended up a politician, a defence minister in

Italy's centre-left government of the 1990s. In between, so far as one could see, came only football. But what football.

Giovanni Rivera made his Serie A début at fifteen. He had been born on 18 August 1943 in Valle San Bartolomeo, in the province of Alessandria, about fifty miles south-west of Milan. Alessandria, then in the top flight, would be his first club, and he made his début at home to Internazionale on 2 June 1959, the penultimate day of the season. Facing the team in third position in the table, Alessandria managed a 1–1 draw. And Rivera was still only a month past his sixteenth birthday when, on the opening day of the 1959–60 season, Milan's other team arrived to begin the defence of their latest championship at the Moccagatta stadium.

This was some Milan. Nils Liedholm, the great Swedish inside forward, was starting the eleventh of his twelve seasons in the red and black stripes; three months earlier he had been lifted on the shoulders of the crowd and carried around San Siro after the team had put seven goals past Udinese without reply in their final home match of the league season. There was Cesare Maldini, who would shortly succeed Liedholm as club captain, destined to lift the European Cup in that capacity and to manage Italy's national team but to become still better known, in the very distant future, as the father of Paolo. Juan Schiaffino, scorer of the first of Uruguay's two goals against Brazil in the final match of the 1950 World Cup, was starting his sixth and final season in Milan's midfield at the age of thirty-four, along with Ernesto Grillo of Argentina. Leading the forward line was the twenty-one-year-old José Altafini, known as 'Mazzola' back home in Brazil when he formed a partnership with Pelé in the national team and still celebrating his remarkable tally of twenty-eight goals in thirty-two Serie A matches in his first season with Milan.

Alessandria, coached by Franco Pedroni, who had played as a defender in Milan's 1954–55 title-winning side, got their season off to a deceptively promising start by beating the champions 3–1, with a hat-trick from their striker, Tacchi, against which the *rossoneri* could manage only a single goal from Altafini. But it was not Tacchi who attracted the attention of Milan's coach, Luigi Bonizzoni, and his technical director, Giuseppe 'Gipo' Viani. When Viani clapped eyes on the slender teenager in Alessandria's forward line, he thought he was seeing double. The resemblance to Schiaffino was uncanny. An approach was made, and Pedroni accompanied Rivera to his medical check-up. After Liedholm and Schiaffino had reassured the club's directors that the boy's slight build would not present an insuperable problem, his future was decided. At the end of the season he would join Milan, for a fee equivalent to around £65,000. When the two clubs met again, at the San Siro in February, Milan would win 3–1; for Alessandria, who were on their way to relegation, Rivera scored a consolation goal four minutes from the end, giving his new fans a taste of the pleasures to come.

Schiaffino had departed by the time Rivera made his début in Milan's No. 10 shirt on 18 September 1960, in a Coppa Italia match against his old club at the Moccagatta. This time the hat-trick went to Altafini as Milan won 5–3. The Brazilian scored again a week later when Rivera made his first league appearance for the club in a 3–0 home win over Catania. The prodigy scored his first goal six weeks later, when Milan travelled to Turin to face Juventus in the Stadio Communale. Holding a 3–0 lead after an hour's play, they hung on to win 4–3 after the home team had mounted a counter-attack, inspired by goals from their own great forwards, Omar Sívori of Argentina and John Charles of Wales. Rivera's goal, Milan's fourth, had made the difference; soon Viani had christened him *Bambino d'Oro*, a nickname often rendered in its English form: the Golden Boy.

Gianni Brera, a respected Italian sports journalist, gave him a second and more ambiguous nickname. To Brera, the teenaged Rivera was *l'abatino* – the young monk, or, by extension, a person not over-endowed with physical courage. True, the Golden Boy was not one to go thundering into tackles or to get involved in midfield scuffles. His slight build and his thoughtful temperament made him a creative player, pure and simple. His job was to interpret the flow of a game and find a way of shaping it in his opponents' half of the field. But he moved with such willowy grace, caressing the ball with so exquisite a touch, that to fault him for a lack of physical commitment would be like criticizing Michelangelo for going through his entire career without designing a municipal sewage system. In his book *Italian Hours* the novelist Henry James wrote, not unapprovingly, of Milan's 'northern reserve, which makes the place rather perhaps the last of the prose capitals than the first of the poetic', but then James was writing fifty years before Rivera's arrival in the city.

On the pitch, a certain aristocratic demeanour gave Rivera his distinction and made him an immediate favourite with supporters of a club that already enjoyed a rich history and a good opinion of itself. Milan Foot-Ball and Cricket Club had been formed in 1899 at a meeting in the Hotel du Nord in which Alfred Ormonde Edwards, an Englishman, was elected president. Their first headquarters was in a wine shop, and their ground was a field where trotting races also took place and which, thirty years later, would be replaced by railway trains trundling in and out of Mussolini's monumental Stazione Centrale. Herbert Kilpin, a Nottingham man, was the captain of the first team to wear the red and black stripes, which included five British players and six Italians. Edwards and Kilpin retained their positions for the first decade of the club's existence, after which Italians took over. By the time the Englishmen stepped down, Milan had won Italy's fledgling championship three times and a schism within the club had led, in 1908, to the formation of a breakaway club, the Football Club Internazionale di Milano, quickly to be known as Inter. Piero Pirelli, the tyre manufacturer, took over the presidency of Milan from Edwards in 1909; his long administration included the opening in 1926 of the club's new ground, San Siro, its four grandstands allowing a capacity of 40,000 spectators. Pirelli was followed in the 1930s by Alberto Rizzoli, Italy's leading publisher and bookseller, whose initial plan for a holiday centre called Milanello, set in wooded countryside halfway between Milan and the Alps, eventually turned into an extraordinarily well-appointed training centre for the footballers, a place where the players of the twenty-first century train during the week, spend the night before home matches, eat well and relax in comfort, receive treatment from doctors and physiotherapists in the world's most advanced sports-medicine centre, and practise their moves on turf minutely prepared to resemble the pitches of their opponents' grounds in forthcoming away fixtures.

Under Rizzoli, however, Milan fell into mediocrity in the 1940s, overshadowed not only by the Fiat-funded Juventus and by a great Torino team but by their own offshoot, Inter. The *rossoneri* would not win a fourth title until 1950–51, when three Swedish internationals – Nils Liedholm, Gunnar Gren and Gunnar Nordahl – galvanized the team, the three of them amassing sixty league goals between them in the season. They won the championship again in 1954–55, after Schiaffino had replaced Gren and Cesare Maldini had arrived from Trieste; once more after Nordahl's departure in 1956–57; and again in 1958–59, with Schiaffino now scoring the goals. And after they had finished second, four points behind Juventus, in Rivera's first season, Nereo Rocco arrived to take charge of the coaching, under Viani's direction.

Now began the golden period of Milan's *rinascimento*. In Rivera's second season they won the title, with the assistance of nine goals in the first ten games of the season – five in open play and four penalties – from Jimmy Greaves, the quicksilver English forward purchased from Chelsea. Greaves nevertheless failed to settle in Italy and was back in London, where he joined Tottenham Hotspur, before Christmas. His place alongside Altafini was filled by a Brazilian, Dino Sani, as Milan cruised to the title, five points ahead of Internazionale. Rivera's ten goals from thirty league matches provided valuable support to Altafini, whose twenty-two made him Italy's joint top scorer. Their success put Milan back into the European Cup, a competition in which they had been threatening to excel.

In 1955–56, the inaugural season of the tournament for champion clubs, they had reached the semi-final but lost by an aggregate score of 6–3 over two legs to Real Madrid, the eventual winners. Two years later they had met the same opponents in a thrilling final in Brussels, going down 3–2 to a goal from Francisco Gento in extra time. In 1960 Benfica had beaten them soundly at home and away in the first round. Now, however, they were ready to become the first Italian club to break the Iberian monopoly. US Luxembourg were their first victims, 14–0 on aggregate with eight goals for Altafini, followed by Alf Ramsey's Ipswich Town, Galatasaray and, in the semi-final, Dundee, for whom Alan Gilzean, later to link up with Greaves in the Tottenham attack, scored a vain winner at home in the second leg before getting himself sent off.

The final was against Benfica, winners in the previous two years, at Wembley, which seemed a good omen for Milan in the light of the club's English ancestry. Wearing an all-white strip that made them resemble Real Madrid, the five-times winners of the trophy, they went behind after eighteen minutes when Eusebio raced through in the inside-right position to collect a pass from José Torres, the tall centre forward, before hitting a perfect shot across Giorgio Ghezzi, the goalkeeper, and inside the far post. Viani and Rocco had dropped a winger, Paolo Barison, in order to stiffen the midfield and specifically to reduce the effectiveness of Mario Coluna, Benfica's captain and midfield hub. The ploy worked,

57

although not without a measure of skulduggery, and gradually Milan began to discomfort the holders. Thirteen minutes into the second half Rivera prodded a short pass that was deflected off a defender's leg into the path of Altafini, who scored with alacrity. Eight minutes later the same duo gave Milan victory, Rivera taking advantage of confusion among Benfica's defenders in the centre circle and sliding a pass through for Altafini, who had timed his break across the halfway line perfectly. The Brazilian hit his first shot against the goalkeeper Costa Pereira, but had better fortune from the rebound. Milan had won their first European trophy, held high by Maldini as their celebrating fans spilled on to the Wembley turf. The Golden Boy, still only nineteen years old, had done his stuff.

A year after Rivera's arrival at San Siro, Milan's other club welcomed their own prodigy. The elder by nine months, Alessandro Mazzola made his début for Internazionale in June 1961, at the age of eighteen, when his team lost 9–1 to Juventus and he scored their solitary goal. There would be only one more appearance in the first team in the following season, but he had become a regular by the time he and Rivera confronted each other in a Milan derby for the first time in February 1963. Mazzola scored in the first minute, and not until twelve minutes from time could the *rossoneri* find an equalizer, through the efforts of Sani. That year Mazzola played twenty-three matches in Serie A and scored ten goals; he was on the way to becoming the star of a side that recaptured their championship from Milan that spring and went on to become one of the most controversial and significant teams of the decade.

Mazzola was what Italians call a *figlio d'arte*: a boy who follows his father's profession. Valentino Mazzola, one of the outstanding Italian footballers of the 1940s, played for his factory team at Alfa Romeo in Turin as a teenager just before the war and for Venezia after being drafted into the Italian navy in 1939. With his new club he won the Coppa Italia in 1942, making his first appearance in Italy's colours the same year and scoring on his international début. A struggle between Torino and Juventus for his services ended in favour of the former, who handed over 200,000 lire and two players to Venezia.

Sandro was born on 8 November 1942, a few weeks after his parents' arrival in Turin, to be joined just over two years later by a baby brother, Ferruccio, named after the president of Torino. With his new club Valentino Mazzola scaled the heights of Italian football, winning the Serie A title in 1942–43 and then again, following two years in which no championship was organized, in 1945–46, 1946–47, 1947–48 and 1948–49, breaking records all the way. In 1947–48, for instance, they beat Milan to the title by an unprecedented nineteen points; the following year the margin was a mere fifteen points. So dominant were Torino that on 11 May 1947 they provided ten of the eleven players who represented Italy against Hungary in Turin and won 3–2, thereby inflicting one of only a very few defeats suffered by Ferenc Puskás's Magyars in the years immediately after the war. Mazzola's influence as captain was immense. 'He alone is half the team,' his teammate Mario Rigamonti said. 'The other half is made up by the rest of us together.' But on 4 May 1949, as the Torino squad was returning home from an exhibition match in Lisbon, their chartered aeroplane crashed into the side of the Superga mountain, which rises above the city of Turin on the far bank of the River Po. Everyone on board – players, coaches, support staff, journalists and aircrew – was killed, leaving only a single first-team player, who had remained behind for treatment to an injury, alive. All Italy mourned, and Turin came to a halt as tens of thousands gathered to watch the funeral. The legend of *Il Grande Torino* was born, along with that of their unforgettable captain.

Valentino Mazzola had divorced his first wife in 1946 and,

after marrying again, gained custody of little Sandro, who was only six years old when his father died. Even at that age, however, he had absorbed lessons from his famous dad; as he grew up, his destiny became obvious. Torino, however, would not be a part of it. There had been certain problems over the club's treatment of the surviving families; even aside from that matter, the son wisely refused to expose himself to such a direct comparison with an incomparable father. He and Ferruccio signed with Internazionale, and although the younger brother would not make an impact, gradually Sandro became every bit as influential in the blue and black stripes of Inter as his father had been in the maroon of Torino.

The club he joined already had a reputation for espousing the defensive tactic known as *catenaccio*, or the 'Swiss bolt'. Instead of four defenders, *catenaccio* proposed the use of five, the extra man operating as a *libero*, or free man, behind the two centre backs, ready to deal with any attacker who managed to make it past his markers. Invented by a Swiss coach, Karl Rappan, it was a formula designed not to make football more enjoyable to watch but to secure results. And its most celebrated prophet was Helenio Herrera, born in Argentina to Spanish immigrants and brought up in Casablanca and Paris, but indelibly associated with Italy and its football.

Herrera arrived from Barcelona in 1960. Inter finished third in his first season, second the next year and first in his third year. By that time he was known as *Il Mago*, the magician, and had built a side full of distinguished players: the full backs Tarcisio Burgnich and Giacinto Facchetti, the elusive Brazilian winger Jair, the veteran midfield general Luis Suárez from Spain (where he had played for Barcelona under Herrera), the tough little sweeper Armando Picchi. And, of course, Mazzola, young and dark and wearing a bandit's moustache, quite tall and skinny and not refined in the manner of Rivera but a cultured player for all that, swift, alert and quite capable of holding his own, as he did in his early days with Inter, at the point of the attack. Eventually Mazzola settled down to invent the game from the inside-right position, but it was he who scored the first and third goals for his side in the 1964 European Cup final, when Inter's 3–1 defeat of Real Madrid in Vienna's Prater stadium enabled them to emulate Milan's feat of the previous season. A year later they repeated the achievement, although there was little applause for the way they beat Benfica on a rainwashed night at San Siro when a shot from Jair passed under Costa Pereira's dive for the only goal of the game. Two years later, when they reached the final again, Jair had gone and Suárez was injured, and they lost to Celtic, a half-fit Mazzola scoring from the penalty spot in reply to goals from Tommy Gemmell and Steve Chalmers for a side whose eleven players all came from within a thirty-mile radius of Glasgow.

By the time Milan won the *scudetto* again, in 1967–68, Rivera was in his second season as captain, having taken over when Maldini left for Torino, leaving, as the club history put it, 'the memory of a gentleman footballer, a player with a clean game, with a sense of style, who nevertheless always observed his defensive duties'. Supervised by Rocco, this was another classic multinational Milan team, and they attacked the 1968–69 European Cup with the tall, cadaverous Fabio Cudicini in goal, the German international Karl-Heinz Schnellinger at left back, Giovanni Trapattoni winning the ball for Rivera in midfield, the experienced Swedish winger Kurt Hamrin and, up front, the duo of the twenty-two-year-old Pierino Prati and the Brazilian veteran Angelo Sormani. In the semi-final at San Siro they beat Manchester United, the holders, 2–0 with goals from Sormani and Hamrin; back at Old Trafford, United's fans believed the chemistry of Charlton, Law and Best would be enough to overturn the deficit. It wasn't, and Milan went through 2–1 on aggregate. In the final, staged in Madrid, they held back football's new wave by thrashing Ajax of Amsterdam, the young Johan Cruyff and all, by four goals to one. There was a hat-trick for Prati, two of the goals coming from Rivera's passes.

Gianni Rivera and Sandro Mazzola had followed parallel paths. In the summer of 1970, however, their destinies became inextricably intertwined when Italy set off for the World Cup finals in Mexico, hoping to add a long-awaited third victory to the triumphs of 1934 and 1938. At eighteen, Rivera had travelled to the 1962 finals in Chile, playing in only one match, a goalless draw with West Germany, as the squad failed to make it to the knockout stages. Both men had gone to England with the *Azzurri* in 1966 and had played together in the 2–0 defeat of Chile in their first match. Mazzola had scored the opening goal and was retained for the next fixture, against the USSR, which Italy lost 1–0. Rivera, left out of that match, rejoined Mazzola for the third and final group game, against North Korea at Middlesbrough's Ayresome Park, expecting a straightforward victory to see them through to the quarter-finals. But it was Rivera who was robbed by Pak Doo-Ik, the Korean inside left, three minutes before half-time, the *Bambino d'Oro* watching in horror as his opponent hit a low cross-shot which left Albertosi helpless in the Italian goal. To the glee of the Middlesbrough crowd, the Italians were out; on arrival back home, they were met with a volley of rotten vegetables.

Ferruccio Valcareggi had taken over as coach after the North Korea debacle, at first in tandem with Herrera, but the arrangement did not last. By the time the 1970 World Cup finals came around he was working alone and had built a highly impressive side largely around the established stars of the city of Milan's two European Cup-winning sides, adding two dangerous attackers, Luigi Riva and Angelo Domenghini, from the Cagliari side that had brought euphoria to Sardinia by winning the Serie A title that spring. A former player, he had begun his career with Trieste, his hometown club, before moving to Fiorentina and, later, Bologna. After a successful return to Florence as coach, he was offered the job with the national team and embarked immediately on a successful campaign in the 1968 European Championships, held in Italy. Valcareggi's team eventually made the most of home advantage, but not until they had eliminated the USSR in Naples on the toss of a coin after extra time had failed to settle a goalless draw, Facchetti calling 'tails' as the referee's coin spun in the air. It was, thank goodness, the only time a major match has been decided in this manner. Italy's excuse was that although Rivera and Mazzola were both on the field when the match kicked off, the former was taken off with an injury in the first half, leaving his teammates a man short for the remainder of the game. Rivera missed the final, in which Italy and Yugoslavia drew 1–1 before the home side took the replay 2–0, with Mazzola prompting from a position behind the strikers. This was a foreshadowing of what was to come in Mexico.

Rivera was unquestionably the more famous of the two, and his smooth acceptance of his own celebrity sometimes inspired less than generous feelings among his contemporaries. But no one doubted his talent. In 1963, aged nineteen, he had been runner-up to Lev Yashin, Russia's great goalkeeper, as *France Football*'s European player of the year. Six years later he won the award, the *Ballon d'Or*, outright, the first Italian to do so, ahead of Gerd Müller and Johan Cruyff. Yet barely a year after that award Valcareggi could not find a place for him in Italy's starting line-up. As he agonized over his belief that the two men could not fit into the same midfield, the coach made plain his preference for the more self-effacing talent of Mazzola. The Internazionale player started in Italy's first two games in Mexico, a pallid 1–0 defeat of Sweden and a dispiriting goalless draw against Uruguay, in which the shared defensive mentality of both sides brought out the worst in each other. Against Israel in the final group match, Valcareggi reacted to a blank scoreboard at half-time by bringing on Rivera to join Mazzola, but the gesture failed to produce the goods.

Frustrated by the inability of Riva and Domenghini to score, and under pressure to make use of Rivera's talent, Valcareggi devised a formula by which he hoped to keep everyone happy. It was called the *staffetta*, the relay, and it involved replacing Mazzola with Rivera at half-time, giving each man forty-five minutes in which to control the match. He tried it for the first time in the quarter-final, against the hosts in Toluca, making the switch at half-time, as scheduled, after an own goal by Javier Guzmán had given Italy a goal to match the one scored by José Luis González in the early minutes. On came Rivera, and suddenly the goals came, too. Riva got a pair, the first of them with a characteristic left-footed shot inside the far post, and Rivera put his own name on the scoresheet after going round the goalkeeper. The *staffetta* was off and running.

Valcareggi stuck to the script in the semi-final against West Germany in Mexico City, although 102,444 witnesses could attest that no one else did. This was one of the most unexpectedly tumultuous matches in the history of the competition. Italy were apparently cruising to a 1–0 victory, thanks to Roberto Boninsegna's eighth-minute goal and the expected quota of cynical defending, when Schnellinger, the former Milan defender, arrived to volley home Jürgen Grabowski's cross in the last minute of normal time. Now Beckenbauer, the victim of many fouls, was playing with an injured shoulder, his arm strapped to his chest. Gerd Müller put the Germans ahead four minutes into extra time, Burgnich equalized four minutes later, and Riva put Italy back into the lead with another typical cross-shot a minute before the end of the first half of extra time, only for Müller to give his team new hope when Rivera, marking the near post at a corner, failed to clear the striker's glancing header and watched it bobble into the net. With ten minutes to go, the Golden Boy set out to repair the damage. From the restart Boninsegna took the ball down the wing and beat Willi Schulz, an ageing defender, before sending in a cross that Rivera, unmarked, met with a calm and precise sidefooted shot into the middle of the goal, outwitting Sepp Maier's desperate dive. As West Germany reeled, Italy prepared to hold on; soon they were in their first World Cup final for thirty-two years.

Rivera's reward was to learn that Valcareggi planned to start the final against Brazil in what had become the customary way, with Mazzola as the midfield general. Given the outcome of the semi-final, he might have expected to have been granted at least forty-five minutes on the biggest stage in world football. But when midsummer's day came, Valcareggi lacked the courage the pursue his own strategy. After Italy and Brazil had come in at half-time with the score locked at 1–1, the coach gave way to the conservatism that so often afflicts Italian football, stifling its creative instincts in the search for success. Mazzola, Italy's most effective player, stayed on the pitch, while Rivera kicked his heels on the bench. Italy were helpless to reverse the momentum of the afternoon as Gérson and Jairzinho scored the goals that Brazil's wonderful football demanded. When a substitute did appear, the first ever in a World Cup final, it was Antonio Juliano, who had no impact on Italy's fortunes. Finally, with six minutes to go and Italy 3–1 down, Valcareggi sent on Rivera. By that time, however, Brazil's momentum had acquired a kind of irresistible moral force; who in the world, apart from 50 million Italians, would have wanted them to lose this match now? And two minutes later Tostão's brilliance allowed Pelé to set up Carlos Alberto for the shot heard around the world, the one that sealed Brazil's third championship. Together on the pitch, where many people believed they should have been all along, Rivera and Mazzola were united in their disappointment.

In West Germany four years later even Valcareggi seemed to agree. The two of them started Italy's opening match of the 1974 finals, against Haiti in Munich, and Rivera scored the first of Italy's three goals after their opponents had taken the lead a minute into the second half, evoking for a few minutes the spectre of North Korea. But this was an ageing and poorly balanced Italy side, and when an exhausted Rivera was substituted after sixty-six minutes of the 1–1 draw with Argentina, it marked the end of his international career; he had become the only Italian to appear in the final rounds of four World Cups. Needing only a draw against Poland, Valcareggi's team lost 2–1 in Rivera's absence and despite a wholehearted display from Mazzola. By 1978's tournament they would both be gone.

Controversy had never frightened Rivera. In the 1960s he attacked the philosophy of Herrera's Internazionale; he abhorred *catenaccio*, and was not afraid to say so. In 1970 he was publicly critical of Walter Mandelli, the supervisor of the *Azzurri*, who had fomented a press campaign to include Mazzola in the side at Rivera's expense. He had taken a leading role in the establishment of a players' union in Italy and, by the mid-1970s, his position at AC Milan was so strong that when the president, Albino Buttichi, talked about swapping him with Claudio Sala, Torino's centre forward, Rivera responded by threatening to retire rather than leave San Siro. In the end it was Buttichi who went, and at one point Rivera was on the brink of accepting the presidency in his place. Instead he reversed his decision, pulled on the team's shirt once more and stayed for a further three seasons. And, as the French say, *il finit en beauté*, leading Milan to the 1978–79 championship, their first for eleven years, and acquiring his third Serie A winners' medal in the process. For his final match at San Siro, against Bologna, so many people turned up that several thousand of them spilled into a section of a stand that had been closed for renovations; when Rivera took a microphone and told them that the match could not start until the section was cleared, they demonstrated their respect for him by moving quietly away. He had appeared in 501 league matches for Milan, scoring 122 goals; in all there had been 658 matches for the club and 164 goals. He had become Milan's *bandiera*, the name given by Italians to a player who symbolizes his club. Years later that honour would pass to the son of Cesare Maldini, but not even the great Paolo, whose career eventually surpassed Rivera's in terms of longevity and trophies, would claim that he did more to adorn Milan's image.

Now Rivera accepted a vice-president's role at the club, which carried an executive function, but over the next few years Milan's fortunes were blighted by a betting scandal, relegation and financial troubles. When the media magnate Silvio Berlusconi took over in 1986, inaugurating a new cycle of success, Rivera declined the suggestion that he might care to make way for the incoming president's men and become chairman of the supporters' club. Instead he left and stood for election to the Italian parliament, where he served for four terms and became a respected under-secretary for defence in the centre-left coalition government headed by Romano Prodi. When his political career drew to a close, as Berlusconi's Forza Italia party gathered strength and took power, he became the host of a popular regional television talk show.

Bobby Charlton scored the only goal of the night, and Denis Law had one chance that he believed crossed the line, but Fabio Cudicini, clad all in black, excelled himself and became the star of the match, at least to Milanisti *and neutrals. Despite being hit on the head by an object thrown from the Stretford End terraces, the gaunt-featured Cudicini extended his telescopic limbs around his goalmouth to such effect that this was the night he earned the nickname of* Il Ragno Nero *(the black spider). Overall, however, it was far from being a classic match, and for that the home team had to bear the majority of the blame. George Best, so outstanding in the final rounds a year earlier against Real Madrid and Benfica, could do little against Milan's efficient marking; there was also a niggly undercurrent set off by the suspicions harboured by British footballers whenever they came up against Italian teams. Only Law, who had spent a season with Torino, was worldly enough to give a resigned smile after Roberto Rosato, his old teammate from the Stadio Filadelfia, had kicked him off the ball or taken a fistful of his shirt and held him down whenever he looked likely to get on the end of a cross or a corner kick from Best or Willie Morgan. The crowd took it all badly and left in a mood of grim resentment that I would recognize more than thirty years later, when the Milan of Paolo Maldini, Andrea Pirlo, Kakà and Hernan Crespo returned to Old Trafford and removed United from the renamed Champions League. While my companions nursed their bitterness on the silent drive home, I hugged a different thought to myself. I had seen Gianni Rivera.*

4 Günter Netzer

Professional footballers were slow to get the message of the revolution wrought on the streets of England, and later around the world, by the Beatles and their followers in the mid-1960s. When Alf Ramsey's team won the World Cup in the last week of July 1966, the pop charts were occupied by Chris Farlowe's 'Out of Time', the Troggs' 'With a Girl Like You' and the Kinks' 'Sunny Afternoon', each representative of a new and freer way of life and the styles of behaviour and appearance that went with it. Yet the players – even the English boys, who had been living for a couple of years amid the exhilarating turmoil of Carnaby Street and *Ready, Steady, Go* – still looked like bank clerks and bus conductors who went home at night and listened to the Light Programme while eating a corned-beef supper washed down with a cup of tea. Not one of them gave the impression that he was in the habit of dancing to the sounds of Motown and Stax, which were filling the country's discotheques. Among the stars of the English first division, George Best's Beatle cut still made him the exception; and his non-conformity was considered so dangerous that Willie Morgan, Manchester United's other winger, once tried to get himself some good publicity through arranging for his picture to be taken for the newspapers while in the barber's chair. By having his own moptop transformed into a short back and sides, Morgan hoped to set a better example to the nation's youth. It must have been his agent's idea; or so one hopes. And although players as uncompromisingly hard as Norman Hunter and Peter Storey eventually let their fringes and sideburns grow, it was not until 1972 that we saw a footballer who looked as cool as Best, and then some. And to back it up, Günter Netzer was fully Best's equal with the ball.

When Netzer orchestrated West Germany's demolition of England at Wembley that year, it was the most traumatic home defeat for the hosts since the 6–3 beating inflicted by the Hungarians nineteen years earlier. And if Puskás's team brought the stately edifice of the English game crashing to the ground, Netzer and his colleagues proved that the subsequent rebuilding work would certainly not withstand the force of an earthquake.

It came as such a seismic shock first of all because Germany – East, West or pre-war – had never won, or even forced a draw, in England. A team representing Hitler's Germany had lost 3–0 at White Hart Lane in 1935, West Germany lost at Wembley in 1954 and 1–0 at the same venue in a friendly in February 1966, and on returning to Wembley five months later they were beaten 4–2 after extra time in the final of the World Cup, allowing English football to experience its greatest triumph. Of course the Germans were accepted as worthy rivals; perhaps the worthiest of all, because (unlike the Italians or the Argentinians, particularly) the game they played was recognizably similar to ours, in speed and style and in its attitude to physical confrontation. But even as Alf Ramsey's reign was drawing to its close, the English were in no doubt about their capacity to win again, and expected to do so when Helmut Schön, the manager in both 1966 and 1970, brought his team to Wembley for the first leg of the quarter-final of the 1972 European Championship, in the days when only the last four gathered for the final rounds in a host country.

So along came Günter Netzer, with his long, dirty-blond hair (like someone attempting to impersonate Brian Jones of the Rolling Stones, but getting the parting wrong), his fashionably abbreviated shorts, which exposed his powerful legs, and his gift for sublime passing, particularly from withdrawn positions and over long distances. (The title of his autobiography,

Aus der Tiefe des Raumes, seems to refer to that particular gift: it translates as 'From the depth of space'.) Most English football fans had never heard of him, not being terribly conversant with the struggle for the soul of German football then going on between his Borussia Mönchengladbach team and Franz Beckenbauer's Bayern Munich. They had memories of Beckenbauer, all right, starting with 1966, when the clean-cut young midfielder had cantered upfield to score twice in his team's opening 5–0 defeat of Switzerland. He scored again in both the quarter-final against Uruguay and the semi-final against the USSR, but in the final he was given the job of marking Bobby Charlton, which meant that neither of them exerted much impact on that historic match. By 1970 he was an even more mature player, although his only goal of the tournament came when, with Germany trailing 2–0 to England in the quarter-final in León, he left Charlton to his own devices, cut past Alan Mullery and shot under the body of the diving Peter Bonetti to set his side on the way to a famous recovery. Other names on the 1972 team sheet were also familiar. Horst-Dieter Höttges, the right back, dated from 1966, as did Sigi Held, the winger, who had won the free kick from which Wolfgang Weber eventually scored the goal that took the final into extra time. The English also had good reason to remember Jürgen Grabowski, the winger sent on as a substitute by Schön in the 1970 match and the provider of the cross from which Gerd Müller hooked home the winner. Müller himself, now established as Europe's deadliest marksman, was present again, as was Sepp Maier, the 1970 goalkeeper. The new names were Paul Breitner at left back, Georg Schwarzenbeck at centre back (partnered by Beckenbauer), and Uli Hoeness and Herbert Wimmer in midfield. And Netzer.

England saw little reason to worry as they approached the kick-off on the evening of Saturday 29 April. They had qualified for the quarter-finals with ease, winning five of their six matches against Greece, Malta and Switzerland. Here was a chance to take revenge for León. Ramsey, too, retained some of the boys of '66: Moore, the captain, still only twenty-five; Gordon Banks and Geoff Hurst, both nearing the end of their careers; Alan Ball; and Martin Peters, well ahead of his career schedule, if one accepted the coach's remark, at the time of the World Cup victory, that he was 'ten years ahead of his time'. Alongside Moore in the back four were Paul Madeley and Norman Hunter of Don Revie's formidable Leeds United and Emlyn Hughes of Bill Shankly's Liverpool; the Manchester City thoroughbred Colin Bell took the place of the retired Bobby Charlton in midfield; and Hurst was flanked by City's Francis Lee and Tottenham's Martin Chivers. Apart from Roy McFarland, required by Brian Clough for an important Derby County fixture two days later, this was Ramsey's first-choice side, and it must have looked good enough to do the job of establishing a lead to take to Berlin two weeks later.

By half-time, when the emerald-green-shirted visitors led 1–0, the England players may have had more than a suspicion that they were facing an unusually distinguished West German side. Subsequently there seems to have been a consensus that it was in fact the best of all time and that this match ushered in its finest flowering. Throughout the first period they repeatedly cut England to pieces, with Netzer at the heart of their strategy. Commanding the centre of midfield, with Wimmer, his skilful Mönchengladbach lieutenant, on one side and Bayern's Hoeness, a strong and direct wing half in the old style, on the other, Netzer showed himself equally capable of directing searching passes to a front-runner and of carrying the ball himself at speed across the rain-slicked surface and into the heart of the opposition, drawing defenders before off-loading the ball to his forwards. Other Germans, too, were drawing attention to their virtues. Although there was nothing unexpected about the menace of Müller and the suaveness of Beckenbauer, at least one of their players seemed to have taken a leap into football's next dimension. With his exaggerated Afro hair and his socks pushed down around his ankles, Paul Breitner lacked nothing in visual distinction to go with the rumours that he was a student of the teachings of Mao Tse-Tung, but he also seemed to be setting new standards in adventurous full-back play, joining the attacks with no sense of inferiority, as Cafu and Roberto Carlos would one day do in Brazil's colours. Breitner was part of the surge towards Total Football, the fruit of Rinus Michels' coaching work at Ajax; this was Germany's response to that Dutch initiative, and already it made England's method look obsolete.

But it was a mistake by the once impeccable Moore that got West Germany on their way with the match half an hour old. Unfathomably, England's captain played the ball to Müller inside his own area and was helpless as the striker switched it to Held, whose quick pass to Hoeness provoked a firm shot that left Banks without a prayer. This was scant reward for forty-five minutes in which the Germans had attacked from every angle, putting together flowing moves that needed only the final touch to bring their due reward.

England did better in the second half, although their football still looked rudimentary by comparison with the stylish stuff the Germans had unveiled before the interval. Yet they got their reward when, with twenty minutes to go, Bell made head-way down the inside-right channel, leaving Netzer loitering in his wake before hitting a powerful low shot that Maier could only palm out to Lee, who nudged it home from point-blank range.

If Ramsey's players imagined that West Germany would set-tle for a draw away from home, they were greatly mistaken. Schön had sent them out in a 4–3–3 formation with a clear attacking intent, and England's equalizer only revived their interest. When Rodney Marsh, on as a substitute for Hurst, lost the ball in the opposition area, the counter-attack came swiftly. Müller prodded the clearance on to Held, who took on Moore in a race towards goal and fell under his tackle as they entered the area. Needing no summons, Netzer stepped forward and knelt down to place the ball on the penalty spot with the care and delicacy of a snooker referee re-spotting the black or Tiger Woods replacing his ball on the green before making a putt. Or, more literally, with exactly the same painstaking routine used thirty years later by David Beckham. Netzer's shot was just about perfect, hit low and hard to the goalkeeper's right. Only Banks's brilliant anticipation allowed him to get both palms to the ball, one behind the other, but even then his effort was good enough only to push it on to the inside of the post on its way into the net.

Back in the lead, West Germany used the last five minutes to seal their win. By the time Hughes failed to control Banks's throw and lost the ball to Held, England were beyond recovery. Hoeness took up possession and found Müller, who twisted between a pair of immobile defenders and, using his marvellous instinct for the geometry of the penalty area, hit a low shot on the turn past Banks's right hand. All around Wembley, and in front of television sets from one end of the country to the other, the message was beginning to sink in. If the Germans could play like this, 1966 meant nothing. England were back where they had been in 1953, watching another nation play the game with an entirely superior technique and grasp of tactics. The ball looked like it belonged to the Germans; to England, it was a stranger. When they tried to control it, it bounced off them. Their passing was banal. By comparison with the economy of a Beckenbauer or a Müller, their physical exertions looked pathetic. And there was, of course, no one remotely like Günter Netzer in the England team, since Netzer was exactly the kind of player that successive England coaches have tried to eliminate from the game by doubting their physical capacity, their competitive instinct, their psychological commitment, their intrinsic worth.

Two weeks later England went to Berlin and sank even lower. Ramsey brought McFarland back into the central defence alongside Moore, pushed Hunter into midfield and paired him with Peter Storey, Arsenal's hatchet man. Needing to score goals and win, the manager had acted according to his own worst instincts. Presumably trying to salvage a shred of English pride by securing a dour draw against more gifted opponents, he unveiled the most negative strategy ever adopted by an England manager, one that showed the consequences of adopting a siege mentality. Those Englishmen who had found it difficult to support their footballers against teams featuring players such as Puskás or Netzer suddenly felt themselves justified. When push came to shove, England reverted to a ghastly stereotype. Now kick-and-run started with kicking your opponent as Storey and Hunter, and others, left their mark on the Germans, and Netzer, in particular. 'The whole England team,' he said afterwards, 'has autographed my leg.'

At the end of a hideous goalless draw, from which England neither sought nor deserved to profit, the Germans were justifiably disdainful of what they had been forced to endure. Beckenbauer's lofty profession of 'disappointment' was even more crushing than his manager's condemnation of 'brutal tackling'. The English football journalists were embarrassed by what Ramsey had wrought in the nation's name. It seemed that when England were faced with the kind of glow that Netzer had cast upon the game, his performance doubling the intensity of the Wembley floodlights, the only response was to retreat. There was nothing to be learnt, it seemed, from such a display.

But then again, even Helmut Schön could not always bring himself to accept the kind of player Günter Netzer represented. The venerable coach treated his expressive style with deep suspicion, as coaches of his ilk always have. What they want is consistency and predictability. They want to know that their carefully prepared tactics are not likely to be upset by the activities of one of their own men. They want things to go according to plan. But players of Netzer's type specialize in the unpredictable; that is what makes them so dangerous. The opposition cannot legislate for their waywardness. No defensive scheme, however sophisticated, is proof against their sudden flights of fancy. By instinct, they know which brick will bring the whole structure crashing down. And sometimes, as is the way of things, their inspiration goes missing. If the genius happens to be a painter or a composer, he simply takes the day off and goes fishing, to return the next day with his imagination refreshed and appetite reawakened. For a footballer, however, the imperatives are different: in a team sport, such respite cannot be permitted. The imagination and the appetite must be summoned at a quarter to eight on a Wednesday night, or the coach's blueprint is so much waste paper.

Netzer might have gone to the 1970 World Cup, had he not been suffering from an injury; only a series of pain-killing injections had allowed him to play through the final weeks of the league season. It seems unlikely, however, that he would have displaced Wolfgang Overath, another veteran of 1966 and a more reliable performer when it came to keeping the midfield ticking over. But by 1972 Netzer's talent had made him impossible to ignore or to discard.

He was born in Mönchengladbach on 14 September 1944, in the cellar of a hospital. Bombing raids were taking place on the town, which lies on the western extremity of Germany, close to the border with Holland. From his first club, FC Mönchengladbach, he moved on to Borussia. There he fell under the influence of Hennes Weisweiler, a coach who had been an obdurate defender during his playing career with Cologne but who, on graduating to the coach's seat, revealed a deep-seated yearning to promote all-out attacking play, fed by his enthusiasm for the English approach. Under Weisweiler, Borussia became synonymous with attractive football that encouraged risk-taking. As assistant to Sepp Herberger, the long-serving coach to the national team, in 1954–55, he might well have succeeded to the job. But he opted for a life in club football, leaving the opportunity to Schön. In 1964 he moved to Mönchengladbach, bringing his enthusiasms to bear on a club whose history stretched back to 1900; by making shrewd use of locally produced young players, he brought them promotion to the Bundesliga in his first season. Down in southern Germany a young Yugoslav coach named Zlatko Cajkovski was doing something very similar with Bayern Munich; promoted in the same season, the two clubs became locked in a rivalry that would occupy West German football fans for the next decade.

Where Cajkovski put his faith in young players such as Beckenbauer, Maier, Schwarzenbeck and Müller, Weisweiler found Vogts, Wimmer, Heynckes and Netzer. As they achieved their first successes, the average age of both teams was twenty-one. But that seemed to be just about the only way in which the two teams resembled each other. In *Tor!*, his history of German football, Ulrich Hesse-Lichtenberger writes about how the rivalry between the two clubs intensified in 1968, when revolutionary politics entered the nation's agenda. Borussia versus Bayern was not a simple question of left versus right or even good versus not-so-good, but the clubs symbolized the mood of polarization at a turbulent time. And, of course, Netzer versus Beckenbauer could certainly be read, very simplistically indeed, as an opposition of two philosophies: inspiration verses efficiency, self-expression versus discipline, hippie versus straight.

Deceptively, Beckenbauer always looked – to English eyes, at least – like the paradigm of the middle-class professional footballer, a species unknown in the British Isles. Yet it was Netzer who came from a comfortable bourgeois family. His father, Christian, was a seed merchant in Mönchengladbach, while his mother, Barbara, ran a corner shop. They had the means to bring their son up in comfort and even to give him and his childhood friends a small piece of land to use as a foot-

79

ball pitch. From that background, Netzer said, came his self-confidence.

Weisweiler and Netzer were not always in accord. The coach wanted the team to race forward at every opportunity, like the English he so admired; the player believed there were times when the team should pause and reflect. Netzer's gift for making an instant appreciation of his colleagues' movements and a technique that allowed him to hit accurate passes over fifty or sixty yards from deep positions meant Borussia were most effective as a counter-attacking force. Thanks in large measure to his inspiration, they won the Bundesliga in 1969–70 and 1970–71, becoming the first club ever to win back-to-back championships in Germany. It was typical of their rivalry that, over the next three seasons, Bayern became the first club to achieve a hat-trick. Once Borussia qualified for the European Cup, however, they proved slow to learn the tricks of winning two-legged ties. Their first opponents in 1970, EPA Larnaca of Cyprus, were dismissed by an aggregate score of 16–0, only for Netzer and his colleagues to go out to Everton after a pair of 1–1 draws, the outcome settled by the new penalty shoot-out system. Having qualified for the tournament once again the following season, they beat Cork Hibernians 7–1 on aggregate in the first round but then found themselves embroiled in one of the most extraordinary ties ever played in the competition. At home, on 21 October 1971, they thrashed Internazionale – the team of defensive specialists, their mastery of *catenaccio* under Helenio Herrera twice making them winners of the competition – by no fewer than seven goals to one in Mönchengladbach's Bökelberg stadium after the Italian team had been reduced to nine men, Netzer scoring twice, with a free kick and a brilliant chip. Yet Borussia were not allowed to enjoy this singular triumph. Roberto Boninsegna, the Italian club's international striker, had been hit in the throat by an empty drink can thrown from among the spectators, leading UEFA to nullify the tie and order it to be replayed in Berlin. The return leg, in Milan, saw Borussia go down 4–2, and when the replayed first leg ended in a goalless draw, Netzer's team were out of the competition.

After missing his chance to make an impact on the international stage in 1970, Netzer was offered an opportunity by the 1972 European Championships. The two quarter-final ties against England had alerted the continent to what it was about to witness in Belgium, where the semi-finals and final would take place. 'We had an incredible squad,' Uli Hoeness remembered, 'with big personalities – Franz Beckenbauer, Günter Netzer, Gerd Müller, Paul Breitner.' Beckenbauer himself believed that the match at Wembley was the turning point in the team's fortunes. 'It was the first time a German team had won on an English ground,' he said. 'It made us think, "Well, if we can beat England at Wembley, we can beat anybody."'

While this may have been rather more of a compliment than England deserved, and may seem distinctly odd to subsequent generations not reared on the expectation of English success, Beckenbauer's view is not to be dismissed. Two years earlier the West German players had tried to persuade Schön to let them take it easy in a group match in Mexico so that they might face Brazil rather than England in the quarter-finals. History must indeed have cast a powerful spell if the Brazil of Pelé, Jairzinho, Gérson, Tostão and Rivelino could be judged less formidable than Ramsey's 1970 squad.

Meeting the host nation in Antwerp in the semi-final of the 1972 European Championships, Netzer produced a master class in the art of No. 10 play. In the first half he chipped the ball to the near post, where Müller jumped in front of his marker, Jean Thissen, to glance a fine header over the goalkeeper, Christian Piot, who had left his line, hesitated and foundered in no man's land. In the second half Netzer launched a typically searching long pass from just inside his own half, finding the gap between Belgium's two central defenders and inviting Müller to glide in from the blind side before swivelling to score with a deceptively simple shot from twelve yards out. These were goals that seemed straightforward but were poetry to anyone relishing the combination of vision and economy that characterized the work of both partners in the creation of these small masterpieces. Belgium secured a consolation goal, but West Germany were through to face the USSR, the winners of the inaugural tournament in 1960 and beaten finalists four years later.

A crowd of 44,000, almost all of whom had made the journey across the German border into Belgium, filled the Heysel stadium in Brussels and saw the Germans take the lead with a goal that summed up many of the virtues of their football. First Beckenbauer made ground into the Soviet Union's half before prodding the ball up to Müller. When the centre forward laid it back, Netzer hit the bar with a screaming volley from twenty yards, his boot striking the ball at about waist height. As the ball came down, a defender's head managed a half clearance. It fell to Erwin Kremers, and the Schalke winger's instant shot from the right-hand edge of area was parried by the Belgian goalkeeper. As it came loose yet again, Müller's uncanny anticipation and positional sense enabled him to chest it down and poke it home from five yards. Herbert Wimmer doubled the lead with a left-foot shot after Netzer had fed Kremers inside the box. When Müller scored the third to complete the victory, the world knew that Schön had come up with his best side yet, and that Günter Netzer had furnished its creative inspiration.

A year later Netzer was on his way to Real Madrid, having negotiated his own deal – 'There are eleven businessmen on the pitch, each looking after his own interests,' he once said – and ready to be anointed as the long-awaited successor to Alfredo di Stéfano. When Barcelona signed Johan Cruyff, Santiago Bernabéu needed to respond in kind. Netzer was the result. With his girlfriend, a beautiful long-haired goldsmith named

Hannelore Girrulat, he posed for photographers in the trophy room of his new club, looking not remotely overawed. He was no supplicant at the court of Santiago Bernabéu. He already had a Lamborghini Miura, just like Rod Stewart's, and a bar and disco called Lovers' Lane in Mönchengladbach. His apartment was full of modern artefacts and his wardrobe bulged with flared hipster slacks, tight crew-neck jumpers and suede jackets cut in the *blouson* style. His hair kept getting longer, and his shorts shorter.

His departure from Mönchengladbach not only exposed his differences with Weisweiler but illustrated his independence. When he told the coach that he was leaving for Spain, Weisweiler responded by omitting him from the starting eleven to play Cologne in the German cup final. With the score at 1–1 in the second half, Weisweiler invited Netzer to leave the bench and join the match. 'They're doing all right without me,' Netzer replied. After ninety minutes, however, when the players were preparing for extra time, he approached his young replacement, Christian Kulik, who was being treated for cramp. Netzer asked Kulik if he would be able to carry on. When the young man said he could not, Netzer took off his track suit. 'Now I am playing,' he told Weisweiler. And within minutes he had advanced from the centre circle, played the ball to Rainer Bonhof, moved into space to collect the return pass and driven a left-foot shot into the net from fifteen yards: a magisterial gesture of farewell to the spectators who had been chanting his name.

The Di Stéfano/Puskás Madrid of the 1950s had been succeeded by the *ye-ye* squad of the 1960s, featuring such younger men as Amancio, Pirri and Sanchís alongside Gento, the only survivor of the first run of five consecutive European Cups; the teams of the 1970s, however, were harder to characterize. And, to begin with, the new relationship did not go well. Netzer and Miguel Muñoz, Madrid's veteran coach, failed to establish a rapport. Initially, the fans were not impressed by the German player's relaxed style and his tendency to play the game at a strolling pace. They were even less impressed when the team finished his first season in eighth place, their lowest position for a quarter of a century. The nadir arrived one night when Barcelona came to Madrid and, conducted by Cruyff at his most imperious, scored five goals without reply. The *gran clásico* had turned into the *noche negra*. A 4–0 victory over Barça in the final of the Copa del Rey at the end of the season was no consolation; both Cruyff and Netzer were absent, preparing for the World Cup.

For the following season Muñoz was replaced by Miljan Miljanic, a Yugoslav coach whose ideas were much more closely attuned to Netzer's philosophy. Paul Breitner arrived, the Maoist of the Bundesliga signing for a club closely identified with the Fascist regime of General Francisco Franco. Miljanic brought in his own fitness trainer, whose ministrations made an immediate impact on a team that needed to find a way of imposing itself on a game. They regained the title in the spring of 1975 and successfully defended it the following season, which began with the old *Generalissimo*'s death.

Madrid's latest successors as kings of Europe were FC Bayern Munich, enjoying a run of three straight wins in the competition. In the European Cup of 1975–76 Netzer and his colleagues beat Dinamo Bucharest, Derby County (losing 4–1 away and winning 5–1 at home) and – as fate would have it – Borussia Mönchengladbach, their away goals giving them a passage to the semi-finals after a 2–2 draw in Germany and a 1–1 draw in Spain. At the first match, in the Bökelberg stadium, Netzer was vigorously booed by the home fans, who resented his defection. Following the return leg, in the Bernabéu, Borussia's players complained that the referee had disallowed two perfectly good goals; such allegations were rife in the competition in the 1970s, particularly when certain Spanish and Italian teams were involved. Nor were their next opponents, Bayern Munich, any happier after their visit to

Madrid. At the end of another 1–1 draw, the home fans attacked the players of the German team and the referee, knocking Gerd Müller out cold in the melee. Bayern settled the account on their own pitch, Müller scoring both goals in a 2–0 win which put them through to the final, where Saint-Etienne failed to prevent them completing the final leg of their hat-trick. A year later Netzer and his colleagues got no further than the second round, where they were eliminated by FC Bruges, while Borussia Mönchengladbach reached the final, only to be beaten by Liverpool.

When Netzer left Madrid, in the summer of 1976, he was close to his thirty-second birthday and his time at the top was over. His international career had ended, in bathetic circumstances, two years earlier. West Germany had carried on from the European Championship success of 1972 to win the World Cup on home soil two years later, Schön retaining the core of the squad as they progressed to the final in Munich's Olympic stadium. Netzer, however, had long since been sidelined, the coach preferring the more reliable skills of Bonhof and the eternal Overath. There would be one appearance in the 1974 World Cup finals, but it could hardly have been less satisfying or less appropriate to a player of such resplendent gifts. In a group match in Hamburg's Volksparkstadion, West and East Germany were playing each other for the first time in their bifurcated history. West Germany, with victories in both their opening matches, were already certain to qualify. Their brothers from the other side of the frontier, however, needed a win. After sixty-nine minutes, with the match goalless, Schön sent on Netzer. Eight minutes later Jürgen Sparwasser broke away to score the winner for the representatives of the communist regime. It was a horribly unattractive match to those with no vested interest, thanks largely to the defensive tactics of East Germany's coach, Georg Buschner, and it hardly seemed an appropriate way for Netzer to say farewell to the *Nationalmannschaft*, after a mere thirty-seven caps and six goals. Had he been in the side a fortnight later, when Schön's selection faced Rinus Michels' Holland in the final, fewer neutrals might have been praying – in vain, as it turned out – on behalf of the Total Football of Johan Cruyff and Johan Neeskens, of Wim van Hanegem and Johnny Rep. Helmut Schön had got it right at last, after the Dutch had mystifyingly failed to press home the advantage conferred by a second-minute penalty, completing his mission thanks to an equalizing penalty from Breitner and a winner from the inevitable Müller. But in his decision to build a side without employing his country's most resplendent, expressive and – let's say it – untypical talent, you would not suggest that he had done football a favour.

When Netzer left Madrid it was for Zürich, where he spent two undemanding seasons with Grasshoppers, the oldest of Switzerland's leading clubs. He won a Swiss league championship medal in that second season, thereby helping the team to qualify for a place in the 1978–79 European Cup. But he was not around when they beat Valetta of Malta 13–3 on aggregate in the first round or, more remarkably, when they beat Real Madrid for a place in the quarter-finals, a 3–1 defeat at the Bernabéu and a 2–0 victory at home taking them through on away goals before they fell to Nottingham Forest, the eventual champions.

In 1978 a new phase of his life began when he became the general manager of Hamburger SV, an important club then struggling to recapture former glories. While he had no interest in coaching, the other elements of managing a football club held considerable appeal. A year earlier Kevin Keegan had been bought from Liverpool and had found the transition difficult. Netzer's predecessor, trying to demonstrate to the public that he was making vigorous efforts to pull the club out of the doldrums, made Keegan's salary public, showing that he was the highest-paid player in the country and thus earning the Englishman the resentment of the entire Bundesliga, opponents and teammates alike. He also broke a promise to find Keegan and his wife a house where they could keep their Old English Sheepdogs; instead the English couple and their pets found themselves quartered on the nineteenth floor of a hotel in the city centre. Nor were matters much better on the pitch. Despite his strenuous efforts to learn the language and integrate himself into his new surroundings, Keegan was not faring well. Certain players refused to pass the ball to him, and he found himself being asked to play in midfield rather than as a striker, the position in which he had made his reputation and where he had just won the European Cup with Liverpool, finishing runner-up to Allan Simonsen of Denmark in the European Player of the Year awards.

Netzer's arrival changed everything. Keegan was restored to his proper position, a new coach instigated a training regime that improved the squad's fitness, and in successive seasons the club went from sixth to second to first in the Bundesliga, their first title in nineteen years and the excuse for a grand parade through the centre of Hamburg. After winning the *Ballon d'Or* two seasons running, Keegan was receiving offers from Juventus and Real Madrid. The one that interested him, however, was the Washington Diplomats in the North American Soccer League, who offered him a quarter of a million dollars for four months' work. His contract with Hamburg was ending but, having helped the club to qualify for the European Cup, he wanted to play in the competition once more. He and Netzer agreed a deal whereby he would spend the summer months in the US and then come back to rejoin Hamburg at the start of the season. When that arrangement was abandoned after the late discovery of a rule barring him, as a NASL player, from competing in the European Cup, Netzer came up with a generous solution that ensured he would not be out of pocket. In exchange for allowing Hamburg to use his name for promotional purposes while he played one last season, he would receive the quarter of a million dollars that the

Diplomats had offered him. Hamburg finished second in the league that season and reached the European Cup final, only to fall to Brian Clough's Nottingham Forest, but Keegan left Germany with warm memories. 'Günter Netzer was one of the most honest and trustworthy men I have ever worked for in football,' Keegan wrote in his own autobiography, a book in which the Englishman seldom erred on the side of sycophancy. 'I am fortunate to have met a lot of principled people in the game, but none was more so than he.' Under Netzer, in Keegan's judgement, Hamburger Sportverein were the only club who fulfilled every promise they had made to him.

Netzer stayed at the Volksparkstadion for eight years, a period in which the club won the championship three times and finished as runners-up on four occasions. And in 1983 his tenure was crowned with success when the team won the European Cup, an honour that had evaded him as a player. With Ernst Happel, who in 1978 had taken FC Bruges to the European Cup final and Holland to a second World Cup final, now in charge of the coaching side, the formidable Manny Kaltz at right back, Felix Magath in midfield and Horst Hrubesch at centre forward, they contrived a 1–0 win in Athens over a Juventus side packed with players who had won the World Cup with Italy a year earlier – Dino Zoff, Marco Tardelli, Claudio Gentile, Gaetano Scirea, Roberto Bettega, Paolo Rossi – and further strengthened by two imports, Michel Platini of France and Zbigniew Boniek of Poland.

Life after football was never going to be a problem for Günter Netzer. When he married Elvira Lang in 1987, their witnesses were Franz Beckenbauer and Mirja Sachs. Mirja was the wife of Günter Sachs, once renowned for being the husband of Brigitte Bardot and for being almost the spitting image of Netzer. At a time when footballers were more or less confined to their own little goldfish bowl, Netzer moved in wider and deeper waters. The index of his autobiography features such names as those of Elke Sommer, Bryan Ferry, Joseph Beuys, Tina Sinatra, Boris Becker, Heinrich Böll, Mick Jagger, Mandy Rice-Davies, Sigmar Polke, Günter Grass and Georg Baselitz. His social and intellectual life apart, Netzer found plenty with which to occupy himself. On the television screen he became a football analyst for German channel RTL. Behind the scenes he acted as a consultant to Germany's successful bid to host the 2006 World Cup, a campaign that reunited him with Beckenbauer, the leader of the bid.

In 2003, after Rudi Völler's hapless Germany had stumbled through a goalless draw with Iceland in Reykjavik, Netzer went on television to describe the performance as representing 'a new low point for German football'. Setting aside the fact that his critic had once been his boyhood idol, Völler produced a vigorous response. And, indeed, the point may have been ill-made. To many, the low point for German football had come twenty-nine years earlier, on the day when, with a World Cup to win, Helmut Schön left Günter Netzer out of his plans.

5 Michel Platini

The French did not actually invent football, although they sometimes act, and very occasionally play, as though they did. But it is to French enthusiasts that we owe the idea and the reality of great international competitions. Baron Pierre de Coubertin created the modern Olympic Games in 1896, of which a football tournament soon formed a significant part. In 1904 Robert Guérin became the first president of FIFA, the governing body of football around the world (he had offered the leadership role to the English but could stimulate no interest in London). Henri Delaunay supervised the organizing of the first World Cup in 1930, naming the trophy after Guérin's successor, Jules Rimet. And it was Gabriel Hanot, a journalist with the daily paper *L'Équipe* and its weekly stablemate *France Football*, who came up with the idea for the European Cup. Professional football existed for more than half a century before France's players showed any signs of understanding its mysteries, but their bureaucrats certainly knew how to lay the foundations for the annual and quadrennial events that have held succeeding generations in their thrall.

In Europe, at least, not much attention is paid to the Intercontinental Cup, nowadays held in Tokyo each year between the holders of the European Cup and the Copa Libertadores. Throughout its chequered forty-year history this competition between the champion clubs of Europe and South America has provided a study in cultural misunderstanding, particularly in the late 1960s, when it was known as the World Club Championship and there were pitched battles between Celtic and Racing Club of Buenos Aires, Manchester United and Estudiantes La Plata, and AC Milan and the same

Estudiantes. By the middle of the 1980s, however, the competition had been renamed, the home-and-away format had been abandoned and a Japanese automobile manufacturer had come up with enough sponsorship money to make it worth a top club's trouble to take a week out of their domestic season.

And it was in the Intercontinental Cup that France's greatest player enjoyed his finest hour. Not in the World Cup, which he graced three times with his talent and which he might, given better luck, have won twice; not in the European Championship, to which he led his national team in an explosion of joy that overflowed the frontiers of France; certainly not in the European Cup, where his triumph was accompanied by one of the deepest tragedies the game has known; but in a competition on the other side of the world, just about as far removed as it was possible to get from football's roots, in a place where few understood the game but where its rise to mass popularity was being propelled by the engines of fashion and commercial exploitation.

'I was at my peak in December 1985,' Michel Platini told Marguerite Duras, the author of *L'Amant* and many other literary novels, during the course of an interview in *Libération*, the French daily newspaper. 'And after that . . .'

There was eloquence in the ellipsis, but the 'after that' barely mattered. In Tokyo's National Stadium on 8 December 1985, in front of 62,000 spectators, many of whom could hardly be expected to comprehend what they were seeing, the thirty-year-old in Juventus's No. 10 shirt produced a performance that touched the heights of football's art. Everything he had promised since his professional début for AS Nancy as a physically underdeveloped seventeen-year-old reached its fruition in this display, so sublime that it remained unspoiled even when his most extravagant moment was overruled by a linesman's flag.

Juventus's opponents were Argentinos Juniors, the club of Diego Armando Maradona's youth (although the little prodigy had passed from their ranks five years earlier). The team from Buenos Aires had just won their national championship for the first time in their history, so qualifying for the Libertadores Cup; in the final they defeated America Cali of Colombia. There were no big names in their side, no players destined to go on to greater fame and fortune across the Atlantic, but they made skilful and combative opponents, and after a goalless first half on a rain-soaked pitch they proved good enough to take the lead twice, through exceptional goals by Carlos Ereros and José 'El Pepe' Castro. In between those two strikes Platini orchestrated an equalizer when he sent a high diagonal ball from the left towards Aldo Serena, who met it as he entered the right-hand corner of the penalty area and was promptly flattened by Jorge Mario Olguín. Platini's penalty was hit, as usual, with the instep of his right boot and aimed low inside the right-hand post.

A few minutes later, just after Castro had blasted Argentinos Juniors back into the lead, the moment arrived that might have defined Platini's qualities for all time. When a Juventus corner kick was half-cleared, Massimo Bonini got his blond head to the ball and nodded it back towards the left-hand side of the penalty area. Platini, standing amid a group of three red-shirted defenders, about fifteen yards from goal, took it on his chest, waited as it dropped and flicked it over his head with the outside of his right ankle before shifting his balance and sending a left-foot volley spearing into the net.

If the Japanese spectators had attended a top-level match every week for the rest of their lives, they would not have seen anything as beautiful, as spontaneous, as breathtakingly skilful or as instinctively calculated to bring pleasure to the man who accomplished it and the people who watched him. It was the essence of Platini, distilled into three or four seconds of action. It was swiftness of appreciation, breadth of imagination, economy of execution. His teammates jumped on him, wanting – for the thousandth time – to show their appreciation of his magical gift and what it had brought them; all, that is, except the two – Serena, the centre forward, and Sergio Brio, the stopper – who were staring in guilty horror at the linesman's raised flag, which correctly indicated that they had been offside at the decisive moment.

Platini, whose football was always illuminated by his sense of humour, took the blow in good spirit. He went over to the touchline, lay down on the grass, put his chin in his hand, held the provocative pose and invited the crowd to share his unspoken thought: 'Well, what more can I do?'

What he could do became clear eight minutes from the end of normal time, when he volleyed a chip across the penalty area into the path of Michael Laudrup, who had sent him the ball and was now rushing to meet the return. The precision of Platini's first-time pass was such that the defence froze solid, the young Dane needing only to control the ball with his first touch, take it round the goalkeeper with his second and clip it into the goal from the tightest of angles with his third. It was the equalizer, and it sent the match into extra time.

When the extra thirty minutes had produced no more goals, Platini rolled down his socks and removed his shin guards. He would be the fifth of the penalty takers. By the time his turn came around, his teammate Stefano Tacconi had saved the attempts of Sergio Batista and José Luis Pavoni. For Juventus, only Aldo Serena had failed to score. If Platini succeeded, his club would be champions. He picked up the ball, rolled it in his hands to remove the streaks of mud and placed it on the spot. A short run-up, a right-foot shot aimed at the same square of rigging, and once again Enrique Bernardo Vidallé, the Argentinian goalkeeper, was helpless. Deprived of his moment of moments, Platini nevertheless had the last word.

Observing him in an airport departure lounge, making his way home from some big European football night or other, you might find it hard to convince a companion that this slightly rumpled, chain-smoking figure had once been the most elegant and admired footballer on earth. But even in his most exalted moments there was always a powerful humanity about Michel François Platini, something that spoke of his shared French and Italian ancestry: a quality of light, of sunshine, of humour, of the giving and the taking of pleasure. Platini, you felt, had the business of football in perspective. The game was something that could engage your loyalty and melt your heart; but it was not, in the end, a matter of supreme importance.

Instead it was, in essence, a matter of satisfying the senses, and sometimes the business of winning and losing could be as irrelevant as taking sides between Cézanne and Matisse. Here is what Platini once said of the experience of going a goal down to Argentina in front of 76,000 people in Buenos Aires' Estadio Monumental during a group match at the 1978 World Cup finals: 'The roar when Luque scored was unbelievable. When Bernard Lacombe and I kicked off again, we both agreed we'd never experienced anything like it. We were almost happy to have conceded the goal just to have heard the noise.' Not to suggest, of course, that he was anything other than a winner. Indeed, just about the only thing in his career that he did not win either as a player or a coach was the competition in which, ten years after his retirement, he served as head of the organizing committee and in which, in 1998, his successors in the French national team swept to immortality: the World Cup.

He was born in the village of Joeuf, near Nancy in the Meurthe-et-Moselle region, in the north-east of France, on 21 June 1955: midsummer's day. His grandfather had been born in the Italian province of Novara and had left for France looking for work and settled there; during Michel's childhood the family often went back to spend a summer holiday among their relatives in the village of Agrate Conturbia, south of Lake Maggiore. As a child he was so small that at school his nickname was 'Raz', derived from *ras-bitume*: asphalt-scraper.

Aldo, his father, played for and later managed AS Nancy-Lorraine; while Michel learned to play in the streets, his father taught him certain lessons, notably this piece of Zen-like wisdom: you must learn to pass the ball, if you want to get it back. One day when Michel was twelve years old the pair of them went off to watch FC Metz, whose star, the hard-shooting, high-living forward Ladislao Kubala, had fled Hungarian communism in 1949. Kubala played for several clubs, most notably Barcelona, where he became the Catalan club's equivalent of Alfredo di Stéfano at Real Madrid, while winning caps for Czechoslovakia and Spain, as well as his native country. Young Michel, not surprisingly, was hooked by the sight of such splendour.

As a teenager he played for AS Joeuf, his local club, with sufficient distinction to raise hopes that football might give him a living. He went for a trial with Metz but failed a respiratory test. Ten times he tried it, but each time the result failed to satisfy the club's exigent medical officer. His heart, the doctor said, was not strong enough. Instead he went to Nancy, his father's club, where he signed an apprentice's contract on 22 June 1972, the day after his seventeenth birthday. Progress was quick, and eleven months later he made his début in the first team, at home to Nîmes in a 3–1 win on 3 May 1973. A month before his eighteenth birthday, he had arrived; two weeks later, away to Olympique Lyonnais, he scored his first goal, and his second, in a 4–2 win. Nancy finished sixth in the French first division that season, in which Platini played five games. A double fracture of his left leg during a match in Nice restricted him to no more than eight appearances the following year, when a final position of eighteenth brought relegation for Nancy. In 1974–75, however, his seventeen goals in thirty-two games helped to propel them back into the top flight before he went off to spend the summer completing his military service.

Twenty-two goals in thirty-eight games the following season won him acclaim and a place in the national team, although there was also another operation on a knee injury suffered during a match at Laval, where he responded to the jeers of the home crowd by scoring a hat-trick. On 27 May 1976, at twenty years old, he made his international début, scoring in a 2–2 draw against Czechoslovakia in the Parc des Princes, near the Bois de Boulogne. That summer he scored in successive matches against Denmark, Bulgaria and the Republic of Ireland before heading for Montreal to take part in the Olympic football tournament with a young squad that also included Jean-François Larios and Patrick Battiston, two future colleagues in the senior ranks. Of their five matches, they won two and drew one. As usual in the days of state-sponsored amateurism, the medals went to East Germany (gold), Poland (silver, with ten members of their 1974 World Cup squad) and the Soviet Union. Brazil placed fourth, while Platini and his colleagues shared fifth place with Iran, Israel and North Korea.

Those who hadn't been paying attention were forced to sit up on 8 February 1978 when France played Italy in Naples and Platini settled the result of the friendly fixture by scoring twice with free kicks, beating the legendary and virtually invincible Dino Zoff. Frequently repeated on television, those strikes made his name around Europe. With his club he won the Coupe de France, scoring the only goal of the final against Nice and receiving the trophy from President Valéry Giscard d'Estaing. In a match at Saint-Etienne the following season, however, he made a challenge in which his ankle was broken in three places; the repairs and subsequent recuperation cost him half of his seventh and final season in the white strip of Nancy, although there were still twelve goals in only eighteen games, two of them in his last appearance at the Stade Marcel-Picot, against Lille.

For 1979–80 he signed with the club that had taken over from Stade de Reims as France's pre-eminent force. Only four years earlier Saint-Etienne had reached the final of the

European Cup, where they lost to Bayern Munich, a year after tasting defeat in the semi-final at the hands of the same opponents. A few weeks into Platini's first season with *les verts* their fanatical supporters were chanting his name when he inspired a 6–0 victory, two of the goals his own, over PSV Eindhoven in the UEFA Cup. In his three seasons at the Stade Geoffroy-Guichard the club finished third, first and second in the first division. In the European Cup of 1981–82, however, they were beaten in the preliminary round by Dinamo Bucharest. Saint-Etienne, it had become clear, could not satisfy his ambition; it was time to take the final step to greatness.

As that season drew to a close Platini was approached by Gianni Agnelli, the patron of Juventus, head of Fiat (the family firm) and a kind of *éminence grise* in Italian society and politics. Known throughout Italy as *l'avvocato* (the lawyer) and for his curious habit of fastening the strap of his watch around the cuff of his hand-made shirts, Agnelli and his older brother Umberto took turns to build the club into the Italian equivalent of Manchester United: a team that drew its support not so much from the home city, Turin, as from other parts of the country, notably the *mezzogiorno* – the poor south, where Serie A teams seldom ventured. Umberto had created the great team of the late 1950s, bringing Omar Sívori from River Plate and John Charles from Leeds United to join an inspirational captain, Giampiero Boniperti. Now *l'avvocato* decided that Platini's gifts would complete a team already containing such stars of the Italian national squad as the indomitable Zoff, the athletic full back Mario Cabrini, the majestic sweeper Gaetano Scirea, the redoubtable wing half Marco Tardelli and the brilliant strikers Roberto Bettega and Paolo Rossi, the latter just returning, at the age of twenty-five, from a two-year suspension imposed for his part in a match-fixing scandal. A further addition was Zbigniew Boniek, probably the finest attacking midfield player ever produced by Poland, purchased from Widzew Łódź.

Platini's contract was up, and he was interested in a move. First he contacted Internazionale, who had tried to sign him from Nancy three years earlier but were thwarted on that occasion by Serie A's imposition of a ban on foreigners. Now they turned him away, telling him that they had filled their only vacancy for a *straniero* by signing the German playmaker Hansi Müller. He was in talks with Arsenal when Agnelli made his approach. Boniperti, now the club's general manager, had travelled to Paris in February to see Platini again get the better of Zoff as France beat Italy 2–0. His recommendation strengthened the resolve of the chairman, who went to Saint-Etienne to watch Platini train. The Italian league had recently announced that clubs would be allowed to hire two foreign players, rather than one, and Agnelli knew who he wanted to play alongside Boniek. It was not Liam Brady, the Irish No. 10 who had performed with distinction in the black and white stripes since his arrival from Arsenal two years earlier. It was the Frenchman. On 30 April 1982, the day of the transfer deadline, Platini and his agent, Bernard Genestar, answered a summons and flew in secret to Turin, where an armour-plated limousine – 'This was the time of the Red Brigades,' Platini would recall – took them to an office near the River Po. There they were joined, as had been pre-arranged, by the head of the French professional footballers' union, who supervised transfer deals, and a clutch of Italian lawyers primed to act on Platini's behalf. Boniperti, however, dismissed the lawyers and the syndicalist. 'We shall make this deal between the two of us,' he announced, and ordered sandwiches.

At Platini's home in Saint-Etienne that afternoon, Claude Bez of Bordeaux was waiting in the hope of persuading him to move to another French club, his own, rather than Arsenal. Platini's wife stalled Bez by telling him her husband was out shopping. At 6 p.m., after three hours of making polite conversation with Christine Platini, Bez could wait no longer and left. Tuning in to Europe 1 on his car radio, however, he heard the news. Platini had signed for Juventus in the biggest move for a French footballer since Raymond Kopa left Stade de Reims for Real Madrid in 1956. Bez called Mme Platini and left a message for Michel's return: 'No hard feelings. Best of luck.'

Once the deal had been agreed, there was a piece of unfinished business. Liam Brady, having been told three days earlier that his contract would be renewed, now had to be informed that he would be on his way. But there was no friction. Two weeks later, when the squad travelled to Catanzaro for the last match of the season and with the championship still in the balance between Juventus and Fiorentina, the Irishman scored the penalty that secured the twentieth *scudetto* in the club's history. Usually the employer gives the employee a leaving present; this time, in a gesture of great generosity, it was the other way round. From Brady's behaviour, Platini could see that he was joining a club whose own conduct encouraged such emotions.

Before he could take residence in Turin, there was the matter of the World Cup. France had played Mexico in the opening game of the very first World Cup, in Montevideo in 1930, winning 4–1; they had reached the quarter-finals on home ground in 1938, losing to Italy; and they had reached the semi-finals in 1958, the team of Raymond Kopa and Just Fontaine beaten 5–2 by a sparkling Brazil and Pelé's hat-trick. Too often, however, they had underperformed, exposing the weakness of their domestic league. And although Michel Hidalgo, their coach, travelled to Spain with perhaps the most gifted group of players assembled in the blue shirts up to that date, under Platini's captaincy, they got off to the worst possible start in their opening Group 4 match against Ron Greenwood's England.

Only twenty-seven seconds had gone when Terry Butcher back-headed Steve Coppell's throw-in from the right-hand touchline and Bryan Robson, England's captain, threw himself into an acrobatic left-footed volley which sent the ball whistling past Jean-Luc Ettori. Gerard Soler, France's left-winger, equalized within half an hour, but in the second half a header from Robson and a simple strike by Paul Mariner secured the win for England. France had played the more cultured football, but England made them appear lacking in character. Kuwait offered them a chance of rehabilitation, and they took it gratefully, goals from Bernard Genghini, Platini, Didier Six and Maxime Bossis giving them a 4–1 win. Six also scored against Czechoslovakia, giving France the draw they needed to go through to the second round, where they met Austria and Northern Ireland in the relatively straightforward Group D. Jean Tigana deputized for the injured Platini in the first match, Genghini taking the free kick that defeated Austria 1–0. The captain was back for the second fixture, in which an incorrect decision to disallow Martin O'Neill's opening strike provided the prelude to another 4–1 win, with two goals each for Alain Giresse and Dominique Rocheteau. Now people were starting to talk about the artistry of the French midfield, in which Platini's brilliance was beautifully complemented by the intelligent bustle of Giresse, the cool ball-winning skills of Tigana and the industry of Genghini. And against West Germany in the Sánchez Pizjuán stadium, Seville, they gave a performance that put the world on the side of French football.

The Germans scored first, the little winger Pierre Littbarski the first to react as Ettori beat out Klaus Fischer's shot. After Bernd Förster impeded Rocheteau, Platini equalized from the penalty spot. That was how it stood after 50 minutes, when Patrick Battiston, a full back, replaced Genghini. Ten minutes later Battiston was in the clear and racing on to Platini's marvellous long ball when Harald 'Toni' Schumacher, the German goalkeeper, came charging out of the penalty area to meet him. Both men were at top speed, but only one of them was interested in the ball. An instant after Battiston had touched it past him, Schumacher – his body tensed for the impact – smashed into the Frenchman. Heavily concussed, with several teeth broken by the goalkeeper's shoulder, Battiston was carried from the pitch by paramedics and given oxygen. Charles Corver, the Dutch referee, had seen nothing wrong in an assault that had made millions around the world gasp in horror. There was no card, not even a free kick, and Schumacher was allowed to continue his business as the shocked French tried to regroup, with Christian Lopez coming on for Battiston. Manuel Amoros hit the bar in the last minute, but not until early in the first period of extra time did Marius Trésor break the deadlock with a fine volley from a Giresse free kick. Giresse himself swiftly profited from Bossis's cut-back to increase the lead, and with twenty minutes left, neutrals everywhere were cheering as France appeared to have secured their place in the final. But, as the Hungarians and the English had learnt in previous years, the West Germans never gave up. Karl-Heinz Rummenigge, their captain, had been injured in the previous match; now he came on as a substitute and, racing into space that Battiston might have occupied, guided home a cross at the near post. Fischer's superb overhead kick took the match to a penalty shoot-out, with the worldwide audience in no doubt about which team was, in the parlance of westerns, wearing the black hats. Justice donned a blindfold, however, as Schumacher saved from Bossis before Horst Hrubesch scored with the last kick to take his team through. France's reserves were given their chance in the third-place play-off match, losing 3–2 to Poland. And for those appalled by Schumacher's assault, there would be a measure of consolation when Alessandro Altobelli humiliated the German goalkeeper as they faced each other with seven minutes of the final to go, the Italian striker going past with disdainful ease to score his side's concluding goal in a very complete 3–1 victory.

As if to deepen the sense of disappointment, Platini's early weeks in Turin were far from easy. He was suffering from a hernia when the season started, and in the spring there would be a double disappointment as Juventus finished runners-up in Serie A and travelled to Athens to lose the final of the European Cup to Hamburg, the only goal scored by Felix Magath. But Platini had given the fans of *La Vecchia Signora* – the old lady, as Juve is known – a good idea of what lay in store. At the end of the season his sixteen league goals had made him Italy's top scorer, and his exploits for club and country secured him the *Ballon d'Or*, ahead of Kenny Dalglish of Liverpool and Allan Simonsen of Vejle BK. He would go on to win both honours three years in a row during his time in Turin, a feat unlikely to be matched.

The following season provided greater satisfaction as he adapted to the rigours of the Italian game and began to explore his relationship with the country of his father's father. 'I'm not in exile,' he said. 'I'm here to rediscover my origins. It's my good fortune to embody two different cultures at the same time.' The club won the league for the twenty-first time, Platini scoring twenty goals. 'When you score goals with Juventus,' he would say, 'the news travels around the world and you really are someone. And that changes your life. The Italians taught me a lot of things. Football is the most important thing in the world there, a bit like wine and cheese are to the French. A Frenchman would travel two hundred kilometres to visit a good vineyard, but an Italian would go twice that distance to see a football match.'

Even the French were enthused, however, when Platini led his country to victory in the 1984 European Championship on home soil, a success that closed the wound inflicted in Seville two years earlier and, although no one knew it at the time, would provide the momentum for further success in later years. With Hidalgo again in charge, the team had undergone one crucial change: in the midfield, Genghini had been replaced by the young Luis Fernandez. Now the string quartet was complete, perfectly harmonized and working to a wonderful collective rhythm. In the group matches, an opening victory over Denmark – the only goal of the match scored by Platini – was followed by a real statement of intent against Belgium. The 50,000 in Nantes' Stade de la Beaujoire were enthralled as France racked up five goals without reply: one for Giresse, one for Fernandez and three for Platini, the last of them the sort of flamboyant header D'Artagnan might have produced, had he been a footballer. Against Yugoslavia, Platini did even better. Again there was a hat-trick, but this time the goals – a left-footed shot under the goalkeeper, a diving header and a right-footed free kick from outside the area – all came in a spell of eighteen minutes, giving France a 3–2 win.

'It was a complete team with a nice playing system,' the captain reflected many years later. 'We had to play good football in our games because if we didn't play well, we didn't win. We didn't have a team capable of sitting back in defence and waiting for the chance to make a counter-attack. But we had eleven players who had good technique and could express themselves. It was a different kind of football in those days, and I loved it.'

And they were loved in return. In the semi-final, against Portugal, the fans in the Stade Vélodrome sang 'La Marseillaise' and then watched as Platini, fouled after twenty-four minutes, got up and dummied a free kick to allow Jean-François Domergue to strike the ball home. Jordão equalized with a fine header, taking the match into extra time, and then scored again with a mis-hit shot as Portugal's gifted ball-players sustained a flood of attacks. With five minutes left, Platini wriggled across the penalty area and fed Domergue, who chipped in his second goal. The match was one minute away from being decided by penalties when Tigana carried the ball into the area, pulled it back from the right and watched as Platini controlled it with a touch of his right boot before battering a shot into the roof of the net. 'Tigana told us that he had never won a match that went to penalties,' Platini said. 'So we knew we had to avoid a shoot-out.'

Suddenly, all France was galvanized as Platini led his team

into the Parc des Princes, to meet Spain in the final. If the match failed to live up to the pulsating excitement of the semifinal, at least it provided the team with the trophy their talents deserved; on this occasion, at least, the manner of the success mattered less. Platini's opening goal came from a twenty-five-yard free kick that seemed to have been intercepted by Luis Arconada before it somehow slid under the Spanish goalkeeper's body and dribbled across the line. Bruno Bellone made it 2–0 when he lifted Tigana's pass over Arconada, and French football finally had something to celebrate.

A year later, however, came the nightmare in the Heysel stadium. On 29 May 1985 Juventus met Liverpool in the European Cup final, and thirty-nine fans were crushed to death against a crumbling wall as the English supporters charged the unprotected Italian enclosures in the hour before kick-off. While the bodies were being laid out and counted, while first-aid workers were helping the injured, the players were in the dressing rooms under the old stadium, knowing that something had happened but unaware of the true nature of the tragedy.

'They asked us to go out and calm the young fans down a bit,' Platini told Marguerite Duras. 'We were the only ones. I mean the eleven Juventus players and the eleven Liverpool players. We were the only people who didn't see the drama. We were getting ready for the match. That meant that what hundreds of millions of people saw, we didn't see.'

Which is why they could respond to the request to start the match. In an atmosphere of unreality, the players went through the motions. When a penalty was awarded in the second half for an offence by the Liverpool defender Gary Gillespie that clearly took place outside the area, and Platini stroked it home, there was nothing more to be said.

'My dream was to play football in front of as many people as possible, for football to be a spectacle, for people to be happy together, to sing,' Platini said. 'Otherwise I don't like crowds.'

Henri Michel had replaced Hidalgo by the time France set off for Mexico in 1986, hoping to repeat their European success on the bigger stage of the World Cup. Still glowing from the praise they had earned in 1984 and from the memory of a run of twelve consecutive victories that year, they were hoping no one would notice that they had still failed to unearth a striker or two to match the contribution of their gilded midfield. Jean-Pierre Papin scored the only goal as they beat humble Canada in their opening match, Fernandez struck in a 1–1 draw with the USSR, and Tigana, Rocheteau and Yannick Stopyra contributed to a 3–0 victory over a very inadequate Hungary. The second round produced a much more significant result as they beat Italy, the defending champions, 2–0. Platini chipped Giovanni Galli, the goalkeeper, and Stopyra scored the second from Tigana's cross.

In the quarter-final they were scheduled to meet Brazil, the three-time champions, on Platini's thirty-first birthday. A splendidly open and competitive game in Guadalajara enthralled 65,000 people, who went away with the bizarre memory of having seen penalties missed by Platini and Zico, two of the greatest strikers of a dead ball in the game's history. Careca gave Brazil the lead early on, Platini equalizing before half-time when he poked home a loose ball. Zico missed from the penalty spot in the second half, and the match went on through extra time into a shoot-out. Sócrates had a casual effort saved by Joel Bats, Platini got under his shot and watched it fly over the bar, Júlio César hit a post, and it was left to a nervous Fernandez to send 125 million Brazilians into a state of despair by putting France through to the last four, where West Germany lay in wait.

After four years, here was an opportunity for revenge. Schumacher was still in the West German goal. But finally this generation of French players was starting to feel the burden of the passing years. The midfield no longer had quite the improvisatory zest that had marked it out in 1984. Platini's tendons were giving him trouble on a regular basis. And when Andreas Brehme's free kick defeated Bats's attempted save after nine minutes, the mood seemed ominous. France no longer had the resources for such a contest. They tried, but a man who might have gone to jail for his assault on Patrick Battiston seemed capable of repelling everything they could throw at him. With two minutes to go, Rudi Völler ran clear with the ball at his feet. Out came Bats, who could have done to Völler exactly what Schumacher had done to Battiston when the German striker lifted the ball over his head. He refrained, allowing Völler to run on and score the goal that put France out and West Germany through to a final against Argentina, where, as in the final against Italy in 1982, Schumacher was again beaten three times as they lost once more.

Again the third-place play-off was left to the reserves, who beat Belgium 4–2 after extra time, with Battiston wearing the *brassard*. Platini's exemplary international career was over. He had played seventy-two matches for France, captaining the team on fifty occasions and scoring forty-one goals, which made him his country's all-time top goalscorer. Back at Juventus he played on for another season, but his best days were behind him. In twenty-nine league matches in 1986–87 there were only two goals, and at the end of the season he announced his retirement. 'Football began for me as a passion,' he told Marguerite Duras, 'but what got me down was going here and there to play matches. In the end I was sick and tired of it.' In his entire league career, shared between three clubs, he had scored 224 goals in 429 games, an average of 0.52 per match.

'The only French player who would have got into the Brazil team of any era, and in any position,' Pelé said, 'was Platini.

He was fantastic. His shooting, his passes, his touch on the ball, his control, his eye, the instinct for goal . . . he had everything.'

And having taken pleasure from being allowed to play the game and score his goals for so many years in front of so many people, Platini attempted to put something back. In 1988 he succeeded to the job of national manager, losing on his début by 3–2 to Yugoslavia in Belgrade in a qualifying match for the 1990 World Cup. Over the next year a series of mediocre performances against Norway, Scotland and Cyprus meant that he was unable to get the squad to the finals. Their form improved in the qualifying matches for the 1992 European Championships, when it seemed that the emergence of Didier Deschamps as the midfield anchor and the partnership of Papin and Eric Cantona up front might help him to re-create the glories of the mid-1980s. When they reached Sweden for the finals, however, a pair of draws against the host nation and England and a defeat by Denmark prefaced the end of Platini's career as a coach. As great creative footballers often discover, the gifts that enable them to control a game from the middle of the pitch do not always translate to the bench.

Instead he took on the role of running the next World Cup, awarded to France in recognition of its triumph, on and off the pitch, in the European Championships of 1984. A splendid new stadium had to be commissioned and built in a northern suburb of Paris; other venues around the country needed to be updated. The French people, seldom gripped by football fever, had to be made aware of the need to welcome the world to a great festival of the sport. Platini turned out to be the ideal choice, a national hero and a football man through and through. 'I regret the absence of Uruguay,' he said when the qualifying stages had been completed. 'They are the only former world champions who didn't make it. And I'm sorry that Portugal won't be here. There are many Portuguese immigrants in France who work very hard and would deserve some happiness.' He would try to ensure, he said, that the World Cup finals remained an event on a human scale – 'without grandeur, able to involve also those who are not crazy about our sport'. As a million people danced in the Champs-Elysées on the night of 12 July 1998, French and foreigners alike celebrating a home victory, his success once again became something for the world to enjoy.

6 Enzo Francescoli

On a warm Tuesday night in late May, with a neon sunset beginning to spread itself over west London, this was more like a trip to a private view at an art museum than a visit to a World Cup warm-up match at the crumbling, piss-stained Wembley stadium. A stroll from the roaring North Circular up to the old twin towers was leading me towards the prospect of a rare appointment with Uruguay, the game's forgotten giants, led by their No. 10, Enzo Francescoli, one of the finest players of his generation.

Both sides were heading for Italia '90, though with contrasting expectations. England, managed for the second World Cup in a row by Bobby Robson, fancied their chances of expunging the memory of Diego Maradona's hand-of-God goal in Mexico City four years earlier. Several of the stars of 1986 were back again, including Gary Lineker, Bryan Robson, Peter Shilton and John Barnes; this time they were joined by the extravagantly talented but temperamentally vulnerable Paul Gascoigne, who appeared to possess the gifts of the real playmaker so long absent from England's ranks (although Lineker, misleadingly, had the No. 10 on his back). Uruguay, coached by Oscar Washington Tabarez, nurtured more limited ambitions. In Mexico they had conformed to the worst modern stereotype of their nation's football. Under Omar Borras, Washington Tabarez's predecessor, they secured a 1–1 draw with West Germany, collapsed to a 6–1 defeat by Denmark after having a man sent off, and were again down to ten men against Scotland when, after just fifty-five seconds (the fastest ever dismissal in the World Cup finals), José Batista fouled Gordon Strachan, although they managed to secure the goalless draw that sent them through to the second round. There, in Puebla's Cuauhtemoc stadium, they were overrun by Maradona's Argentina, although it took only a single goal to decide the match and remove the champions of 1930 and 1950.

Probably more than a few of the England fans occupying the Wembley grandstands when Uruguay made their entrance were ignorant of the fact that the visitors were representing a nation that had won the World Cup as many times as West Germany and twice as many times as England itself. Only Italy and Brazil, with three each, had won more. How did such a tiny nation, with a population of 2 million in 1930 and barely 3 million sixty years later, and insignificant in practically every other dimension, with the possible exceptions of the meat-packing industry and the art of the *bolo*, achieve such a feat? And why were they not more successful now? Perhaps the match at Wembley would provide an answer. It would at least provide a glimpse of Francescoli.

Known to his nation, and to the fans of his clubs in Argentina and France, as *El Príncipe*, or *Le Prince*, Francescoli was a player with whom I had fallen in love on the slenderest of evidence. That happens, although it used to happen much more often in the days before Rupert Murdoch discovered that football attracted audiences to his satellite channel and television and started conveying live matches most nights of the week, not just from the various English competitions but from all the corners of Europe and even, if you were willing to stay up all night, from South America and elsewhere.

Back in the pre-Murdoch era, it was like being on rationing. Only during the finals of a World Cup or when an English club played in Europe was there a chance to see the celebrated artists of other nations in action. So when a Pelé or a Netzer did something amazing, it tended to stick in the memory. Nowadays we are so accustomed to our weekly dose of Serie A and La Liga that we take the magic of a Ronaldinho or a Kakà almost for granted. Although no less enjoyable, the experience fails to convey the aura of rarity and exoticism that once sur-rounded the appearance of a Gento or an Altafini.

Like George Eastham or Osvaldo Ardiles, Francescoli was a player I loved at first sight. In such relationships, bonds of admiration, affection and concern transcend loyalties to club or nation. In the best sense, they are disinterested. A whole dimension of football's beauty seemed to be embodied in Francescoli's slender, flowing movement, in the consideration he gave to every pass, in the clarity of the geometry he imposed on the game. Maybe he wasn't one of the very greatest foot-ballers of all time. And, unlike George Best, George Weah or Ryan Giggs, he had the chance to play on the World Cup stage, yet made little impression. But I would have paid money to see him whenever and wherever he was performing, simply to be in touch with those qualities of extreme elegance and percep-tion that are given to few footballers. Francescoli was one of those players who could invest the game with a balletic grace, without undermining its competitiveness or physicality. Just as interesting to me, he represented the late – perhaps the last – flowering of creative talent from a country that had been the first to dominate international football before entering a decline which he would prove powerless to reverse.

Uruguay's national team has two nicknames. The first, *La Celeste*, honours the sky-blue flag; the second, *Las Charrúas*, refers to the tribe of Indian hunter-gatherers who occupied the land before the Spanish arrived in the sixteenth century. As was the case with their South American neighbours, football arrived in Uruguay in the late nineteenth century, as a pastime imported by British workers. William Poole, an English profes-sor at Montevideo University, was the founder of Albion Football Club in 1886; five years later, Englishmen employed by the Central Uruguayan Railway formed a club that eventu-ally became known, after the district in which its ground was situated, as Peñarol. A national football association was founded in 1900, and on 16 May 1901 a Uruguayan representative side met their Argentinian counterparts in Montevideo in the first international match to be played outside the British Isles; the visitors won 3–2, and there were still British names on the team sheets of both sides. In 1910 the same nations competed in the final of what was effectively, although unofficially, the first South American championship; again Argentina were the winners, this time by 4–1. Uruguay's goal was scored by the most celebrated of their early players, José Piendibene, who was still around in 1916 to provide inspiration when his country won the first official staging of the competition, beating Chile 4–0 with a side that included two players of African descent: Isabelino Gradín and Juan Delgado, each the great-grandson of slaves.

Among Piendibene's last appearances was a 6–0 win over Brazil in Viña del Mar, said to be the first away win in international football. He had retired, however, by the time Uruguay began their astonishing and surprisingly lengthy period of dominance in international football. Led by the defender José Nasazzi, they travelled to Paris for the 1924 Olympic Games as the only representatives of South America. There they beat Yugoslavia, the United States, France and Holland before defeating Switzerland 3–0 in the final – watched by a crowd of 60,000 in the Stade Colombes – to win the gold medal in the football tournament, the first full-scale global contest for national teams. In front of a midfield known as 'the iron curtain', Pedro Petrone scored eight of their goals, with four from Héctor Scarone. Parisian society was particularly taken by the team's black midfield player, José Leandro Andrade, who could run half the length of the field with the ball bobbling on his head. In *Passion of the People?*, a study of South American football, Tony Mason quotes the verdict of the French journalist Gabriel Hanot, in *Le Miroir des Sports*: 'It is the best of the twenty-two teams that has won the championship . . . The principal quality of the victors was a marvellous virtuosity in receiving the ball, controlling it and using it. They have such a complete technique that they also have the necessary leisure to note the position of partners and teammates. They do not stand still, waiting for a pass. They are on the move, away from markers, to make it easy for teammates . . . They created a beautiful football, elegant but at the same time varied, rapid, powerful and effective . . . These fine athletes . . . are to the English professionals as Arab thoroughbreds next to farm horses . . .' Hanot sounded like a man who had seen the future.

Four years later in Amsterdam a similar Uruguay team repeated their achievement. Petrone scored four and Scarone two as they beat Holland, Germany and Italy on their way to the final. This time they met Argentina in a match their neighbours expected to win; they had, after all, faced each other more than a hundred times in the twenty-seven years since their first encounter, and the balance of results was firmly in Argentina's favour. Carlos Gardel, the great tango singer, serenaded the Argentinian dressing room before the kick-off. Having drawn the match 1–1 in front of 40,000 in Amsterdam, however, Uruguay won the replay 2–1, Scarone securing the decisive goal as his teammates kept out their opponents with a display of iron-clad defending.

These highly successful Olympic tournaments were the direct forerunners of the World Cup, and their success prompted Henri Delaunay, the secretary of FIFA, to urge the notion on his compatriot Jules Rimet, the governing body's president. It can be said, therefore, that Uruguay were the champions of the world in 1924 and 1928, making them the legitimate choice to host the inaugural World Cup in 1930, which they approached with a justified sense of confidence expressed in the building of a new national football stadium in a Montevideo park. The imposing 80,000-capacity Centenario stadium received its name in celebration of the anniversary of the formal independence of the country that had been known simply as *La Banda Oriental* – the East Bank (of the Rio de la

Plata) – before José Artigas, the country's revolutionary leader, fought to free it from the occupying forces in the early years of the nineteenth century.

Weather conditions delayed the building work, which meant that the stadium was not ready for the start of the tournament. Europe sent France, Yugoslavia, Belgium and Romania; there was no sign of Germany, England, Italy, Hungary or Spain, even though Uruguay had issued invitations and pledged to pay the expenses of the competing teams. Argentina, Mexico, Chile, Bolivia, Brazil, Paraguay, the United States and Peru joined the hosts as representatives of the Americas. The early fixtures were played in lesser stadiums before, in their own first match, Uruguay inaugurated the still-unfinished Centenario by beating Peru 1–0 in front of 57,000 people. Three days later, with the building work still going on, 70,000 were admitted to see a 4–0 win over Romania, which took Uruguay through to the semi-final. Again Europe's representatives were cut down, Pedro Cea scoring a hat-trick in a 6–1 victory over Yugoslavia in front of 79,000. Argentina beat the United States in the other semi-final, setting up a meeting between the old rivals.

National and political tensions, plus a death threat to Argentina's best player, the defender Luisito Monti, persuaded the authorities to reduce the stadium's capacity: the recorded attendance for the first ever World Cup final would be 68,346. In the preceding days every ferry from Buenos Aires to Montevideo had been oversubscribed; each was cheered on its departure by fans waving banners. Once again the great Gardel turned up in the dressing room and sang in the hope of inspiring his fellow countrymen. Uruguay scored first, through Pablo Dorado, but Carlos Peucelle equalized for Argentina, who then took the lead through Guillermo Stábile. By half-time Argentina's inventiveness had given them a clear advantage. After the interval, however, Uruguay knuckled down and started to impose themselves. Cea equalized after fifty-seven minutes, Santos Iriarte gave them the lead with a shot from long range eleven minutes later, and with a minute left to play Héctor Castro sealed the victory with a looping header. Nasazzi stepped up to become the first recipient of the newly fashioned gold trophy, named after Rimet. While Montevideo erupted in triumph, across the water there were shocked silences in the squares of Buenos Aires, Rosario, Córdoba and other cities, where crowds had massed to listen to the progress of the match via tannoys; in the capital, the Uruguayan consulate was stoned and there were a couple of shootings.

Curiously, Uruguay declined the opportunity to defend their title when the second World Cup was held in Italy four years later, and were absent again in France in 1938; on both occasions, Italy won the trophy. The reasons for the decision are obscured by time: some say it was a sulky response to the poor European turnout in 1930; others that the arrival of full-scale professionalism in Uruguayan football in 1932 created damaging internal conflicts. But Uruguay were present and correct in Brazil in 1950, for the first post-war World Cup, in which the thirteen entrants were organized into four mini-leagues from which the winners would emerge to play a round-robin series for the title. The hosts were the firm favourites, having recently obliterated all opposition while winning the Copa América, scoring forty-three goals in six matches and conceding four. Uruguay, for example, had been crushed 5–1.

Again, a new stadium was not quite ready for the opening match; at the Maracanã in Rio de Janeiro the capacity was halved and only 81,000 witnessed Brazil starting as they intended to go on by burying Mexico 4–0; a draw against Switzerland and a win over Yugoslavia saw them safely through. Spain, Sweden and Uruguay were the other qualifiers for the final round, the champions of 1930 having beaten Bolivia 8–0 in the only first-round match they were required to play. Their 2–2 draw with Spain and a late winner in a 3–2 victory over Sweden combined with wins for Brazil against Sweden and Spain to turn the last match of the final group into the contest that would decide the tournament. This time, with Brazil needing only a draw to take the trophy, the Maracanã was packed to overflowing. A hundred and seventy-three thousand was the official figure, but at least another 30,000 appeared to have found their way into the gleaming bowl.

They were rewarded with the sight of Brazil's skilful forwards – Friaça, Zizinho, Ademir, Jair and Chico – launching themselves at a defence marshalled by Uruguay's outstanding captain, Obdulio Varela, a centre half with attacking inclinations. Ademir had already scored eight goals in the competition, and Brazil would register thirty shots on goal in the ninety minutes of the final, but the game was still goalless at half-time. When Friaça gave his team the lead with a cross-shot two minutes after the interval, the crowd assumed that an avalanche was on its way. Varela, however, had other ideas. At his instigation Uruguay began to move forward, and gradually the strength of their own attacking players became apparent. Crucial in this match was the supremacy of Alcide Ghiggia, the outside right, over Bigode, his marker. But ranged alongside Ghiggia were Oscar Omar Miguez, the Peñarol centre forward, and Juan Alberto Schiaffino, the No. 10. Miguez had scored a hat-trick in the opening match against Bolivia and two more against Sweden, while Schiaffino had a pair against Bolivia, and Ghiggia had scored a goal in each of their three matches. Now their quality was re-emphasized. After sixty-five minutes Varela brought the ball out of defence and fed the hunched, moustachioed Ghiggia, wide on the right. Easily beating Bigode on the outside, Ghiggia sent in a cross that Schiaffino, completely unmarked, struck home. With seventy-eight minutes gone Julio Pérez, Uruguay's inside right, fed Ghiggia, who this time angled his run towards goal and sent a bobbling shot between the goalkeeper and the near post. After a further dozen minutes of frantic but fruitless attacking by the home side, the final whistle sounded and all Brazil was plunged into mourning. The trophy was going back to Montevideo.

It nearly stayed there in 1954, too, when Schiaffino was the undoubted star of a team that travelled to Switzerland and beat Czechoslovakia, Scotland and England before meeting Hungary in the semi-final. Ferenc Púskas, maimed by a West German defender, was absent from this match, but so were Miguez and Varela, two of Uruguay's key players. They missed a classic. Juan Eduardo Hohberg scored two goals for the South Americans, both from Schiaffino's knife-like passes, to take the match into extra time, but a pair of headers from Sándor Kocsis helped the Magyars to a 4–2 win.

Schiaffino went straight to Italy, where he joined AC Milan. In his first league match, a 4–0 win over Triestina, he scored twice. That season gave him the first of three Serie A championship medals; he stayed six seasons at San Siro, until he was thirty-five years old, making 171 appearances and scoring sixty goals. When he left for Roma, in the summer of 1960, the transition was seamless: in came Gianni Rivera, a No. 10 of matching elegance.

For Uruguay, it took a generation to find a replacement. While winning the Copa América again in 1956 and 1959, they failed to qualify for the World Cup in 1958 and were eliminated in the first round in Chile in 1962. Four years later, at Wembley, a dreadful goalless draw with Alf Ramsey's England provided the gloomiest possible start to the tournament before a 2–1 win over France and a draw with Mexico, also goalless, took them through to a quarter-final match with West Germany. There, in Sheffield, after Uruguay had been reduced to nine men by two dismissals early in the second half, they lost 4–0 to the accompaniment of complaints from both sides about the opposition's violence and histrionics.

A year later they again won the Copa América, beating Antonio Rattín's Argentina in the deciding match, but Uruguay's reputation for physical play had already begun to obscure the memory of the talented footballers who had brought them two world championships. The problem could be summed up in one word: *garra*. It is a term that stands for the spirit of aggression believed by Uruguayans to be at the core of their temperament; on the football field its signs can cross the frontier of mere resolution to take the form of persistent fouling, often of the most infuriating kind. As early as 1953, when England were on a summer tour of Latin America, their players complained, after losing 2–1 in the Centenario, of Uruguay's 'hacking, hitting, shirt-pulling and hauling on every hand-hold they could find'. Cultural differences offer a partial explanation. In the game against West Germany at Hillsborough in 1966, for instance, Uruguay were justified in believing that important decisions had gone against them. Their answer, however, came not with the sort of creative attacking football that might have been the response from Schiaffino and Ghiggia but with trips, bodychecks, slaps and raised studs jabbed into the leg of Helmut Haller, whose play-acting had infuriated them.

It may have been no coincidence that a country which had spent most of the twentieth century as a prosperous democracy, its citizens enjoying a minimum wage, free medical care and nationalized utilities, was becoming enmeshed in a bitter conflict between the government and a guerrilla army. The Tupamaros began as a vehicle for the protests of leftist revolutionaries, many of them middle-class students; by the end of the 1960s, however, their repertoire had expanded to the kidnapping and murder of foreign diplomats and aid officials, along with a sideline in bank robberies. In 1973 the country's generals responded by seizing power, dissolving the legislature and declaring a state of emergency. Four years later the US withdrew economic aid and Amnesty International announced that Uruguay's jails held 5,000 political prisoners. Nevertheless, by 1978 the Tupamaros had been more or less eliminated, and in 1984 free elections were held once again.

During the period of darkness, which paralleled the rule of

the military junta in neighbouring Argentina, the increasingly defensive, almost paranoid nature of the football played by the national team deepened the impression of a nation at odds with itself. In Mexico in 1970 their coach, Juan Eduardo Hohberg, was asked to account for their unappealingly cautious approach to the matches in the group stage. The two-goal hero of the 1954 semi-final brusquely retorted that it wasn't his job to think like the crowd. In the quarter-finals Uruguay's rough tactics kept the Soviet Union at bay and a goal three minutes from the end of extra time gave them the victory. Amazingly, they took the lead against Brazil after seventeen minutes of their semi-final, through Luis Cubilla, but Clodoaldo equalized just before half-time, and second-half goals from Jairzinho and Roberto Rivelino put the world back on its proper axis.

There was more to come in West Germany in the 1974 World Cup finals, when they had a man sent off in a rancorous 2–0 defeat by Holland's Total Footballers, drew 1–1 with Bulgaria in the same stadium and fell 3–0 to Sweden in Düsseldorf. It would be their last appearance in the finals for twelve years. The effectiveness of the *garra* seemed to have found its limits, or perhaps it had turned in on itself, finding new expression in the political battles being fought within the country.

When they returned to the World Cup finals, in 1986, it was not just as citizens of a revived democracy but as a team with an authentic star in their midst. Proof of just how good Enzo Francescoli was comes in the estimation of a player who went on to enjoy a far greater fame around the world: when Zinédine Zidane was a boy in Marseille, supporting the local team, *Le Prince* was his hero. Years later, when Zidane's wife gave birth to their first child, there was only one choice of forename: the boy became another Enzo.

Writing in 1997, the Uruguayan novelist Eduardo Galeano

located the poignancy of Francescoli's talent in the broader context of the nation's football history. 'Uruguay's success at the '24 and '28 Olympics, and at the 1930 and 1950 World Cups, owed a larger debt to the government's policy of building sports fields around the country to promote physical education,' he wrote. 'Now all that remains of the state's social calling, and of football, is nostalgia. Several players, for example the very subtle Enzo Francescoli, have managed to inherit and renovate the old arts, but in general Uruguayan football is a far cry from what it used to be. Ever fewer children play it and ever fewer men play it gracefully. Nevertheless there is no Uruguayan who does not consider himself a PhD in tactics and strategy, and a scholar of its history. Uruguayans' passion for football comes from those days long ago, and its deep roots are still visible. Every time the national team plays, no matter against whom, the country holds its breath. Politicians, singers and street vendors shut their mouths, lovers suspend their caresses, and flies stop flying.'

Enzo Francescoli Uriarte was born in Barrio Capurro, a district of Uruguay's capital city, on 12 November 1961. In childhood he played for Cadys Juniors, a local team, and at fourteen he joined the junior section of Montevideo Wanderers. Founded in 1902, Wanderers had been among the early giants of the Uruguayan game but were eventually relegated to the status of supporting cast to the country's big two clubs, Peñarol (Francescoli's childhood favourites) and Nacional. At nineteen he made his senior début in the club's magpie stripes, the first of seventy-four appearances in which he scored a total of twenty goals. In 1981 he took part in the South American junior championship, winning the award for the best player of the tournament. Two years later he was part of the senior team who beat Brazil to secure the Copa América, scoring the first goal of the two-legged final in a 2–0 win over Brazil in Montevideo and keeping his place as they travelled to Salvador to secure a 1–1 draw. It was all more than enough to bring him to the attention of Club Atlético River Plate, Argentina's resplendent *millonarios*, who paid Wanderers $360,000 for his services. His first goal for the club, on 24 April 1983, gave them an away win against Ferrocarril Oeste. Two years later he was the top *goleador* and player of the year in the Argentinian league. A championship winners' medal in 1985–86, and another season at the top of the league's scoring chart, meant that he had secured a permanent place in the affections of River's fans.

In 1986, after taking part in Uruguay's desperately disappointing World Cup campaign, the effects of Argentina's ailing economy forced a move to Europe. He had played 113 games for River Plate, scoring sixty-eight goals, and had lived up to the legend of Walter Gómez, another Uruguayan forward who had won a place in the hearts of River Plate's supporters thirty years earlier. A few months after Francescoli left them, the *millonarios* would go on to win the Copa Libertadores for the first time; his work in getting them into the competition was not forgotten.

Whereas most South American stars were lured to Italy or Spain, Francescoli headed for Racing Club de Paris, founded in the 1930s but now reconstituted under the name Matra Racing, with sponsorship from a company manufacturing missiles, sports cars and Formula One engines. The project was not built on the firmest foundations; within three years the team would be relegated, the name Matra disappearing from football as suddenly as it had arrived. In the national shirt, however, a second Copa América came Francescoli's way in 1987, Uruguay beating Maradona's Argentina in the semi-final and Chile in the final, both matches held in the familiar surroundings of River Plate's Estadio Monumental and both won by a single goal.

After the meltdown in Paris, and having scored thirty-six goals in eighty-nine appearances for Matra Racing, in the summer of 1989 he moved south to Olympique de Marseille, where Bernard Tapie, the extrovert president, had already funded a championship-winning side and now seemed willing to pay any price to bring the European Cup to the passionate supporters who thronged the Stade Vélodrome. There Francescoli encountered an all-star side including the prolific striker Jean-Pierre Papin, the Ghanaian forward Abedi Pelé, the powerful stopper Basile Boli, the efficient midfielder Didier Deschamps and the stoop-shouldered, deceptively casual English winger Chris Waddle.

'It was a funny time,' Waddle recalled. 'In the forwards there were Papin, Pelé, me and Philippe Vercruysse, and then Tapie bought Francescoli because he wanted another player who would score a lot of goals. Papin was scoring twenty or twenty-five a season, Pelé would get a dozen and I'd get six or seven. He wanted another player who could get the same as Papin was getting. Enzo was a nice guy, very easy-going. He'd been the South American superstar before Maradona came along, but he was very down to earth and helpful and popular with all the other players. He liked the odd cigarette; typical South American. He had fantastic ability, of course. He wasn't the quickest player in the world, but he had good balance, good vision and, as all great players have, good awareness. He knew how to pass the ball to the right side of a player. He came from a background where football is played at close quarters: a lot of little one-twos in tight areas. English players would probably say, "It's too tight – play it long." But he'd want to use his skill to get himself out of that sort of position. I enjoyed playing with him because that's the way I like to play myself. And, like a lot of the South Americans, he could look after himself on the pitch. If someone was being a little bit naughty with him, he knew all the tricks and he'd bide his time. It was the way he'd been brought up.'

So Francescoli, in the eyes of the ambitious Tapie, was supposed to provide the final piece of the jigsaw. 'In certain games,' Waddle said, 'it worked. In others, not. The way we operated, the ball would come to me from Deschamps or one of the other midfield players and I'd get it to Papin or Pelé. When Enzo came in, he probably didn't get as much of the ball as he wanted. If Papin had been injured for a spell, Enzo would probably have relished it and made the most of the opportunity. But it didn't happen.'

The critical moment came when Marseille reached the semi-final of the European Cup in the spring of 1990. Benfica were the opponents, and the first leg was in the Vélodrome. 'We went 2–1 up,' Waddle remembered. 'Then we had three or four more good chances to score, and Enzo missed the lot. That got him a mixed reception from the spectators, and from Tapie.' Benfica won by the only goal in Lisbon and went through to the final.

'His time with us might have been the hardest of his whole career,' Waddle said. 'Marseille didn't see the best of him.'

By the time Francescoli arrived in London with the Uruguay squad in May 1990, he had cleared his locker at the Vélodrome, and he and Waddle were no longer teammates. After scoring eleven goals in twenty-eight games for Marseille, Francescoli was on his way to Sardinia, where he would spend three seasons with Cagliari, newly returned to Italy's Serie A.

That night in a half-full Wembley he strolled around with lethal grace, dispensing thoroughbred passes at acute and unexpected angles. England came into the match on an unbeaten run of seventeen games, stretching back to the 1988 European championships; it was the foundation on which they built their hopes for Italia '90. After twenty-seven minutes, however, Francescoli carried the ball up the middle and delivered a perfectly weighted pass to Antonio Alzamendi on the left wing. Alzamendi checked back and crossed with his right foot for Santiago Ostolaza to run clear of his marker and send a header looping over the stranded Peter Shilton. Six minutes into the second half England's fans perked up when Stuart

Pearce, fed by Paul Gascoigne's long diagonal ball, crossed to John Barnes, who cushioned the ball on his chest before scoring with an emphatic left-footed half-volley. Just after the hour, however, Uruguay regained the lead when José Perdomo's free kick from twenty-five yards swerved around the defensive wall and exposed every one of Shilton's forty years as the veteran goalkeeper pushed the ball into the net. England's streak was at an end, although in Italy they would ride their luck all the way to the semi-final.

For Uruguay, Italia '90 may have been less spectacular but at least it represented an improvement on the unpleasantness in Mexico four years earlier. With Francescoli wearing the captain's armband and leaving the goal-scoring role to Perdomo, Alzamendi, Rubén Sosa and the young Daniel Fonseca, once again they did just enough in the group matches – a goalless draw with Spain, a 3–1 defeat by Belgium and a 1–0 win over South Korea – to earn their passage to the second round. There, in Rome's Olympic stadium, in a meeting of the nations who, between them, won the first four World Cup tournaments, they were eliminated by the hosts, losing 2–0 to goals from Salvatore Schillaci and Aldo Serena. At twenty-eight years of age, Enzo Francescoli had played in his last World Cup.

If there are no second chapters in American lives, F. Scott Fitzgerald's celebrated axiom does not seem to apply to Uruguayans. Nor does the familiar adage, 'Never go back.' When his peaceful years in Sardinia were over, Cagliari having finished fourteenth, thirteenth and sixth in the table during his three seasons, Francescoli spent a year helping to keep Torino in Serie A's top ten. And then, aged thirty-three, he returned to River Plate, the scene of his greatest triumphs. Such a choice might have ended in ignominy, trampling on the image he had lodged in the collective memory during his first stint with the club; instead it provided a luminous coda to his career.

During Francescoli's eight-year absence, Argentina's national league had been split into two annual championships:

the *Apertura* (opening) and the *Clausura* (closing), run consecutively. Over the course of the next three and a half years, starting in 1994, Francescoli played in seven of these competitions, winning four of them, plus the Copa Libertadores in 1996, and scoring forty-seven goals in eighty-four appearances during his second stint with one of the world's great clubs. Back in the colours of Uruguay, there was also a third Copa América triumph, when the *Charrúas* held Brazil 1–1 before winning on penalties in the 1995 final.

In February 1998 he announced his retirement. At a gala match, held eighteen months later, his farewell to River Plate was something to see. A familiar chant of '*Uruguayo! Uruguayo!*' rang around a packed Estadio Monumental as he appeared for the last time in the famous white shirt with the scarlet sash, confronting his choice of opponent: his boyhood idols, Peñarol of Montevideo. Among the spectators were the presidents of Argentina, Carlos Menem, and of Uruguay, Julio María Sanguinetti. Walter Gómez, the compatriot whose club goal-scoring record he had taken, kicked off. A crowd of 80,000 had come to say goodbye to a player who had never even looked like winning a World Cup but whose value, in the eyes of his admirers, had little to do with cups or medals.

A River Plate fan posted an eloquent valediction on a website after that final match in Buenos Aires, his adopted home during those years. The correspondent describes those big eyes, that slender frame, the opaque shyness, the austere speech. '*Cristalino, frontal, recto, llano, de una sola palabra*' – crystalline, face-on, upright, straightforward, of few words (although, like most translations, an English rendering seems somehow to miss the point). The fan continues: 'No one has ever heard him say anything aggressive. No one has ever trapped him in a scandal. There have been no long nights. No compromising photographs with underworld figures. No ostentation. Francescoli remains an example. *Es el Príncipe de fútbol. Y de la vida.*' A prince of football, and of life.

7 Diego Maradona

A testimonial match in north London, one evening twenty years ago. The crowd is so big and the queues at the turnstiles so long that the kick-off is delayed by almost half an hour to enable all the spectators to take their places. They are there to say a fond farewell to Osvaldo Ardiles, the little Argentinian midfielder who arrived at White Hart Lane in 1978, accompanied by his compatriot Ricardo Villa, just a few weeks after their triumph in the World Cup finals. The burly, moustachioed Villa, almost a caricature of the English idea of the hulking, brooding gaucho, would score an unforgettable goal in an FA Cup final, one of the best ever seen at Wembley, but it was the slight Ardiles who won a place in the hearts of Tottenham Hotspur's supporters for the darting wit and unflagging commitment with which he played the game. And tonight, after suffering a series of injuries, he is bidding farewell to his adopted home with a match in which Spurs are meeting Internazionale of Milan, albeit an Inter shorn of their most famous players, such as Alessandro Altobelli and Giuseppe Bergomi, who are at a training camp in preparation for Italy's imminent attempt to defend the World Cup.

The centre of attention, however, is not a hero of the 1978 or the 1982 finals. It is the man who, within the month, will win the World Cup for his country virtually single-handedly. Diego Armando Maradona has arrived from Naples to put on the white shirt of Tottenham and add an extra layer of lustre to his former international teammate's benefit night. Along with the genuine affection felt for Ardiles in this part of London, Maradona's presence must be the reason for an attendance that stretches the old ground to its capacity. At this stage the British still love Maradona, after seeing him score a wonderful goal in a friendly against Scotland at Hampden Park in 1979 and almost score another in another friendly against England at Wembley a year later. There is also a widespread sense of residual sympathy for the brutal treatment he received from defenders in Spain during the 1982 World Cup. The war over the ownership of the Falkland Islands, or Las Malvinas, is ended and banished from most British minds (although not, as it turns out, from the Argentinian consciousness). The spectators at White Hart Lane have no reason to suspect that Maradona will soon, again single-handedly, become English football's nemesis.

Ardiles, it becomes clear, can do little more than hobble around the pitch. There will be none of those incisive runs that once took him hurdling over the challenges of clumsier men, to be followed by the stiletto thrust of a goal-making pass. He will last barely a quarter of an hour before withdrawing to the sidelines. So all the attention is on Maradona, and on his partnership with Glenn Hoddle, Tottenham's home-produced midfield star and golden boy.

Perhaps five minutes have elapsed when the willowy Hoddle, sitting deep in his own half, receives the ball, raises his eyes and lofts a fifty-yard pass upfield. Maradona doesn't need to move an inch. As he stands with his back to goal, the ball hits him on the chest with such accuracy that he might have had a bull's eye painted on his shirt. He stuns the ball with instinctive precision, but it has not even dropped on to his toe before he is looking back down the pitch at the man who delivered the pass, putting his hands together to applaud the artistry and the execution of the service. In that moment, you can see how much Diego Maradona loves football, wherever it takes place and whoever is playing it.

We remember two faces. First, the face of the curly-haired little boy, ten or eleven years old, with sad eyes, like a child extra from Pasolini's *Gospel According to St Matthew*, looking straight at the camera and saying: 'I have two dreams. One is to play in the World Cup. The other is to be the champion.' Second, the face of the man who has just scored a goal against Greece in Boston during the 1994 World Cup finals: again he confronts the camera, but this time those eyes are wild with some sort of fathomless and inexplicable rage. He is staring, glaring, daring the world to deny his genius. His mouth is screaming. Four days later, after Argentina's second match, against Nigeria, he is selected for a post-match dope test and led away by a Green Cross nurse. After a further four days the analysis comes comes back from the laboratory: 'Ephedrine, Metephredine, Phenylpropanolamine = Norephredine (listed substances); Pseudoephedrine, Norpseudoephedrine (substances are not listed, but from the chemical content and biological effect similar to the Ephedrine and Norephedrine, could possibly be metabolites) . . .' That 2–1 victory over Nigeria was Diego Maradona's twenty-first World Cup match, and it turned out to be his last.

This was a man who made celebrities even of the defenders who marked him. How many would otherwise remember Claudio Gentile and Andoni Goikoetxea? On 29 June 1982 there was Gentile, the hard man of the Italian rearguard, taking the job of restricting Maradona's activities in their second-round match at the 1982 World Cup finals so seriously that he followed him around Barcelona's Sarriá stadium for ninety minutes, wrapped around his opponent closer than a piece of clingfilm around a sandwich. In his script for the official film of that tournament, Stan Hey coined the widely quoted phrase about Gentile not bothering to wait until the final whistle to swap shirts with his opponent. The Italian held, he nudged, he tugged, he shoved, he kicked. Maradona dodged, twisted, turned and wriggled, but he could never break free. Argentina lost 2–1. Italy went on to win the World Cup.

Just over a year later, on 24 September 1983, there was

Goikoetxea, the Basque who broke Maradona's left ankle in a match between Barcelona and Athletic de Bilbao. This was the start of Maradona's second season at the Camp Nou, and Barça were winning 3–0 when he went to pick up a loose ball in the centre circle. As he touched the ball, the defender's left leg stretched from behind and caught him. Maradona said he heard a sound like a piece of wood breaking. There would be an operation, and he would be out of the game for three months. He came back in January, and at the end of the season Barcelona met Bilbao again in the final of the Copa del Rey, with King Juan Carlos in attendance. Goikoetxea, Maradona claimed, seemed to fancy finishing what he had started in September. The match descended into a full-scale brawl, with players aiming waist-high kicks at each other all over the pitch. It was blood-curdlingly hideous, even worse than anything seen in those legendary rumbles between British and Argentinian teams in the world club championship in the late 1960s. As he used his knee to make vigorous contact with the Bilbao goalkeeper's face, Maradona showed he had a talent for that, too.

Where did it come from, all that rage? From being told, at an early age, that he was a genius, and from being treated as a superstar not just before the use of the term had been extended to famous footballers but before his temperament had developed the necessary coping mechanisms. From being a poor boy surrounded by rich men who showered him with money before he had learnt the discretion required to avoid getting carried away with it. From looking like an aboriginal kid from some wild back-country out there beyond the pampas. From being left out of the 1978 World Cup finals by a compassionate and clear-headed manager, César Luis Menotti, who felt that he was still too young to bear the burden of Argentina's imperative need to win the competition on home soil at a time when, on one side, the generals were exerting pressure and, on the other, the people were begging for some form of deliverance. From constant exposure to the incompetence of men such as Nicolae Rainea, the Romanian referee who permitted Gentile to suffocate his talent with such profound cynicism when, four years later, he did make it to the World Cup finals. From finding an adoptive home at La Bombonera, the chocolate box, the stadium of Boca Juniors, where he and his club's fans fell into a mutual embrace founded on a raucous denial of moderation. From a natural affinity, in fact, for excess.

Two of the best books about Maradona, Jimmy Burns's 1996 portrait and the player's own autobiography, published in 2000, are both contained within covers depicting him on his knees, with his hands clasped and his eyes raised in prayer. Yet this is a man whose most famous moments on the pitch include one of the most blatant – and unrepented, to say the least – examples of cheating ever seen in a world tournament, a man whose addiction to cocaine shortened his career and almost cost him his life, a man whose social dalliances with the gangs of Naples became the stuff of legend, a man who for a long time refused to acknowledge the existence of a son born out of wedlock, even after a DNA test had proved his paternity. No wonder Diego Armando Maradona prays, you might say. But for what? And what does he think is God's view of him?

What he did, we might surmise, was spend his career mining every ounce of slight and insult for the fuel it provided, for the rage it ignited. Growing up inside a particular culture, Maradona came to believe that passion was an essential ingredient of his art, the equal of his technical virtuosity. So when Argentina met England in the quarter-finals of the 1986 World Cup, he found a use for the resentment stored since Alf Ramsey's description, twenty years earlier, of his fellow countrymen as 'animals', for the ill-feeling generated by the violent meetings between Manchester United and Estudiantes de la Plata three years later, and for the bloody memory of the more recent war in the south Atlantic. The fact that generals, politicians and diplomats were to blame was immaterial: he identified with the boys on the *Belgrano*, burning and drowning to the cheers of the British press. The *Sun* had bellowed: 'Gotcha!' That was his riposte, too, as he raised his fist to punch the ball over Peter Shilton's belated jump.

All of this had a firm basis in Argentina's feeling of historic mistreatment at the hands of the British, who had spent most of the nineteenth and twentieth century exploiting the country's resources and owning its railways, banks, docks and department stores, as well as lending it the lineaments of a culture. Argentina was an independent nation, but by the time of the First World War more than half of her trade was conducted with Britain – 'a colonial relationship', as the historian David Downing put it, 'in all but name'. A fondness for polo and afternoon tea were among the more obvious examples of English habits taking root in Argentinian soil. Footballs, too, came in the baggage of British sailors and railway workers. When a football league became established in Argentina, its foundations had been laid by the British headmaster of Buenos Aires' English High School. After the great depression of the early 1930s, however, Britain negotiated a new trade treaty which put the already limping Argentinian economy at a severe disadvantage. When the nationalist General Juan Perón took over the presidency in the wake of the Second World War, with a promise to release the urban working class from its chains, the British government viewed him with grave suspicion.

To Diego Maradona, football's British roots were immaterial, of no consequence. They might never have existed, except to provide the satisfaction of knowing that the pupils were now capable of humiliating and destroying the teachers. And by the time he kicked a ball for the first time, the game had been naturalized. It had an Argentinian nationality, symbolized in a style of play known as *la nuestra*, which means 'our thing'. *La nuestra* was based on flamboyant dribbling, on the development of sleight of foot, on tricks. By the middle of the century it was to English football as the tango was to the fox-trot: blessed with greater degrees of grace, romance and gesture, along with an undertone of violence. Its great masterpiece was the *gambeta*, a slaloming dribble between defenders.

If you want to find Maradona's forerunner, look no further than Omar Enrique Sívori, whose coffin was carried through the streets of San Nicolas, his home town, after his death from cancer at the age of sixty-nine in the early weeks of 2005. Almost fifty years earlier he had formed, with Antonio Valentín Angelillo, the centre forward, and Humberto Maschio, the inside right, a three-pronged Argentinian attack variously celebrated as the Trio of Death and the Angels with Dirty Faces. Together they scored twenty of the twenty-five goals in seven games that gave Argentina the Copa América in Peru in the spring of 1957. A few weeks later the three, all in their early twenties, were sold to Italian clubs, Sívori going from River Plate to Juventus, Angelillo from Boca Juniors to Internazionale and Maschio to Bologna. The Argentinian football association's policy prevented them from being picked again for the national team, which meant they missed the trip to Sweden in 1958, and their country's hopes of winning the World Cup for the first time were significantly reduced.

Umberto Agnelli had paid 160 million lire to take Sívori to Juventus, where he discovered new associates of equal merit: Giampiero Boniperti, the team's captain, who moved from inside forward to playmaker to accommodate the new arrival, and John Charles, the giant Welshman who, uniquely at this level of football, was equally happy at centre forward and centre half. Together they won three championships and earned a special place in the club's Valhalla. Very quickly, too, Sívori was given an Italian passport, allowing him to play for the *Azzurri*. Sívori's nine caps for his adopted country yielded eight goals and he appeared alongside the eighteen-year-old Gianni Rivera and José Altafini (a Brazilian with an Italian passport) in the unsuccessful World Cup campaign in Chile in 1962.

Whereas Charles was noted for his sportsmanship, Sívori was a tricky little devil who liked to drive his marker to distraction. 'I've lost a teammate, a friend, an angel,' Angelillo said when he heard of his old colleague's death, but not many Italian defenders of the era would choose the last of those terms. The *tunnel* – the Italian term for the nutmeg, the trick of humiliating an opponent by pushing the ball between his legs and running around him to collect it on the other side – was his speciality, along with the expression of a volatile temperament. 'He was only small but he was a hard man who more than punched his weight,' Charles wrote in his autobiography. 'He was an explosive little man who would flare up in an instant and was never afraid to kick a defender or two. He had a strong temper and would react not only when he was kicked but also when I was kicked. He knew I would not retaliate and he would take it upon himself to dig back for me. He was a great player and he wasn't afraid to tell anyone so, on or off the pitch.'

To many spectators he was known by his Spanish nickname, *El Cabezón*: the big-head. But he was not alone in his high opinion of his own abilities. According to Sandro Mazzola, who played against him for Internazionale, Sívori was the man who defined the new role of *trequartista* in Italian football: the player who occupies what is now called the 'hole' behind the main striker. And as he reflected on the great man's death, Mazzola was quite clear in his opinion. 'Sívori was greater than Diego Maradona,' he said, which sounded like the highest compliment a man could pay.

Omar Sívori's *tunnel* was among the catalogue of tricks and techniques on which Argentinian football prided itself. This reliance on finesse was what distinguished it not just from European football but even from the game as it was played in neighbouring Uruguay, whose tall, blond players were derided for their undue reliance on strength, and from the blend that had evolved in Brazil, where a spirit of improvisation cast a different light on technical skill. The *amasada* (drag-back), the *bicicleta* (bicycle kick), the *sombrerito* (lifting the ball over a player and running round him to collect it) and the *marianela* (a kind of prototype of the Cruyff turn) were in use long before Europe adopted them. The *chileña* (scissor kick), as its name suggests, had originated on the other side of the South American landmass. But it was the *gambeta* that was the special skill of Argentina's footballers: part slalom, part ballet, this was the dribble that propelled an urchin through a crowd of would-be tacklers, keeping the ball under close control even on uneven surfaces that could boast not a blade of grass, enabling them to carry the ball from one end of the pitch to the other and to plant it between the sticks or bottles or piles of jerseys that denoted the opposition's goal.

These were the skills developed by boys who played in the alleys, on waste ground, playing wall passes off real walls, learning to maintain possession of the ball in the most hostile circumstances; the skills, in fact, that became the language of Diego Armando Maradona, starting during his infancy in Villa Fiorito, a poor district of Avellaneda, a suburb of Buenos Aires. His parents, Diego and Dalma, had come from Esquina, a fishing village on the bank of the River Corrientes, in the north-east of Argentina, not far from the border with Paraguay. There Don Diego had earned a living by rowing a boat across the water, ferrying cows to and from their pasture and fishing for his family's supper. In 1955, with their two daughters, he and Dalma made their way to Villa Fiorito, where the father found work in a bone-meal factory and his wife gave birth to six more children. Diego Armando, the fifth of the total of eight and the first of three boys, was born on 30 October 1960 in a hospital named after Eva Perón. On his third birthday he received a present of an old-fashioned leather ball, given by a cousin; he learnt about what it was for and what it could do on waste ground around Villa Fiorito, where the family lived without running water, electricity or sanitation in a series of improvised shanties made of corrugated iron, bricks and cardboard, the 'rooms' separated by strips of sacking.

His father was a keen amateur footballer, renowned for his ferocious shooting. He played for a local club called Estrella Roja, or Red Star, on whose scrubby pitch the young Diego practised with his friends. When the boy was nine he was told about a trial to be held by Argentinos Juniors, a league club whose ground was a two-hour bus ride away. There he caught the eye of the coach in charge of Los Cebollitas, a sort of preparatory squad intended to feed the club with a supply of players ready to sign youth forms at the prescribed age of fourteen. During Maradona's time as a player with Los Cebollitas they won 136 matches in a row, thanks in great measure to his goals. The No. 10 shirt was already his. Before his eleventh birthday, the Buenos Aires daily paper *Clarín* declared him a star of the future. Soon he was being invited to perform his ball-juggling tricks on television shows and at half-time in Argentinos Juniors' first-division matches. When Los Cebollitas beat their young equivalents from River Plate, the president of Argentina's grandest club made an unsuccessful offer to buy him at any price. In his autobiography, *El Diego*, Maradona says that a goal in that match was the forerunner of the one with which he would kill off England's hopes at the World Cup in 1986: he dribbled past seven opponents and scored. He was twelve years old. At fifteen the club gave him a rent-free apartment – the first of the material inducements that would be pressed on him over the next twenty years.

Ten days before his sixteenth birthday he took his place on the substitutes' bench at La Paternal, Argentinos Juniors' stadium, for a senior league match against Talleres de Córdoba. In his red shirt with a white diagonal stripe, and a No. 16 on his back, he came on in the second half, when his team were a goal down. They lost, but within a month he had scored his first goals as a first-team player and had become the sensation of Argentinian football. And within a further two months he was called up to the national youth squad, with whom he played practice matches against the senior stars, quickly catching the eye of Menotti, the long-haired, chain-smoking, socialist coach who was preparing Argentina for their assault on the World Cup the following summer. Menotti – *El Flaco*, the Thin Man – gave him his senior international début in a friendly against Hungary at La Bombonera on 27 February 1977: in twenty minutes as a substitute for the striker Leopoldo Luque he could contribute little more than a good impression to a 5–1 victory in which Daniel Bertoni, one of his heroes, scored a hat-trick.

Nevertheless, Menotti left him out of the World Cup party when the squad of twenty-five was reduced to the final twenty-two. There were five men who could play in the No. 10 position, and one of them had to go. Daniel Valencia, Ricardo Villa, Norberto Alonso and Ricardo Enrique Bochini stayed. Maradona went. Menotti told the sixteen-year-old not to worry because he would play many more World Cups, and in time Maradona would dry his teenage tears and recognize the value of the coach's vision. (Sixteen years later Carlos Alberto Parreira would do the same with Ronaldo, leaving the teenager on the bench as Brazil won their fourth World Cup; after the mysterious business of his fainting fit before the 1998 final in Paris, Ronaldo eventually secured his winners' medal with two goals in Yokohama in 2002.) At the time, however, it was the hardest news to take, made no easier by his attendance at two of Argentina's matches in the Estadio Monumental, the 1–0 defeat by Italy in the group stage and the 3–1 victory over Holland in the final, when a blizzard of confetti floated down on the nation's heroes.

While, deep down, he could never truly forgive Menotti, Maradona also revered him. In 1979 the coach took Argentina's junior side to the inaugural World Youth Cup in

Japan, where Maradona led a victorious campaign which excited the country almost as much as the seniors had a year earlier. Wearing the captain's armband, he scored the last goal – from a free kick – in the climactic 3–1 victory over the Soviet Union. Immediately afterwards he joined the senior squad, flying off to score his first international goal at that level against Scotland at Hampden Park. Three weeks later he was scoring against the Rest of the World in the Monumental, in a match arranged to celebrate the anniversary of the World Cup victory; he could only think, Why was I not playing then?

'Where I come from,' Maradona wrote in his autobiography, 'our hearts belonged to Boca.' Situated along the Riachuelo, a waterway leading off the Rio de la Plata bordered by meat-packing plants and warehouses, La Boca – 'the mouth' – is the dockyard of Buenos Aires, the equivalent of the old waterfronts of Liverpool, Marseille and Naples. Originally the majority of its inhabitants were French Basques, followed by a larger wave of Italian immigrants, mostly economic refugees from the poorer regions: the mountains of Abruzzo, the parched lands of Calabria and Basilicata. Founded in 1905, the football club borrowed its distinctive blue and gold colours from the flag those first players saw flying from a Swedish ship at anchor. Avellaneda, an industrial suburb, lies next to La Boca; the working class provided the club with its support, and at the beginning of 1981 the call for which Maradona had been waiting came from La Bombonera.

He had already scored the hundredth goal in the colours of his first club and had instructed his business manager, Jorge Cyterszpiler, to reject an offer from River Plate, whose stadium was in Palermo, a leafy quarter of the city, whose following numbered members of the middle class and the professions, and whose material resources were such that they were known as *los millonarios*. Instead, he was waiting for the invitation to join a club which was suffering at the bottom of the league and which, in a time of national financial meltdown, could barely manage to pay its players.

Since Boca could not afford a straight transfer fee, it was agreed that Maradona would be taken on a year's loan for a fee of $4 million, plus half a dozen players deemed superfluous to requirements. A full transfer would follow. Maradona's share should have been $600,000, but in place of cash he was persuaded to take a number of new apartments; unfortunately, the proper documentation failed to materialize, and anyway the flats were so poorly constructed that they turned out to be virtually unsaleable. Nevertheless, Maradona was delighted to pull on the blue and gold strip at last, and as the goals flowed he developed a rapport with fans who recognized one of their own, a player whose feats incarnated their dreams and desires with an unusual directness. Within a few weeks he travelled with Boca to River Plate's stadium, where he dominated the *superclásico*, as the derby is known, scoring the first of his team's three unanswered goals by controlling a cross at the far post and deliberately beating two heroes of the World Cup team, the goalkeeper Ubaldo Fillol and the left back Alberto Tarantini, before sliding the ball home.

The Metropolitan championship came Maradona's way in that first season with Boca, but River Plate beat his club to the title in the National championship. And by the end of the year it was already certain that he would be on his way again, thanks to the continuing catastrophe that was the national economy. Even a series of friendlies in Europe and Africa was not enough to help Boca pay their bills, and by the time the Argentina squad flew to Spain for the 1982 World Cup, a deal between Maradona's manager and Barcelona had already been agreed: this time the fee was $8 million, more than half of it going to Argentinos Juniors, with a chance that real money might actually change hands.

After a subdued Argentina, once again coached by Menotti, lost their first group match to Belgium, Maradona scored his first World Cup goals in a 4–1 defeat of Hungary. While beating El Salvador 2–0 he got a taste of the kind of physical unpleasantness that would be waiting for him in the second round, where he and his teammates were scheduled to meet Italy and Brazil, with only one of the three to go through to the semi-finals. On behalf of Italy, Gentile took on the job of asphyxiating the twenty-one-year-old. It says everything about the match that, despite the presence of such players as Maradona, Mario Kempes, Ossie Ardiles, Paolo Rossi and Giancarlo Antognoni, all three goals were scored by defenders: Marco Tardelli and Antonio Cabrini for Italy, Daniel Passarella for Argentina. And having fallen to football's darker forces, in their next match Maradona and his teammates were undone by the sheer brilliance of Brazil, led by Sócrates de Souza and animated by Paulo Roberto Falcão, Zico, Éder de Assis and Toninho Cerezo. Three goals down and with only six minutes to go, Maradona could hold in his frustration no longer: beaten by Falcão, he lashed out and kicked the nearest Brazilian, who turned out to be João Batista, a substitute. For Maradona and, a few minutes later, for Argentina, the World Cup was over.

Within the month, however, he had been presented to the Catalan public in Camp Nou, and the next phase of his career had begun. Without a league title in nine years, Barcelona paired Maradona with Bernd Schuster, the German playmaker, in the hope of challenging Real Madrid, but the appeal of Las Ramblas and the city's good-time atmosphere soon began to exert a destructive influence. Barcelona, Maradona said later, was where he first sampled cocaine, and although his addiction would become much more pronounced after his move to Italy, already his professional discipline was starting to slip. Courtiers began to attend to him at his villa, and when he was injured he demanded the services of his personal physicians rather than the club's medical staff. He missed games while recovering from a bout of hepatitis. Even the replacement of the head coach, Udo Lattek, by Menotti for Maradona's second season could not significantly improve the situation. Maradona was pleased when Lattek's morning training sessions were replaced by a more congenial schedule that required the players to turn up for work at three o'clock in the afternoon, but in the fourth match of that second season, against Bilbao, Andoni Goikoetxea's tackle inflicted such severe damage to the tendons of his left ankle that he would not play for three months. In the third game after his return, against Bilbao in the San Mamés stadium, more than fifty fouls were committed and he scored both his side's goals as Barcelona won 2–1. The last vestigial hope of honours under Menotti disappeared when Manchester United knocked them out of the European Cup Winners' Cup; for both Argentinians, their days in Catalunya were numbered.

By the time Terry Venables arrived from England to replace Menotti, the club had already agreed a deal with Napoli; the player, his finances in ruins after two years of wild spending, was keen for an injection of cash and a fresh start. After making a quick assessment of the position, Venables agreed to the move and began re-laying the club's foundations in preparation for a campaign that would bring the league title back to Barcelona. For Maradona, the move worked equally well. Having deflected an approach from the aristocrats of Juventus, he found his new Boca on the Bay of Naples: a rowdy, colourful setting in which metropolitan sophistication had no place and where he would find himself enfolded in the adoring embrace of supporters who, like the fans in La Bombonera, saw in him their own reflection.

Founded in 1931, SSC Napoli had never won the Italian championship. On the day of Maradona's arrival, 5 July 1984, more than 70,000 crammed into the San Paolo stadium to greet him. He arrived, like the statue of Christ flying over the rooftops of Rome in the opening sequence of Fellini's *La Dolce Vita*, by helicopter, descending from the heavens to be met by scenes of pandemonium that would last, on and off, for seven years.

Sívori had preceded him in Naples by just over twenty years, arriving from Juventus at the same time as the club signed another great but ageing forward, José Altafini, from AC Milan. For nothing more than playing a part in a victory over Roma in the league, the club struck a special gold medal for Sívori. Until the arrival of Maradona, however, they had done no more than come close to capturing the championship, usually being edged out by Sívori's former club. By the time Maradona arrived they had fought off relegation for three seasons in a row, a fact of which he was apparently unaware when he was deciding his future. They were, he later estimated, a Serie B team masquerading as a top-flight outfit. After a poor start to that first year his efforts hauled Napoli up to eighth in the final standings, his fourteen goals placing him third in the table of Serie A's top scorers, behind Michel Platini of Juventus and Alessandro Altobelli of Internazionale. The following season he lifted the club up to third place in the table, but still he could only watch as Juventus and Roma battled for the title.

As the 1986 World Cup approached, his life was running at a dangerous speed. Cocaine, women, parties and Ferraris vied with football for his affections. His incessant demands had irritated Corrado Ferlaino, the club's president. His weight began to increase as he lost his appetite for training. Cyterszpiler, whose investments had turned his earnings to dust, left the camp, to be replaced by a new manager, Guillermo Cóppola. Another departure, even more operatic in its emotional intensity, was that of Claudia Villafane, Maradona's girlfriend since his teenage years and the mother of his two daughters; her replacements were numberless and often nameless, although one of them, a twenty-year-old woman named Cristina Sinagra, appeared to occupy a special place. She was swiftly ejected, however, when she announced that she was pregnant with his child. His denial failed to silence her. When the Argentina squad touched down on Mexican soil and faced a forest of cameras and microphones, the first question to their captain was a request for his reaction to Cristina's announcement, at her own press conference in Naples, that he was the father of her son, due to be born in two months' time.

Replacing the cultured, thoughtful Menotti as Argentina's head coach was a man of very different instincts, one who seemed to engage in a battle with Menotti for the very soul of Argentinian football. Carlos Bilardo had been a member of the notorious Estudiantes de la Plata side of the 1960s, and in terms of their philosophies the two men were as directly opposed as Bernardino Rivadavia and Juan Manuel de Rosas, the democrat and the tyrant who battled over the future of the nascent republic of Argentina in the early nineteenth century. In his time as coach of Huracán, before he took over the national side, Menotti had established a reputation for promoting a progressive, expressive brand of football. With Estudiantes, Bilardo had mimicked the cynical brutality of Rosas's *colorados*, the red-shirted gauchos who rode in from the pampas to make history of Rivadavia's civilized style of government.

René Houseman, one of the heroes of 1978, once observed: 'Menotti would say, "Get on the field and invent." That's all. He didn't say "mark" or "run". Just "invent".' By contrast, for Bilardo the experience of winning trophies with his club had persuaded him that invention could only take place once the prime objective, the destruction of the opposition's forces, had been achieved. 'I'll never approve of the way Estudiantes played,' Antonio Rattín, the captain of Boca Juniors, said. 'No one wanted to play them. They fought, they bit, they wouldn't let opponents play, yet they were the champions of America and the world.' Bilardo knew how vehemently they were disliked. 'But over the years people had to admit that the team had integrity and got results,' he said. 'People like success. Very few fans like lyrical football. They might say they like a football spectacle, but when their team is one–nil up they long for the final whistle.'

In Mexico, however, his own captain once again became the target of the tactics Bilardo had favoured. First the South Koreans tripped and nudged Maradona as he guided Argentina to a 3–1 win in their opening group game, creating all three goals for Jorge Valdano and Oscar Ruggeri. Against Italy in the next match he was marked by his friend and club colleague Salvatore Bagni, and scored the equalizer in a one-all draw. Argentina's third opponents, Bulgaria, knew that a narrow defeat would allow them to qualify for the next round and were happy to pack their defence and lose 2–0. In the second round Argentina met Uruguay, their old rivals, who were smarting from a FIFA fine and reprimand after turning their final group match against Scotland into a masterclass in the art of time-wasting while achieving their desired goalless draw. Maradona spent most of his time avoiding waist-high Uruguayan tackles, began the move that ended with Pedro Pasculli scoring the only goal of the match and steered his side to safety through the electric storm that punctuated the second half. The result took them to a meeting with the bitterest enemy of all.

Maradona was only five years old when England won the 1966 World Cup, but his analysis of that victory was shared by every single one of his fellow countrymen. 'Financially,' he would say, 'it was important that the home team won.' The populations of Argentina and Uruguay were united in the belief that the German who refereed England vs Argentina and the Englishman who refereed West Germany vs Uruguay in the 1966 quarter-finals had been appointed specifically to ensure that the South American teams made no further progress. When Antonio Rattín, Argentina's captain, was sent off after thirty minutes' play at Wembley, apparently for disputing Rudolf Kreitlein's decision, their worst fears were confirmed. Rattín remembered chocolate being thrown at him by the English crowd as, after his arguments had held up the game for eight minutes, he made his way to the tunnel. As he passed the corner post, topped by a small Union Jack, he fingered the flag thoughtfully.

But the ingrained Argentinian dislike of the English went back much further than that. In 1806 ten warships under the command of Sir Home Popham invaded Buenos Aires, looting the government treasury and sending the spoils back to London before a citizen army launched a successful counter-attack. General John Whitelocke, who lost a quarter of his 12,000 men in an attempt to break the siege, was impressed by the fervour of the resistance. 'Every male inhabitant, whether free or slave, fought with a resolution and perseverance which could not have been expected, even from the enthusiasm of religion and national prejudice, or the most inveterate and implacable hostility,' he wrote. And since Wembley, of course, there had been not just the famous battles between Manchester United and Estudiantes but also the Falklands War in 1982. In the build-up to the quarter-final in Mexico City's Azteca Stadium on 22 June 1986, both teams were asked repeatedly about the effect of those military hostilities on their attitude to the forthcoming match. All denied that the conflict between Thatcher and Galtieri held any lingering relevance. Maradona, at least, was lying. 'This was revenge,' he said many years later. 'It was like recovering a little bit of the Malvinas.'

The satisfaction could not have been greater when, after fifty-one minutes of an excruciatingly tense match, he stole the first goal with a piece of cheating that ripped the heart out of the English. Leaping above the slow-starting Peter Shilton, he got his left fist to Steve Hodge's sliced clearance, and the only people in the world who did not see it were Ali Bennaceur, the Tunisian referee, and his linesman. Four minutes later, with the

English still flattened with horror at the injustice of it all, he picked up the ball inside his own half. What happened in the next ten and a half seconds constituted, by common consent, one of the greatest goals ever scored. First he turned through 180 degrees before slipping between Peter Beardsley and Peter Reid. He accelerated inside Terry Butcher, held off Terry Fenwick, waited until Shilton had bought the merest hint of a dummy, and then, with Butcher closing in for a last-ditch tackle, slid the ball home with the cold economy of a back-street assassin. Glenn Hoddle, applauded by Maradona at White Hart Lane a few weeks earlier, could only stand and watch in horrified admiration.

Two factors prevented Maradona's second goal against England from being considered the equal of Jairzinho's success against the same opponents sixteen years earlier. First, football is a team game, and this was a solo performance, while the move that defeated Bobby Moore's England represented collective invention in its highest form. Second, as several observers pointed out, it was devalued by the shattering effect on English morale and concentration of Maradona's blatant cheating only four minutes earlier. But it meant that, with thirty-five minutes to go, the game was effectively over, despite an English revival inspired by the wingers Chris Waddle and John Barnes, belatedly sent on as substitutes. A Barnes cross was touched home by Gary Lineker, who then came close to scoring an equalizer. But Argentina were through to meet Belgium in the semi-final, where Maradona did the same again: two goals in the Azteca, this time without reply, the first with a perfectly timed flick of his foot, the second with an unstoppable burst of acceleration through the massed defence that rivalled his second effort against England, although without the surrounding melodrama.

West Germany reached the final with an undistinguished team under the management of Franz Beckenbauer, who knew the limitations of the resources at his disposal. Lothar

Matthäus, his best player, was given the job of shackling Maradona, which was perhaps why Argentina's captain contributed to neither of the goals, by José Luis Brown and Valdano, that put them two up with an hour gone. Then came the typical German recovery, goals by Karl-Heinz Rummenigge and Rudi Völler bringing them level with less than ten minutes to play. Untypically, however, Beckenbauer's team failed to bolt the door and wait for the extra half-hour that might have allowed them to grind out a win. Maradona, finally, found a killer pass to Jorge Burruchaga, who ran in from the right to shoot across the static Toni Schumacher. Maradona had not scored in the final but his five goals in the tournament put him one behind Gary Lineker of England and level with Emilio Butragueño of Spain and Careca of Brazil, his Napoli colleague. And this time there was no military government waiting in the Casa Rosada to use the triumph as a political weapon.

But 29 June 1986 was not the day Diego Maradona would describe as the greatest of his life. That occurred almost a year later, on 10 May 1987, when the race for the Serie A title reached its climax and the championship finally came to Naples. Needing only a point against Fiorentina at San Paolo, Maradona set up Andrea Carnevale for the opening goal, watched the teenaged Roberto Baggio equalize with his first goal in Serie A, and then helped his teammates play out time until 86,000 people and thousands more in the streets outside could give vent to an explosion of joy and relief. 'Maradona didn't do this,' he added. 'God did it.' As if only God's achievements could surpass those of Maradona. And, anyway, the fans had seen it for themselves; they knew where the responsibility lay.

Three years later the championship would be won for a second time. In between times Maradona turned down an ardent appeal from Silvio Berlusconi, the media tycoon, to join his allstar AC Milan side. And in 1989 he led Napoli to the UEFA

Cup final, where they met VfB Stuttgart over two legs. At home, after Stuttgart had taken the lead, Maradona drove his teammates to a 2–1 victory. Away, in the Neckar Stadium, Ricardo Alemão scored for the Italian side before Jürgen Klinsmann pulled a goal back. Ciro Ferrara, the great Naples-born defender, scored from Maradona's headed cross before the interval, and on the hour, having resisted enormous pressure from the home side, Maradona set up Antonio Careca for the goal that opened up a three-goal advantage on aggregate. Though Stuttgart scored twice more, Napoli hung on to win 5–4 over the two legs. It was the club's first and only European trophy, and once again the genius of the golden boy had secured it for his new congregation of *descamisados*.

It was in Naples, however, that his life really came apart. When, in November 1989, he finally married his hometown sweetheart, Claudia Villafane, it was hardly a sign of encroaching stability. Their lavish ceremony mimicked the celebrations preferred by African dictators, establishing a template for subsequent caricatures of the domestic lives of over-rewarded footballers. Marriage did nothing to curb his behaviour. His circle of friends expanded to include, and eventually to be dominated by, members of the Camorra, the Neapolitan equivalent of the Sicilian Mafia; it was no coincidence that his consumption of drugs increased exponentially. Cristina Sinagra and her infant son, also christened Diego, were ignored. And although in 1987 he had signed a five-year extension to his contract, by the time of Napoli's second title his increasingly erratic and wilful behaviour had damaged his relationships with the club's directors and management beyond repair.

During Italia '90 he made one of his biggest mistakes. Assuming that his two championships had forged a bond with the Neapolitan people which transcended national loyalties, he invited them to abandon Italy and support Argentina when the two teams met, as luck would have it, at San Paolo with a place in the final at stake. It was the gesture that strained his relationship with his adopted home to breaking point.

Bilardo's team had started their defence of the title on the worst possible note, losing by the only goal of the match to Cameroon in front of a crowd of 73,000 at San Siro. Two Africans were sent off in the second half as they protected the lead given to them when François Omam Biyick's header slipped through the hands of Nery Pumpido, but Maradona was suffering from the effects of an injury to his left foot, inflicted during a warm-up match, and could do nothing to salvage the holders' pride. The largely Milanese crowd, which only weeks earlier had been edged out of the title race by Maradona's Napoli, now had the chance to revel in his discomfiture. Maradona's reaction, however, was magnificently sarcastic. Having shaken the hand of every opponent, he told reporters: 'I am proud to have played a part in the people of Milan putting aside their racism for a day to cheer on Cameroon.'

In Naples for their second match, Argentina again benefited from having an opponent sent off, this time a Russian. Pumpido, however, had already left the field with a broken leg, to be replaced by Sergio Goycochea. The hand of Maradona again took a part, clearing Oleg Kuznetsov's flick off the line; once more the officials saw nothing amiss. Pedro Troglio and Burruchaga scored the goals that righted Bilardo's ship. A 1–1 draw with Romania five days later carried them into the second round, although 52,000 Neapolitans saw their hero overshadowed by another small, dark No. 10 with occasional weight problems: Gheorghe Hagi, the man known as 'the Maradona of the Carpathians'.

Brazil were the opponents in the last sixteen, and 61,000 turned up to watch at Turin's new Stadio delle Alpi. With Napoli's Alemão and Careca leading their attack, Brazil charged at Argentina from the kick-off, with Maradona apparently powerless as they poured forward. But their failure to convert their chances proved fatal after eighty-one minutes when Maradona took possession in the centre circle, beat four defenders on a run that rolled back the years, and fed Claudio Caniggia, the speedy winger, who drove the ball past Claudio Taffarel for the winner. Ricardo Gomes, Brazil's captain, was sent off two minutes later. A fine Yugoslav side, inspired by Robert Prosinecki and Dejan Savicevic, and making light of the first-half expulsion of Refik Sabanadzovic, held Argentina to a goalless draw after 120 minutes in the quarter-final in Florence before losing 3–2 on penalties, with Maradona's own weak effort saved by Tomislav Ivkovic.

Then came the drama of a meeting between Italy and Argentina in the semi-final, with Napoli's stadium as the setting. Maradona's appeal to the locals was based on sentiments belonging to the previous century. What, he asked them, has Italy – meaning the power centres of the north – ever done for you? By supporting Argentina they could demonstrate their independence from the neglectful establishment. Some responded to his call; most did not. The rest of Italy was enraged by his presumption. Their team, however, failed to back up the sentiments with the necessary deeds. Salvatore Schillaci, the surprise of the tournament, opened the scoring in the first half, Caniggia equalizing after an hour. Ricardo Giusti was sent off for a foul on Baggio in extra time, and Argentina won the shoot-out 4–3, with Maradona converting his side's final effort before Aldo Serena's miss settled the tie and eliminated the hosts.

To most fans around the world, Brazil, Yugoslavia or Italy would have made better opponents for Argentina in Rome's Stadio Olimpico. Yet again, however, West Germany had scrapped their way to a final that few remember with pleasure. Argentina had four players suspended, including Caniggia, their most potent scorer, and lost two more, substitute Pedro Monzón and Gustavo Dezotti, to red cards in the second half; after concentrating almost wholly on using any means possible to keep the Germans out of their penalty area, they achieved the ignominious feat of becoming the first side not to score in a World Cup final. Maradona was subdued by the close attentions of Guido Buchwald, and a dismal match was settled by Andreas Brehme's penalty six minutes from time, leaving millions around the globe grateful to be spared extra time and yet another shoot-out.

Even after Maradona had dried his copious tears, he found a return to normality impossible. There were flashes of the old brilliance in his performances for Napoli in the autumn of 1990, but his self-indulgence was reaching new levels and his appearances at the training ground were increasingly sporadic. The pleas of his teammates fell on ears that were listening to other, more seductive music. A couple of weeks before his thirtieth birthday, he announced his retirement from international football. When he withdrew himself from consideration on the eve of Napoli's match against Fiorentina, after a night of wild partying, the club's management finally turned against him. The sudden appearance of a supergrass with tales of the involvement of Maradona and Cóppola in a cocaine-dealing racket darkened the waters swirling around the head of the former golden boy. After years of being sheltered by the club from Serie A's post-match dope tests, finally the protection was withdrawn. On 17 March 1991, after Napoli had defeated Bari 1–0 at home with a goal from the young Gianfranco Zola, Maradona was called to provide a sample. A week later the result came through and the world was told that traces of cocaine had been discovered in his urine. Banned by the Italian football association, within days he was on a private plane back to Argentina.

He had further to fall before redemption arrived. In Buenos Aires he was arrested at a friend's apartment and taken away in handcuffs, and a judge ordered him to undergo treatment for his addiction. He played in a couple of charity games in

Argentina and tried to get the suspension lifted. When it ended, in June 1992, he began the process of severing his links with Napoli and, after rejecting Bernard Tapie's invitation to join Olympique de Marseille, flew back across the Atlantic to join Sevilla, where Bilardo, the head coach, had persuaded his employers to pay Napoli a fee of $7 million. There would be twenty-six appearances, a mere five goals and the now familiar stories of colourful night-time behaviour. When Bilardo substituted him during a match against Burgos, old enmities surfaced. 'I'm going to have this out with Bilardo, man to man,' he said. 'If, that is, Bilardo is a man.' It was his last appearance in a Sevilla shirt and he returned home, without a club.

At his country villa outside Buenos Aires, bloated and confused, he tried to put his life back together, without measurable success. Goaded by photographers massed outside his front gate, he retaliated by firing at them with an air rifle. Headlines around the world recorded his latest shame, but the clemency of the authorities, encouraged by the Argentinian president, Carlos Menem, kept him out of jail, requiring only a payment of a substantial fine and damages to those who had suffered pellet wounds.

And yet, in time of need, once again the nation turned its eyes to him. When Colombia arrived in Buenos Aires and beat a Maradona-less Argentina 5–0 in a qualifying match for the 1994 World Cup, the outcry became irresistible. No matter that Pelé himself had predicted that the team of Carlos Valderrama, Freddy Rincón and Faustino Asprilla would triumph in the finals in the United States; no matter that Maradona had said he would not play for Alfio Basile, Argentina's new head coach, even 'if he came begging on his knees'; the crowd had chanted Maradona's name throughout the second half. The next issue of *El Gráfico*, Argentina's weekly sports magazine, appeared with a black cover. In response to the outpouring of public emotion, he travelled to the city of Rosario, two hundred miles from his home, and signed with Newell's Old Boys. There he would get himself back to fitness in preparation for a return to the national colours.

Unflatteringly nicknamed *Los Leprosos*, the lepers, Newell's Old Boys were not even the most famous team in Rosario. Founded in 1903 by the former pupils of Isaac Newell's Anglo-Argentine Commercial School, they had lived in the shadow of Rosario Central, formed in 1899 by workers of the Central Argentine Railway Company and the favoured team of Che Guevara, who was born and raised in the city. 'Don't do it, Diego,' the historian Osvaldo Bayer pleaded in his column in the local newspaper, *La Capital*. 'Think about those of us whose faith is vested, man and boy, in Rosario Central. Don't make us turn our backs on you. Don't play against the glorious blue and yellows. Che is looking down from heaven on you . . .'

While his manager negotiated with the club, which paid a fee of $4 million for his registration and pledged a weekly sum of $25,000 to the player, Maradona spent several weeks training with the squad of Chacarito Juniors. His weight fell from 92 to 77 kg and the only man who knew how it had been done was Daniel Cerrini, his trainer, who put him on a crash diet and made extensive use of food supplements. When he arrived in Rosario, 30,000 people turned up to watch his first training session in the red and black shirt. 'I wanted to hug them all, one by one,' he said. 'It's like starting to live again.' His first match, a hastily arranged friendly against Emelec, of Ecuador, took place in a stadium packed to the rafters, with fans climbing the floodlight pylons to get a view, so there was much hilarity in the press box when the official attendance, for a stadium with a capacity of 30,000, was given as a shade over 21,000, with receipts of just over half a million dollars from tickets costing $50 for seats and $20 for the terraces. 'A bad night for the taxman,' somebody sniggered. But a good one for Diego. According to a newspaper report, he had 102 touches during the game, completed sixty-two passes and had five shots on goal, including an extravagant bicycle kick. In the seventieth minute he carried the ball across the face of the goal from left to right before paralyzing Emilio Valencia, Emelec's goal-keeper, with a right-footed shot that flew in a tantalizing arc and entered the goal just inside the angle of bar and post. 'I felt very good,' he said afterwards, attending his press conference in a loud green jacket, with diamonds winking from the gold ring in his left earlobe, his cheekbones looking sharp enough to cut paper. 'Of course I'm short of fitness, but I'll get there. Little by little, day by day.' As the fans made their way home, many of them wearing red and black shirts bearing the No. 10, they were performing a new song. 'Let's have a minute's silence for Rosario Central,' they bellowed. 'They're already as good as dead.'

That turned out to be wishful thinking. The adventure in Rosario lasted only a few weeks; the town wasn't big enough for him. But it did its job. Basile brought him back into the national squad and qualification was achieved, thanks to a deflected shot in a play-off against Australia. In their opening match at the finals, in Boston's Foxboro stadium, Gabriel Batistuta scored a hat-trick as Argentina beat Greece 4–0; the other goal came from the captain, Diego Armando Maradona, whose maniacal reaction to his success seemed to be that of a man not entirely in possession of his senses. Four days later came the news of the positive dope test, with its implied message about how all that weight had been lost, and the end of his career in international football.

'They've killed me,' he exclaimed. Banned for a further fifteen months by FIFA, he believed that he was being paid back for criticisms levelled in earlier years at the world governing body, such as his claim in 1990 that the World Cup draw was rigged. Unable to play for a living, he tried his hand at management, first with the lowly Deportivo Mandiyu and then with Racing Club, one of the great names of Argentinian football. Not surprisingly, his tenure at both clubs was brief and explosive. Unable to hold his tongue when a refereeing decision went against his players, he suffered touchline bans. When Mandiyu were relegated, he called one official 'a liar and a thief'. Frustrated by the inability of lesser players to meet the standards he required, he grew distracted. One of the distractions, also short-lived, was the creation of an international players' trade union; at the press conference to launch the project he was joined by Eric Cantona, Gianluca Vialli and George Weah. Cantona had once claimed: 'In the course of time it will be said that Maradona was to football what Rimbaud was to poetry and Mozart was to music.' But if Che Guevara was looking down from heaven on this gathering, hoping to see the beginning of a successful campaign for players' rights, the great revolutionary witnessed only a bunch of rich men perpetrating a farce.

Always there was turmoil, always there were cameras and microphones. He seemed to need it all, to detest it and to devour it at the same time. When he paid for his wife to have her breasts surgically enhanced, he appeared on the steps of the clinic after the operation to meet the waiting media. '*Sus lolas son barbaras,*' he announced with a smile of pride that contrived to look more like a leer. In translation: her tits are amazing.

Once his suspension had expired there remained only a final fling in the shirt of Boca Juniors, a sentimental return in his thirty-seventh year. It ended, on 24 August 1997, with another positive test for cocaine, after which he was told by an Argentinian specialist that he faced death if he continued to use the drug.

It took him another two years to recognize the truth of that prediction. A heart attack on holiday in the Uruguyan resort of Punta del Este drove him into the arms of Fidel Castro, *el commandante en jefe*, who put Cuba's excellent medical facilities at his disposal. Accompanied by his parents, his wife and his daughters, Maradona entered a specialist centre and did his best to rid himself of the addiction.

While he struggled, he received pieces of evidence that he had not been forgotten. In his honour, Napoli retired the No. 10 shirt. After polling fans around the world via the internet, FIFA made a special award to Pelé and Maradona, two such contrasting figures, as the greatest players of the millennium; it was rumoured that Maradona had won the popular vote by a landslide, prompting the governing body to appoint a committee of experts who would vote in favour of the Brazilian, thus permitting a joint award. And on 10 November 2001, as the climax to a special Maradona day, Argentina played a testimonial match in La Bombonera against a Rest of the World XI including René Higuita, the Colombian goalkeeper, Ciro Ferrara, his old comrade from Napoli, Hristo Stoichkov, another founder member of the abortive players' union, Cantona, Matthäus, Valderrama, Careca, Enzo Francescoli of Uruguay and Davor Šuker of Croatia. Maradona, now almost as wide as he was tall, played forty-five minutes for each side, with his teammates ceaselessly trying to set up scoring chances for a man who once needed no help in that respect, not even from God. More than 60,000 packed the stadium, singing and chanting and going crazy in the second half when he finally put a penalty kick past Higuita before turning away and pulling off his Argentina shirt to reveal the colours of Boca Juniors underneath. The noise shook the whole city; it really was the end.

Some feared the end of football would mean the end of his life. And two and a half years later, on 18 April 2004, as a sweaty, corpulent Maradona was watching Boca from a VIP box, shouting and gesturing at the players in his usual manner, he suddenly slumped to his knees and keeled over. While paramedics manoeuvred his forty-three-year-old body, now weighing 122 kg – almost twenty stone – on to a stretcher and carried him down to an ambulance, the news began to travel around the world. As he lay in an intensive care room in the Suizo-Argentina clinic, obituaries were prepared. Buenos Aires went into a state of suspended animation, praying and preparing to mourn. Cars flew the national flag and hooted as they passed the clinic; ordinary people gathered outside, holding candles. Inside, doctors were noting that his heart was functioning at barely a third of its capacity.

Three days later he came off the critical list and the recovery began. He returned to Cuba for further treatment to wean him off cocaine, which had been his support and escape for almost twenty years. In Colombia – the source, ironically, of the substance he had so rigorously abused – he submitted to the knife of a surgeon, who put a staple in his stomach to curb his eating. Soon his scales no longer read 122 kg but something very close to 74 kg, which was his fighting weight in his prime. He accepted a post as technical director of Boca Juniors. Claudia was back at his side, albeit on a platonic basis, according to a clearly regretful Maradona. He began hosting a chat show on Argentinian television, titled *La Noche del Diez* (*The Night of the 10*), during which he provided another rationalization for the hand-ball goal against England: 'He who robs a thief gets a hundred years of pardons,' he said. When the only rival to his pre-eminence among history's great players appeared as a guest, Maradona was asked which of the two was the greater and came up with the perfect reply: 'My mother thinks I was. Pelé's mother thinks he was.' Then came an offer to appear on a weekly show in Rome, *Ballando con le Stelle* (*Dancing with the Stars*). In this he could be seen performing the waltz, the samba and the tango with Miss Italy and other lissom partners. It was quite a success, reviving memories of the days when Serie A danced to his irresistible tune. Only a few weeks into the series, however, Maradona failed to arrive on his regular transatlantic flight from Buenos Aires. Nor, it transpired, would he be appearing again any time soon. The Italian taxman wanted $21 million, said to be owing from his days in Naples.

Buenos Aires possesses two big cemeteries. The neoclassical portals of the first, La Recoleta, stand next to a fine park in the fashionable north-west of the city, shaded by luxuriant trees and surrounded by expensive residences. Here is where, in the words of Jorge Luis Borges, 'old sweetnesses, old rigours meet and are one'. La Recoleta contains the remains of the country's dignitaries and founding fathers, such as Admiral Guillermo (William) Brown, born in Foxford, County Mayo, in 1777: *'Inglés de origen, Argentino por sus servicios.'* Eva Perón is buried there, in the vault of the Duarte family, always with drying and fading flowers tucked behind its grille by worshippers, along with keepsakes. There is a life-size bronze of the boxer Luis Angel Firpo, who was known as the Wild Bull of the Pampas and almost became the first Latin American to win the heavyweight championship of the world when he felled Jack Dempsey in the opening minutes of their fight in New York in 1923, before Dempsey got up to take ample revenge in the second round. Firpo eventually retired to become a car dealer and a rancher; he died in 1960, aged sixty-six, and his statue is accompanied by a tender inscription from his widow: *'Luis amor mío, gracias por haberme amado tanto / que Dios todo poderosa ponga / Luz y paz en tu silencio – Lourdes.'* Light and peace in your silence. Maybe one day Diego Armando Maradona will rest there, too. But they should really lay him down in the other garden of death, La Chacarita, on the west side of town.

This is the people's cemetery, built after the yellow-fever epidemic of the 1870s and now filled with row after row of unnotables. There are exceptions, including Ángel Labruna and Adolfo Pedernera, two members of the celebrated River Plate forward line of the late 1940s, an attack so irresistible that it became known as *La Máquina* (the machine); at the age of forty Labruna was called out of retirement to lead Argentina in the 1958 World Cup, while Pedernera later managed the national team. But the most remarkable tomb is that of Carlos Gardel, the great tango singer, whose body was brought home after his death in a plane crash in Medellin, Colombia, in 1935. Gardel was a combination of Rudolph Valentino, Maurice Chevalier and Frank Sinatra, and his handsome statue sings for eternity, surrounded by plaques sent by Gardel societies from Lima to Lisbon. At weekends, *Porteños* (natives of Buenos Aires) visiting family graves pause to lay a flower at his feet or to light a cigarette and place it between his waiting fingers, crafted to accept just such a tribute. Gardel, his fans say, sings better every day. But La Chacarita makes no pretences. Here, Borges wrote, 'A hard vegetation, purgatorial rubbish / inured to damnation, / batters your long line of walls / as though nothing were sure but corruption; a slum / hurls its fiery life at your feet / in gutters shot through with a low flame of mud, / or stands, dazed and unwilling, in the sound of accordions / or the bleating of carnival horns.'

And this is where the poet heard a voice, accompanied by a guitar, singing these words:

> *La muerte es vida vivida*
> *La vida es muerte que viene.*

Death is life lived away / Life is death coming on.

Light and peace, Diego. May they be yours when the time comes. But not silence. You wouldn't know how to handle that.

8 Roberto Baggio

When Italy's twenty-two players were given a day off in Paris during the 1998 World Cup finals, they made their plans and split up into groups. Some of the older ones, including Paolo Maldini, Giuseppe Bergomi and Billy Costacurta, spent the day with their families. Demetrio Albertini, Alessandro Nesta, Gianluca Pagliuca, Enrico Chiesa and Gianluigi Buffon went on a shopping expedition. A third group, including Alessandro Del Piero, Roberto Di Matteo, Filippo Inzaghi, Christian Vieri, Fabio Cannavaro and Luigi Di Biagio, decided to experience the fibre-glass fantasies of Disneyland Paris. And one man went to visit the local Buddhist centre.

That man, of course, was Roberto Baggio. A fine teammate, popular with his colleagues, a conscientious and inspiring captain during his final seasons in the top flight of Italian league football, Baggio is nevertheless among the most striking examples of the sort of No. 10 who stands alone – sometimes in majesty, sometimes in a less enviable form of isolation. His great career, which encompassed twenty-two years as a professional footballer and enabled him to participate in three World Cups, was marked not only by the sincere affection of fans throughout the world but by the feeling that he never quite made full use of the marvellous gifts that made themselves apparent while he was still a child, and which never left him. The blame could be shared between the series of seven major knee operations that began when he was barely out of his teens and the distrust that coaches often display towards an individualist. And even when he was committing his heart and his soul and his sweat to the team, Baggio was always an individualist.

Some would even suggest that the defining moment of his

career came on 17 July 1994, when he stood in front of the ball at the Rose Bowl in Pasadena, waiting under a harsh sun to take the penalty kick that would keep Italy in the final of the World Cup. Watched by a global audience numbering in the hundreds of millions, he had never been more alone in his life.

Two of his teammates had already failed during the penalty contest that followed a goalless stalemate lasting a hundred and twenty minutes. Franco Baresi had missed the target, Daniele Massaro had seen his shot saved, and Brazil led the shoot-out 3–2, with one attempt left for each side. Baggio, who had injured his thigh so badly in the previous match that his doctor had advised him to sit out the final, looked exhausted as he gathered himself for one last effort. He took his usual short run-up, applied the instep of his right boot to the ball, and watched it fly over Claudio Taffarel's crossbar. As Brazil's gold-shirted players embraced and danced across the pitch, Baggio put his hands on his knees and bowed his head in recognition of his historic failure. Seldom has sport seemed more randomly vindictive; nothing he had done in his career justified humiliation on such a vast scale.

He was marked out from the start. His professional début came at fifteen, in the colours of Vicenza, his local league club, then playing in Serie C1, the third division of the Italian league. Twenty-two years later he was applauded from the field by 80,000 fans in a packed San Siro stadium, his career at an end after 452 appearances and 205 goals (an astonishing eighty-five of them decisive) in Serie A, plus fifty-six appearances and twenty-seven goals for Italy. He was making his final appearance for Brescia, the club at which he spent his last four years, but it was the fans of AC Milan, amid the celebrations of their own club's seventeenth championship season, who rose to give him an ovation as he walked through a latticework of sunshine and shadow to the touchline after eighty-four minutes of play and out of football for ever.

He had played for Milan a few years earlier, without success. His heart had not seemed to be in it. His £7.7 million transfer from Juventus had been arranged between the owners of the two clubs, Juve's Gianni Agnelli and Milan's Silvio Berlusconi, and was rumoured to have its origin mostly in Berlusconi's desire to make a big-name signing that would give a spectacular push to the election campaign of his political party, Forza Italia. For Baggio, noted for the honesty and transparency of his approach to life and football, even an indirect participation in the games of such men must have been an uncomfortable experience.

One of eight children, he was born to Fiorindo Baggio, a shopkeeper, and his wife Matilde on 18 February 1967 in the small town of Caldogno, north of Vicenza, the prosperous hometown of Palladio, the great sixteenth-century architect, and more recently a centre for the textile and computer industries. Roberto showed his interest in football from an early age; often his father would have to mount his bike at dusk to go searching for the boy, who would be off somewhere playing with his ball. At nine, Roberto's promise was noticed by the coach of Caldogno, Gian Piero Zenere, and in 1982, after he had scored six goals against Leva, he was introduced to the Vicenza club by a scout, Antonio Mora, who persuaded the larger outfit to reward Caldogno with a fee of around £300.

He played in one league game at fifteen, and in six more the following season under a new coach, Bruno Giorgi, who saw him score his first league goal. In February 1984 he received national recognition when he was called up to play for Italy's U16s, but it was during the following season that he blossomed, playing twenty-nine games in Serie C1 and scoring twelve goals, with two more goals in five appearances in the Coppa Italia. His achievement contributed to promotion to Serie B for Vicenza and, on 3 May 1985, a transfer to Fiorentina and Serie A for Baggio.

Two days after signing his contract, however, he suffered a ruptured cruciate ligament in his right knee, an injury so severe that it seemed possible the eighteen-year-old's career was over before it had properly begun. Instead, Fiorentina's management kept faith and sent him to France for an operation performed by Gilles Bousquet, a specialist in sports medicine whose Bellevue clinic in Saint-Etienne was becoming well known. Roberto Bettega, the Juventus and Italy striker, had been the first celebrated footballer to benefit from Bousquet's expertise, followed by Pietropaolo Virdis and others. Baggio spent a week in the clinic, worked hard at his recovery when he returned home, and was rewarded when his new club eased him gently back into action. In December, however, he was back in Saint-Etienne with a torn meniscus. Once again, despite a gloomy prognosis, Baggio refused to entertain negative thoughts. 'Roberto showed the strength of his character,' the doctor later said. 'He was never sorry for himself.' Back in Italy, his lengthy convalescence was supervised by Carlo Vittori, the physiotherapist who had worked with Pietro Mennea, Italy's Olympic 200 metres champion at the 1980 games in Moscow. The ministrations worked and Baggio was back in time to make his Serie A début in September against Sampdoria; he played a further five matches in the championship that season, scoring his first league goal against Napoli on 10 May 1987.

Few years in his life were to be more pivotal than the one in which he turned twenty-one. During the 1987–88 season, with Fiorentina now coached by a young Swede named Sven-Göran Eriksson, he made twenty-nine league appearances and seven in the Coppa Italia, scoring nine times. He also grew his hair and tied it at the back, establishing the image that led to his nickname of *Il Codino Divino* – the sacred ponytail. Those things, the goals and the hairstyle, were what the public was starting to notice. Perhaps more significant for Baggio himself, however, was a decision that had nothing to do with football;

nothing obvious, anyway. This was the year he converted to Buddhism.

Few prominent professional footballers have shown much inclination to involve themselves in movements aimed at changing the world. There was Paul Breitner, the Bayern Munich and West Germany full back who teamed a spectacular Afro with a Zapata moustache, refused to sing 'Deutschland Über Alles' before international matches and displayed Maoist tendencies at a time when the members of the Baader-Meinhof gang were wreaking havoc throughout Germany. And there was Sócrates, the Brazilian playmaker of the 1980s, a qualified doctor whose left-wing views, less tied to the momentary zeitgeist than those of Breitner, found an application in a movement which aimed to change the way Brazilian football was run. So successful in the short term that his club, Corinthians, won the São Paulo state championship with the word *Democracia* on the backs of the players' shirts, the movement led Sócrates into involvement with the more general desire to remove Brazil's military government and restore democracy. Breitner and Sócrates apart, when it comes to linking football with a consciousness of the state of the wider world, and particularly its less privileged inhabitants, we are left with the cosmetic charity work undertaken by today's superstars in order to broaden their appeal, often at the behest of their agents and in collaboration with commercial sponsors seeking to ameliorate the image-tarnishing effects of global corporatism.

Baggio's commitment, made when he was barely twenty-one, appears to have been of a very different order. The movement he joined, called Soka Gakkai, was founded in 1930 by Tsunesaburo Makiguchi, a Japanese educator and philosopher who, as the society's history puts it, 'emphasized the importance of critical thinking over rote learning and self-motivation over blind obedience'. His warnings against his country's growing militarism and against the use of religion to deify the emperor led to his imprisonment during the Second World War, along with his protégé, Josei Toda, and nineteen of their colleagues, on an Orwellian charge of 'thought crime'. Makiguchi, suffering from malnutrition, died in jail before Japan's defeat, aged seventy-three, but Toda emerged to supervise the resumption of the society's activities.

Its name translates as Society for the Creation of Value, and it has branches in seventy-nine countries and members in about 120 more, although it does not list them publicly. 'Certain countries,' it says, 'for religious, social or political reasons, may be sensitive to having us announce publicly that there are Buddhists practising in their borders.' Soka Gakkai International, established in 1970 as the movement's popularity began to spread, now claims more than 12 million members around the world, all of them devoted to 'a practical philosophy of individual empowerment and inner transformation that enables people to develop themselves and take responsibility for their lives'. Soka Gakkai's adherents 'strive in their everyday lives to develop the ability to live with confidence, to create value in any circumstances and to contribute to the well-being of friends, family and community. The promotion of peace, culture and education is central to SGI's activities.' Its projects include humanitarian relief projects, an ecological research centre in Brazil, peace forums and touring exhibitions on the subject of human rights.

Makiguchi founded Soka Gakkai in 1930, two years after he had discovered the teachings of Nichirin, a thirteenth-century Buddhist monk who, like Makiguchi himself, often found himself in conflict with authority, particularly over the abuse of the education system to serve the interests of Japan's ruling élite. Nichirin's petition *On Establishing the Correct Teaching for the Peace of the Land*, published in 1260, provoked the establishment's anger; some of his followers were murdered and Nichirin himself narrowly avoided assassination on several occasions. In 1271 he was arrested and sentenced to death, but his execution was called off when his guards saw a bright light in the night sky and took it to be a divine signal. He spent the rest of his life in exile on the island of Sado, where he survived a harsh climate and occupied himself with writing epistles to his followers on the mainland.

Some of these contained the core of his teaching, which centres on the importance of the Lotus Sutra, one of the most important of Mahayana Buddhism's sacred scriptures. Concentrating on the study of the 'Buddha nature', it teaches that enlightenment is attainable by all people, irrespective of gender, social class, age or educational privilege. A reformist movement, Mahayana Buddhism promotes the ideal of the bodhisattva, the seeker after enlightenment who blends an enjoyment of life with work to relieve suffering and bring joy to others. 'The path of a bodhisattva is not an otherworldly undertaking for people with unique gifts of compassion or wisdom,' Soka Gakkai's teachers say. 'Rather, the qualities of the bodhisattva are inherent in the lives of ordinary men and women, and the purpose of Buddhist practice is to strengthen these qualities until compassion becomes the basis of all our actions.' A twice-daily chant based on the Japanese translation of the Lotus Sutra's title, *Nam-myoho-renge-kyo*, remains the 'primary practice' of Soka Gakkai's membership.

The point is to shape one's own karma in the ascent to Buddhahood. 'By carrying out the correct practice of Buddhism one is able to bring their individual life into harmony with the greater life of the universe,' the teachings continue. 'The result of this is that one is able to experience greater wisdom, courage, life force and compassion. The process of inner spiritual transformation or "human revolution" leads to not only individual empowerment but is the surest way to direct humankind's energies towards creating a peaceful and prosperous world.'

*

Baggio's first call to join the senior international side came in November 1988, when he joined the squad for a friendly against Holland in Rome's Stadio Olimpico. His début came the following April, when Azeglio Vicini, the head coach, put him into the starting line-up against Uruguay in Verona. After twenty minutes he gave his side the lead with a right-footed free kick taken from just outside the area and swung over a six-man defensive wall to curl inside a post. Italy led until two minutes from time, when Aguilera produced an equalizer. Back in Caldogno at the end of another very promising season, he married his childhood sweetheart.

A total of seventeen goals from thirty-two appearances in the 1989–90 Serie A season proved him to be a goalscorer of the highest class and consistency. Fiorentina had also qualified for the UEFA Cup, and Baggio played a significant part in their progress to the final, where they lost to Juventus. The disappointment of Fiorentina's fans turned to anguish and anger when it was learnt that Baggio would be taking off the club's violet shirt at the end of the season to put on Juventus's magpie stripes. But near-riotous demonstrations in the city centre and outside the stadium changed nothing.

Sempre nel mio cuore, the Italian valediction goes – you'll always be in my heart. And this time the club was not just in the fans' hearts but also in that of the player, too.When Juventus met Fiorentina the following season, Baggio refused to take a penalty for his new club. And when he left the pitch at the end of the match, a violet scarf was draped around his neck. The supporters knew that this was a player for whom affection and loyalty were more than skin-deep, even if he had been forced to recognize the brute realities of football's marketplace.

His first World Cup came in 1990, when Italy enjoyed the benefit of home advantage in their attempt to win the tournament for the fourth time. Vicini's squad included Giuseppe Bergomi, Franco Baresi, Gianluca Vialli, Roberto Donadoni, the teenage defender Paolo Maldini and a virtually unknown Sicilian striker, Salvatore 'Toto' Schillaci, who came on as a substitute after seventy-five barren minutes of their opening group match against Austria in Rome and, within four minutes, had thumped home the winner with his forehead.

Baggio watched that one from the bench in the Stadio Olimpico, and he was still there when Italy beat the United States 1–0 with a goal from Giuseppe Giannini, AS Roma's slender playmaker. But when they met Czechoslovakia in the match that would decide who won the group, Vicini made the bold decision to start the match with Schillaci and Baggio up front, displacing Vialli and Andrea Carnevale. Italy looked like a proper team for the first time in the competition, and Vicini's judgement was vindicated first when the wild-eyed Schillaci opened the scoring with another header after nine minutes, and again when Baggio doubled the lead to complete the score-line twelve minutes from time. After playing a one-two with Giannini, he beat two defenders on his way to hitting his shot past Jan Stejskal for a goal that many believed to be the best of the entire tournament.

He was less prominent in Italy's second-round match against Uruguay, a 2–0 victory won with goals from Schillaci, who was rapidly making himself the star of the finals, and Aldo Serena. Against the Republic of Ireland in the quarter-final it was Baggio's run, leaving three beaten defenders in his wake, that set up Donadoni for the shot which, parried by Packie Bonner, gave Schillaci the chance to knock home the rebound and advance his reputation still further.

For Baggio, however, there was severe disappointment when Vicini told him that he would not be starting the semi-final against Argentina in Naples. 'He said I looked tired,' Baggio remembered. 'But I was twenty-three! I would have eaten grass to play.' The inevitable Schillaci, partnered by Vialli, gave Italy the lead after seventeen minutes with a tap-in, but Vicini's side went into their shell and received their due reward after sixty-seven minutes when Claudio Caniggia back-headed Argentina's equalizer, the first goal conceded by Italy in eleven matches. Baggio was brought on for Giannini with a quarter of an hour of normal time to go, and in the second half of extra time Ricardo Giusti was sent off for bringing him down before the match went to a penalty shoot-out. Baresi converted Italy's first effort, followed with success by Baggio and Luigi De Agostini, but misses by Donadoni and Serena meant that Argentina would be going to Rome to meet West Germany in a final that turned out to be the worst in the tournament's history.

Twenty-seven goals in thirty-seven matches during his first season with Juventus, surpassing even his average during his last two seasons with Fiorentina, made Baggio a favourite among the fans in the new Stadio delle Alpi, even though the coach, Gigi Maifredi, was not the most sympathetic of tactical mentors and the team finished an unsatisfactory seventh in the league. Midway through the season, Baggio's wife gave birth to their first child, a daughter whom they named Valentina.

The return of Giovanni Trapattoni in Maifredi's place the following year made life easier for Baggio. In the three years of Trapattoni's second spell in charge, Juventus finished second, fourth and second in Serie A. In 1992–93, the second of those seasons, they also won the UEFA Cup, a side including Baggio, Vialli, Andreas Möller, Jürgen Kohler and Angelo Peruzzi beating Borussia Dortmund 3–1 away and 3–0 at home in the two-legged final. Baggio had scored six goals in nine games on the way to a victory that set the seal on his own personal *annus mirabilis*, at the end of which he was named both FIFA's World Player of the Year and UEFA's European Player of the Year.

With Diego Maradona in serious decline, Ronaldo still just a rumour and the late-blooming Zinédine Zidane yet to make his appearance on the world stage, this was Baggio's time. For a while he was unquestionably the world's pre-eminent footballer, the successor to Pelé, Cruyff and Platini as the repository of the game's finest arts, the model for any child in the process of falling in love with the game.

This state of affairs lasted until the 1994 World Cup finals in the United States, to which Italy travelled with great hopes of success under Arrigo Sacchi, who had introduced the 'pressing' game with such success while in charge of AC Milan. Italy's optimism was increased by the knowledge that they would be playing their group matches in New Jersey and Washington, where they would be encouraged by vast numbers of fans of Italian-American descent. Baggio crossed the Atlantic in particularly good spirits; his wife, Andreina, had just delivered a second child, named Mattia.

Unfortunately for Italy, the Republic of Ireland benefited from the same home-away-from-home advantage. In the Giants Stadium on 18 June there were many thousands of Irish-Americans among the 74,826 who watched Jack Charlton's team of strays and mongrels inflict a 1–0 defeat on Sacchi's pampered thoroughbreds. Ray Houghton scored the goal, chesting down Baresi's poor clearance and sending a long-range volley over the horrified Gianluca Pagliuca in the twelfth minute. With only little Beppe Signori stationed ahead of a web of five blue-shirted midfielders, and with a coach clearly unable to re-create the attacking zest that three great Dutchmen – Ruud Gullit, Marco van Basten and Frank Rijkaard – had bestowed upon his Milan team, Italy subsided to a defeat barely less discreditable in the eyes of their fans back home than the one suffered at the hands of North Korea at Goodison Park in 1966.

Worse seemed likely to follow when Pagliuca was sent off for a foul on Øyvind Leonhardsen after twenty-one minutes of their next match, against Norway. Needing to withdraw an outfield player in order to put on his substitute goalkeeper, Luca Marchegiani, Sacchi shocked all of Italy by removing Baggio. From the midfield, the coach could have selected Nicola Berti, Demetrio Albertini or Dino Baggio (unrelated), all players of markedly lesser talent. Or he could have withdrawn one of the two strikers, Signori or Pierluigi Casiraghi. But no, the message seemed clear: in a moment of crisis, Roberto Baggio was a luxury item. And this time Sacchi's gamble paid off, as Dino Baggio headed the only goal of the game with twenty-one minutes left to play, foiling Norway's attempt to hold out for a point against ten men.

In the final group game, played in Washington's RFK Stadium, Baggio was restored to the line-up and Italy drew with Mexico 1–1, with a goal by Daniele Massaro, a half-time substitute for Casiraghi. All four Group E teams finished level on points, the first time this had happened in the history of the competition. Norway, who had scored one goal and conceded one in their three games, were eliminated while the other three went on to the second phase.

Sacchi kept faith with Baggio for the match against Nigeria in Boston, and it was as well he did. As usual, Italy suffered before they could celebrate. Emmanuel Amunike opened the scoring after a corner had bounced off Maldini in the twenty-sixth minute. Then Gianfranco Zola, who had come on in place of Signori, was unjustly sent off with a quarter of an hour to go. Two minutes from time, however, Roberto Mussi won the ball, fed Baggio, and watched the No. 10 despatch it through a gap between defender and goalkeeper with a shot that sacrificed power in favour of an audacious precision. Late in the first half of extra time the Nigerian defender Augustine Eguavoen fouled Antonio Benarrivo, and Baggio's penalty kick went in off the post to take Italy into the quarter-finals.

Both Baggios scored for Italy against Spain in Boston, Dino after twenty-six minutes and Roberto after eighty-eight. In between, José Luis Caminero equalized with a deflected shot and Mauro Tassotti was fortunate not to concede a penalty for an elbow in the face of Luis Enrique (for which he subsequently received an eight-match international ban). The outcome of a match between two tense teams was settled when

Signori, under pressure, bravely smuggled the ball to Baggio, who beat Andoni Zubizarreta, the Spanish goalkeeper, from a narrow angle.

Italy's semi-final against Bulgaria might be said to represent the zenith of Baggio's career. More specifically, the goal with which he opened the scoring after twenty minutes could stand as a signature moment, a piece of play providing a vignette of the skill, imagination and courage that had taken him to the pinnacle of the world game. Under the gaze of 77,094 fans in the Giants Stadium, he accepted the ball from a throw-in on the left, turning one tight-marking defender in the same movement before beating another as he ran across the face of the penalty area. Finally, he curled a perfectly weighted right-foot shot around Trifon Ivanov, the giant centre back, and past the groping left hand of Borislav Mikhailov, the goalkeeper.

If that was a moment of superlative individualism, his second goal, two minutes later, required the assistance of a colleague, young Albertini's chip into the inside-right channel encouraging him to turn and hit a left-foot volley past Mikhailov. Hristo Stoichkov, Bulgaria's totemic striker, cut Italy's lead with a penalty a minute before the interval, but Sacchi's team held out comfortably – with the exception of Baggio, who pulled a hamstring in the second half and was replaced by Signori with twenty minutes to go.

The four days before the final were spent in intense physiotherapy on the injured leg. The *Azzurri* were already suffering casualties – Baresi was due to return after an operation to cure a knee injury suffered against the Irish, and Costacurta was suspended – and Baggio's presence in the Rose Bowl on 17 July would be crucial to their hopes of success against Brazil. Not only did he make it to the kick-off, he was still on the field two and a half hours later, at the end of the protracted penalty shoot-out. But his contribution was measurably reduced and that, in a poor final which finished scoreless at the end of extra time, may have made a significant difference to the outcome.

In a match between two countries that had both won the title three times, Baggio and his Brazilian rival Romario were charged with the responsibility for scoring the goals that would ensure a classic encounter. In the furnace-like heat of a summer Sunday afternoon in the Pasadena Valley, however, both men could only fire blanks. On the one occasion he escaped the attentions of the outstanding Baresi, the Brazilian striker missed an open goal. And when the Italian genius played a one-two with Massaro to find a clear shooting position, his weak shot was easily gathered by Claudio Taffarel. Then came the fateful finale, in which Baggio's penalty soared into the crowd while Romario's went in off a post. In 1970 Italy had lost a goal-rich final to a Brazil side whose brilliant individuals were setting new standards in collective play; now they flew back across the Atlantic in a mood of disappointment deepened by the knowledge that, against relatively undistinguished opposition, they had failed to do themselves justice. In Baggio's case, an acceptance of the role of blind fate was hardly enough to soften the blow.

He would have to wait four more years for another chance. His fifth and final season at Juventus coincided not just with the arrival of a new manager, Marcello Lippi, and a long-awaited victory in the championship but also, more fatefully, with the appearance in the squad of Alessandro Del Piero, a prodigy with a claim to the No. 10 shirt. Acquired from Padova the previous summer, Del Piero was still in his teens at the start of the championship season, but his exploits made him the new golden boy, an immediate and lasting favourite with the club's patriarchs, the brothers Umberto and Gianni Agnelli. His right foot was as sweet as Baggio's, and when he took free kicks, his success rate was so spectacular that the *Gazzetta dello Sport* began referring to the area just outside the penalty box as the 'Del Piero zone', publishing elaborate diagrams to illustrate his near infallibility. He was young, fresh and good-looking, with eyes so darkly shadowed that they seemed to have been underscored with kohl, and the crowd loved him from the start.

His arrival cast a shadow over Baggio, who left Juventus in the summer of 1995 in a deal designed not just to ease the passage of Del Piero into a permanent starting role but to give Berlusconi the superstar he felt he needed to attract voters and to boost a Milan squad whose trio of Dutch stars had melted away. The arrival of Baggio could not halt Milan's disintegration, however; he never seemed to hit it off with Fabio Capello, the coach. There were fifty-one league appearances in two seasons, but only twelve goals for a team that had lost its identity. Only a couple of seasons earlier, they had compiled a record good enough to allow them to be known as the *Invincibili*. Now players and coaches were coming and going with little rhyme or reason. Oscar Washington Tabarez succeeded Capello, and Sacchi was recalled when Tabarez proved to be a disaster. No one was surprised when, in the summer of 1997, Baggio was deemed surplus to requirements and left to join the comparatively humble Bologna. Founded in 1909, his new club had won the league seven times, but not since 1964. By the time Baggio arrived they had grown accustomed to a life spent on the brink of relegation.

The deal had been done by Bologna's general managers, without the knowledge of the coach, Renzo Ulivieri. There were problems to begin with, but they were overcome when Ulivieri saw that his new acquisition could make a significant impact on the team. In his single season with the club, Baggio made thirty Serie A appearances and scored twenty-two goals. At the age of thirty-one, this represented a grand *risorgimento*; the joy in Bologna was matched by the pleasure felt around Italy that a player who had given so much to clubs and country had not been driven into obscurity by the effects of injuries and the ageing process.

It was enough to win him a popular return to the national

squad in time for the 1998 World Cup, to which they travelled under the guidance of Cesare Maldini, the father of Paolo. A barrage of newspaper articles and opinion polls had persuaded Maldini to restore Baggio to the colours. Now, however, Baggio was seen as Del Piero's understudy, a luxury player who might be brought on to work a little of his old magic if things were going badly.

He started only one game in the tournament, Italy's first group match, against Chile. The *Azzurri* were 2–1 down with two minutes left and facing an ignominious start to their campaign when they were awarded a penalty. As Baggio stepped up to take it, the tension rose. In a moment of high drama, with spectators and television viewers – and no doubt Baggio himself, not to mention his teammates and their coach – recalling the disaster at the Rose Bowl four years earlier, he slotted it safely home. It gave Italy a 2–2 draw and got them off to a respectable start. Baggio's reward was to be relegated to the bench for the remainder of France '98.

The coach's misjudgement became obvious when Italy reached the quarter-finals, where they met the hosts in the Stade de France, the magnificent new stadium in Saint-Denis. After sixty-six minutes, with the score at 0–0, the coach withdrew Del Piero and sent on Baggio. Before long the veteran provoked Laurent Blanc, the experienced and unflappable central defender, into conceding a free kick outside the area. Baggio took it himself, curled it carefully on to Luigi Di Biagio's head and watched the ball slide wide of the post. Three minutes later he played Francesco Moriero in down the right, only to see Bixente Lizarazu make a tremendous interception. As the clock ticked past ninety minutes, his lovely trap and cross allowed Gianluca Pessotto to unleash a drive straight at Fabien Barthez. And as Hugh Dallas, the Scottish referee, was preparing to blow for the end of normal time, Baggio carried the ball into the area, only for Marcel Desailly to cut out his pass to Christian Vieri. In less than twenty-five minutes he had achieved more for Italy than Del Piero had managed in the whole tournament, and the good work seemed likely to continue in the first half of extra time, when he met Demetrio Albertini's chip at the near post with a volley of the utmost delicacy that floated narrowly wide. Thereafter, however, he subsided, along with the rest of the game, as both sides waited for the inevitable shoot-out from the penalty spot.

His turn came early. Zinédine Zidane opened the sequence, scoring with a low shot past Gianluca Pagliuca's right hand. Again Baggio did not flinch. Stepping up, he hit his shot low into the opposite corner, past Barthez's left hand. Redemption of a sort, yet it was not enough. Lizarazu missed for France, but so did Albertini and Di Biagio for Italy. The hosts were through and the *Azzurri* were on the way home to more questions and recriminations.

When Baggio returned to Italy, his haul of nine goals in three World Cups making him Italy's all-time leading scorer in the final stages of the competition, it was to sign on with yet another new club. His rebirth at Bologna had brought about a return to the city of Milan, although this time to Internazionale, another club with a proud history, vast ambitions and a large number of problems. Massimo Moratti, the president, was constantly changing coaches and adding players in an attempt to match the achievement of his father, Angelo, under whose stewardship, and that of the Argentinian coach Helenio Herrera, the *Nerazzurri* had won the European Cup in 1964 and 1965. Despite the presence of Ronaldo and Vieri up front, Blanc in defence and Angelo Peruzzi in goal, nothing much was achieved. Injuries affected Baggio's first season but he still managed ten goals in twenty-three matches in the league and also scored in Champions League meetings with Sturm Graz and Real Madrid. When Marcello Lippi arrived to coach the team for Baggio's second season, however, it was not good news. Ronaldo could manage only five league matches all season as he struggled to overcome a serious knee injury, and Baggio did little better: seven Serie A starts and eleven appearances from the substitutes' bench, with a return of four goals, constituted a severe disappointment. Inter reached the final of the Coppa Italia, but although Baggio played in both matches, he was replaced by Iván Zamorano in the first leg and by Alvaro Recoba in the second, and Inter went down 2–1 on aggregate.

After two seasons at Inter, the *Codino Divino* took on an increasingly bedraggled look as all the good work achieved at Bologna seemed to come undone. But there was to be one more throw of the dice. When Moratti decided to discard him, Baggio headed along the Via Emilia to Brescia, a town best known within sport for providing the start and finish of the Mille Miglia, the legendary race for sports cars. There, in the modest Stadio Mario Rigamonti, under the direction first of Carlo Mazzone and then Giovanni De Biasi, Baggio discovered the same kind of environment that had been so helpful to him in Bologna three years earlier. His knees had taken such punishment that he would wake up on the morning of a match praying for rain and a soft pitch. But with teammates such as Jonathan Bachini, Dario Hubner, Pavel Srnicek and the Brazilian midfielder Matuzalem, he spent four years filling the ground to its 27,500 capacity and bringing Brescia Calcio, founded in 1911, to a position of solid respectability in Serie A, scoring forty-four goals in the blue shirt with its distinctive white 'V' across the chest.

When the time finally came to end his career, on the last day of the 2003–04 season, fate arranged the perfect setting. On a fine mid-May afternoon, all important issues had been settled and nothing could distract attention from the significance of his departure. Against Lazio a week earlier he had delighted Brescia's home fans by tricking his way past Fernando Couto on the edge of the area and guiding a cool left-foot shot inside the post to give his side victory. It was his twefth and final goal of a season in which he played thirty-eight league games and during which he became only the fifth man in history to score 200 goals in Serie A, after Silvio Piola, Gunnar Nordahl, José Altafini and Giuseppe Meazza – in other words, the only man to accomplish that feat in the past quarter century. Now, for the last of those thirty-eight games, he returned to the San Siro, where Milan's capacity crowd put out banners that bade him a fond farewell, chanted his name constantly and applauded his every touch. The home side paid him an unwitting compliment by fielding three brilliant playmakers during the course of the match: the great Portuguese veteran Manuel Rui Costa, the Brazilian starlet Kakà and the young Italian international Andrea Pirlo, who had learnt much from Baggio while on loan at Brescia a couple of seasons earlier. This time Baggio failed to add to his scoring record. The deep-lying Matuzalem registered both Brescia's goals in response to Milan's four, but Baggio, his ponytail now greying, provided the precisely angled return pass that allowed the Brazilian to volley a spectacular second goal from outside the penalty area.

In the eighty-fourth minute the signal came from the bench, and Baggio began the walk to the touchline. The spectators, anticipating the moment, bathed him in the warmest of ovations. As he removed his armband, Paolo Maldini, Milan's captain and his teammate in three World Cups, gave him an embrace full of affection and admiration. And when Baggio crossed the touchline, heading off into history, he embraced the occupants of both benches before turning and heading for the tunnel at the north-east corner of the ground, the cheers resounding in his ears until he disappeared into the darkness for the last time, leaving behind the endless discussion on whether, in his glittering and eventful career, he had truly fulfilled himself.

'Italy loved you, Baggino,' somebody wrote, 'but it also obscured and humiliated you.' As he chanted his Buddhist mantra that night, it is a fair bet that Roberto Baggio's mind was clear of regrets.

*

A few weeks later, at a theatre in the town of Besançon in France, an opera titled *Orfeo Baggio*, with words by Mario Morisi and music by Valerio Gonzales, received its world première. On stage a man in one of Baggio's Brescia No. 10 shirts defended himself against police interrogators accusing him of the rape and murder of a female librarian. 'It is an allegory,' the theatre's publicity document said. 'In a world threatened by chaos (G8 at Genoa, the Twin Towers, the Middle East), how can dreams and beauty survive? In time of war, don't they, too, become enemies of the state? And aren't those who refuse to mobilize against the enemy, who try to hold back the stream of dominant thought and refuse to bend to the monopoly of money and power, also the enemy?'

Morisi, French-born but with Italian antecedents, had travelled to Caldogno, Baggio's home town, to research the project, with the aid of a Stendhal grant from the French foreign ministry. Why choose a famous footballer as the vehicle for his allegory? 'To compare Baggio to Orpheus might seem provocative,' Morisi said, 'but in truth the two myths have many affinities. Both were enchanters of the masses – Orpheus with the lyre, Baggio with the ball. Both descended to the underworld in search of the impossible.'

Based in part on Baggio's own words, taken from interviews down the years, Morisi's libretto contains the following stanza:

> Give me back my football
> Without it, I do not exist
> Without my football, I can say nothing.

It's a sentiment that is true of many great players, sadly enough, yet it is not at all relevant to Roberto Baggio, whose footballing tragedies were even more memorable than his many triumphs but who seemed to have reached an understanding that however important the game might have seemed, it was not, after all, a matter of life and death.

9 Dennis Bergkamp

This, to be truthful, is the one selection I wasn't sure about. The one that made me think hard about Dejan Savicevic and his hallucinatory goal against Barcelona for Milan in the 4–0 win in Athens at the 1994 European Cup final. Or about Johnny Haynes and the memory of seeing him slide a perfect pass through the centre of the Nottingham Forest defence for Allan Clarke to score a goal that silenced the City Ground one afternoon in the 1960s. Or about Teófilo Cubillas, such a delight in the 1970 World Cup finals. Or about Jay Jay Okocha, the only man who could do a step-over with both feet simultaneously off the ground, his body seeming to veer in both directions at once. Or about Enzo Scifo, the Belgian wizard with Italian ancestry. Or about dear, daft Gazza. Or, of course, about the marvellous Zico, who played the game in a kind of golden aura and who may well be the one whose absence from these pages is most widely deplored. But then I spent a day watching film of Dennis Bergkamp in action, thinking about all the things I'd seen him do and remembering the words of Arsène Wenger when they were in the process of winning their first English League-and-Cup double together in 1998: 'A great player is one who makes his team win. Anything else is just talk.' And I resolved to send my apologies to Messrs Savicevic, Haynes, Cubillas, Okocha, Scifo, Gascoigne and Zico.

When the immortal Tom Finney, the most artful of English footballers, was asked to select a team from all the foreign players who have plied their trade in the English league, Bergkamp was among his choices. Few would disagree. Soon after his arrival in 1996 it was obvious that Bergkamp would be an adornment to the Premier League. Over a period of ten years, he distinguished himself in three dimensions: his goal-scoring, his general artistry and the air of quiet serenity with which he went about his job.

I got a hint of the latter attribute in the last weeks of 1992, when I went to Amsterdam to talk to him. He was twenty-three years old at the time, in his sixth season in the Ajax first team, and about to become the object of vast bids from Europe's biggest clubs. After getting the all-clear from his head coach, the beady-eyed Louis van Gaal, I waited for him in the players' restaurant. Training had finished for the day, and he was with the physiotherapist. When he appeared, the thing that struck me was how ordinary he looked. In his nondescript beige sweater, his chain-store stone-washed jeans and his conservative neo-rockabilly quiff, he could have been a trainee tax inspector relaxing after a game of squash. He ordered a glass of milk and a sticky bun, which hardly added to the sense of drama.

We talked about the possibility of a move to Italy, where so many of his former Ajax teammates were to be found: Marco van Basten and Frank Rijkaard at AC Milan, Aron Winter at Lazio, Johnny van't Schip at Genoa. Indeed, on the other side of the restaurant the young winger Bryan Roy was saying his farewells to various colleagues; he was on his way to join Foggia and had been clearing his locker. And now the giants of Serie A were said to be manoeuvring into position to secure Bergkamp's signature.

He mentioned that he had a girlfriend, Henrita, but that he still lived with his parents – 'in the old-fashioned way', he added with a little smile. He liked staying at home. 'I don't necessarily have to get out and party,' he said. 'And it doesn't have to be like that. Look at Milan, at Gullit or Van Basten or Rijkaard, and compare them with Ronald Koeman at Barcelona. It's a big difference. Koeman is very much with his family, nice and quiet, he's never in the gossip papers. I think I could be like him.'

A couple of days earlier I had travelled to Rotterdam to watch Ajax play in Feyenoord's raucous tin drum of a stadium. With the youngsters Edgar Davids and Marc Overmars raiding down the wings, the visitors won 3–0, and Bergkamp made two of the goals. But it was something he did after twenty-five minutes, when the match was still scoreless, that caught my attention. Out on the left-hand touchline, inside his own half, he picked up the ball and tricked his marker with a wonderfully deft turn before racing into Feyenoord's territory and making for the penalty area. Outpacing a second defender, he carried the ball wide of yet another opponent and past the goalkeeper before flicking it across the face of the goal with the outside of his right foot. He missed by inches, but it had been an electrifying glimpse of his potential.

The next day I rang Bobby Robson, then coaching at Sporting Lisbon. Robson knew Bergkamp well from his time with PSV in Eindhoven. People were saying, I told him, that Bergkamp was about to fetch a price of £20 million (this was 1993, remember, a time when £3 million could take Alan Shearer from Southampton to Blackburn Rovers). 'Well,' Robson replied, 'I can tell you that this boy is as good as anything in Europe at the moment. He's a terrific player. A *terrific* player.' Yes, but 20 million quid's worth of terrific player? What makes him worth that much? 'Many qualities. He scores goals, but he's not just a striker. He's got good movement, and he makes his runs from deep in midfield. He's strong, too, so he can make a lot of those runs. He takes the ball easily on either side, he's got a lovely first touch, and he's a cool finisher. He can hit it or he can slot it, and he's good at making the choice. He can head the ball. He's like Greaves or Law or Maradona – you think you've got him under control, and over eighty-five minutes maybe you have, but then he'll give you the slip and knock it in, and there's nothing at all you can do about it. And he's a good team player. He works for other people, not just for himself. Even when he doesn't score, you'll find that his contribution to the match was considerable. And he's got an ideal temperament. He's a super boy, a good athlete, and I'm told he lives well. Everything about him is absolutely right.' So might somebody be justified in laying out the 20 million? 'Who's to say? Probably. It's all relative. In two years' time, 3 million for Alan Shearer might look like chicken-feed. All you can say is that Dennis Bergkamp is a great player to have in your team.'

A dozen years later you would not find a football fan in England ready to disagree with a single word of Robson's analysis.

Dennis Nicolaas Maria Bergkamp was born in Amsterdam on 10 May 1969, eighteen days before Ajax, the city's most famous club, reached the final of the European Cup for the first time; they lost 4–1 that night in Madrid, going down, despite the presence of the young Johan Cruyff, to the AC Milan team that had deprived Manchester United of the opportunity to defend their title.

The child's father was an electrician who played for a local amateur club, Wilskracht; he named the last of his four sons after one of his heroes, Denis Law, the Scottish striker who wore Manchester United's No. 10 shirt. The discrepancy in the spelling ('It's the only difference between us,' Bergkamp told me, with a grin) came at the insistence of an Amsterdam registrar, who thought he knew the correct form of the name. The family lived in a working-class neighbourhood with upwardly mobile aspirations, and Dennis, who had played with a football since he could walk, soon started to appear in Wilskracht's junior teams. But when Ajax, famed for their scouting and youth coaching system, began to notice the talent of the Bergkamp brothers, their father discouraged the club's interest; he felt Ajax were too snooty, and anyway he was a fan of Feyenoord, having spent a year working in Rotterdam. Eventually three of the brothers moved away from football:

the oldest became a chartered accountant, the second a bio-chemist and the third a computer programmer with KLM, the Dutch airline. In Dennis's case, however, the overtures paid off, and at the age of eleven he began to combine his interest in mathematics with evenings at the Ajax academy, a model for all the similar organizations that would grow up around the world over the next twenty years.

Under Rinus Michels, whose promotion of the progressive gospel of Total Football had taken Ajax to a glittering hat-trick of European Cup victories in 1971, 1972 and 1973, every team at the club, from the nine-year-olds to the seniors, played the same fluid 3–4–3 system. In order to give them the right kind of flexibility and a broader vision of the game, and per-haps also to eradicate any hint of prior conditioning, the younger players were made to play in all the outfield positions, with right-footers taking their turn on the left side, and vice versa. 'They made us play everywhere,' Bergkamp said. 'At right back, for instance, not really so that you'd learn how to defend, but so you'd know what a right back was thinking.' By the rudimentary standards of the day, the tuition was extensive and profound. 'At most clubs they only do the basic things, but at Ajax you're learning how to score, how to give a pass, you're playing without goals and learning how to find a free player, at a very young age.'

Cruyff, still playing in the first team, was an object of admi-ration for Ajax's youngsters, and Bergkamp was no exception. His real idol, however, was an Englishman, although not from one of the clubs he visited when his father regularly took the family on holidays to East Anglia, where they would go to look at the stadiums of Norwich City and Ipswich Town. 'We always watched English matches on television,' he said. 'It's nice to watch, it's always a spectacle, always a real game. We looked forward to the Cup final each year. I became a sup-porter of Tottenham Hotspur, because my oldest brother was always shouting, "Look at that!" and it always turned out to be Glenn Hoddle who had done something brilliant. I was a centre forward then, but I followed him for three or four years, and I tried to get some of the techniques he was using into my own play. Like when the ball would come high, he could get it with one leg in the air' – he mimed bringing the ball down from chest height – 'and make a pass with the other foot in a tenth of a second. That was unbelievable.'

Ajax's coaching staff appreciated the skills of the adolescent Bergkamp, but they were concerned about his comparative physical frailty. Nor did they believe that his seemingly passive approach would be suited to senior football. A career in physiotherapy appeared to beckon. When he was sixteen, however, Cruyff returned to the club as its head coach, and within a year Bergkamp had made the leap of which all young footballers dream. Cruyff, who occasionally took training sessions with the juniors, recognized his special qualities and put him in the reserves. And then, one Saturday in December 1986, he was pulled off at half-time and told to make himself ready to join the first-team squad for the following day's home game against Roda JC Kerkrade. In the old Ajax stadium, he sat on the bench for seventy minutes before Cruyff sent him on as a substitute for Rob Witschge. 'At first,' he remembered, 'I was very nervous. I went to the right wing, which was where I played for the youth team. And when I got into the game, it was OK.' At which point the career in physiotherapy was put on permanent hold.

Eventually he came in from the right wing and assumed the position he was born to play, which is known to the Dutch as 'shadow striker'. He played twenty or so games in partnership with Van Basten before the great centre forward left for Milan, assumed a more prominent role thereafter and gradually became a part of the Ajax scenery. During six seasons with the club, first under Cruyff and then Van Gaal, there would be 103 goals in 187 league matches, a Dutch championship winners' medal in 1990, the Dutch Cup in 1987 and

1993, the European Cup Winners' Cup in 1987 (coming on as a substitute in the 1–0 victory over Lokomotiv Leipzig in the final, three days before his eighteenth birthday) and the UEFA Cup in 1992 (beating Torino on away goals). By 1988 he was a regular in the international side and in 1992 he scored three goals for Holland in the European Championship finals. And just as Van Basten's career in Milan was drawing to an injury-hastened close, so Bergkamp – the Netherlands' player of the year in 1991–92, when he scored twenty-four league goals – became the next Ajax star to be linked with a lucrative move south. It was his own club president, indeed, who put the £20-million valuation on his head.

In the end they settled for the £12.5 million offered by the other Milanese club, Internazionale. Bergkamp listened to their proposal and believed what he was told. The club had not won the Serie A title since 1988–89, they told him; now was the time to break away from the old defensive outlook associated with Helenio Herrera, who had brought them two European Cups in the mid-1960s by sticking to the creed of *catenaccio*. He, Dennis Bergkamp, would be the fulcrum of the club's new attacking policy. To keep him company, they would also buy his friend Wim Jonk, a shrewd midfield player. The whole team would be built around him.

When he got there, however, he found that a club does not shed its skin quite so easily. Nothing, in essence, had changed. Worst of all, his fellow striker, the Uruguayan international Rubén Sosa, had not been brought up on the Ajax philosophy of providing constant support for teammates. Nor had he been told about the club's new attitude. In Sosa's eyes, there was only one goalscorer at Internazionale, and it was him. If giving the ball to Bergkamp meant that someone else might score a goal for the team, then he would rather not part company with it. The consequences could be seen in the league table. Inter finished thirteenth in Bergkamp's first season, resulting in the departure of the coach, Osvaldo Bagnoli. He was replaced for the following year by Ottavio Bianchi, but the football seldom rose above the mediocre and sixth place in the final standings hardly represented a fulfilment of the club's ambitions. A victory in the UEFA Cup, overcoming Casino Strasbourg in the two-legged final, scarcely registered in Italy, where only the European Cup counts. Bergkamp had grown deeply unhappy; while scoring a meagre eleven goals in fifty-two appearances, the only thing he had learnt was how to defend himself against man-markers whose scruples were few. The disenchantment was mutual; his Italian critics believed that he had never got to grips with the problem of unlocking massed defences, Italian-style. At the end of the 1994–95 season Internazionale were ready, in footballing argot, to move him on.

Easier to say than to do, of course. His reputation was shot. He was damaged goods. As far as the outside world was concerned, he had gone to the sternest arena in football and failed the test. When Arsenal moved in to buy him, for a cut-price £7.5 million, there was little competition. Indeed, Inter's president remarked that the purchasing club would be lucky if he scored ten goals for them in the next season. The Highbury fans were not thrilled by the news.

The question of who instigated the move remains a mystery. Bruce Rioch was the manager, but it is said that Arsène Wenger, then with Grampus Eight in Japan, was already in touch with David Dein, Arsenal's powerful vice-president, and that the Frenchman had recommended Bergkamp to Dein in the strongest possible terms. A year after Bergkamp's arrival, Wenger would take over from Rioch at Highbury. Conclusions, shall we say, were drawn.

The challenge of taking on English defences turned out to suit Bergkamp very well: they pushed higher up the field, looking for an offside decision, leaving space behind them into which he could direct his passes and make his runs. Nevertheless, it took him seven games to score his first goal, and mutters of disquiet had already been heard from a perennially critical set of fans before he changed the complexion of their response to him by putting the first one away with a right-footed volley against Southampton at Highbury on 29 September 1995. Attentive spectators noted the way he leaned while hitting the shot, making the perfect body shape. A run at the defence and a drive from twenty-two yards gave him a second goal that same afternoon, and there was a hint of the young maths wizard in the way the powerful shot went in off the inside of the right-hand post, as if that had been his intention. 'I had every confidence that Dennis would produce performances for the team,' Rioch said. 'It took him a few games to get a goal, but when they came, they were worth waiting for.' Although Arsenal would finish no higher than fifth that season, Bergkamp had already begun to show the range of his finishing. A left-footed drive against Barnsley, a left-footed half-volley against Spurs, a free kick, a header, a curler hit with the outside of his right foot past Mark Bosnich, a brilliant right-footed shot meeting Lee Dixon's deep cross on the half-volley: it was the beginning of a highlights reel that would encompass a century of goals for the club.

Wenger's arrival changed everything at Highbury, not least the circumstances in which they trained and the way they went about their preparation. Bergkamp was not among those most urgently in need of the new manager's insistence on a carefully planned diet and on the use of the new science of plyometrics to increase the suppleness of his footballers, but he was certainly among the beneficiaries. Always lean, now he took on the aspect of a greyhound. He continued to score regularly through Wenger's first season, but it was in 1997–98 that he came into his own. While Arsenal captured the double of the Premier League title and the FA Cup, Bergkamp claimed the Player of the Year awards from both the Professional Footballers' Association – the judgement of his peers – and the Football Writers' Association. It was the season in which his goals came first, second and third in one of *Match of the Day*'s goal of the month awards – an unprecedented feat. One of those goals, the concluding part of a hat-trick against Leicester City, came when, lurking on the left-hand side of the penalty area, he cushioned a long diagonal ball from midfield with his right instep, kept it up with his left instep as he turned inside a puzzled defender, pushed it forward with his right foot as it fell and then opened his body to steer a shot with the side of the same foot past the goalkeeper's left hand and inside the far post.

A perfect goal, but not quite a perfect footballer. Even some Arsenal fans were displeased by the amount of time that Bergkamp spent complaining when he was the victim of fouls, real or imagined. His own view of the matter provided a thoughtful explanation of a forward's mental processes. 'I accept that I do quite often sit on the ground after a foul, with my hands in the air, calling on the referee to make a decision my way,' he observed. 'It must be frustrating for the fans when they see that because even though I've been fouled, they must wish I could just get on with it. But it's just so frustrating because you have the whole picture of the move in your head and then you get pushed or pulled and no one sees it.'

Not many could see the whole picture of a move as clearly as Bergkamp, and his ability to form productive relationships with a succession of partners was also becoming evident. In his first season at Arsenal there had been the effervescent Ian Wright, a pure goalscorer who revelled in Bergkamp's intelligent play. Then, from France, came Nicolas Anelka, the enigmatic teenager who rarely smiled as he scored his goals but also proved to be a genuinely altruistic teammate, taking pleasure in the success he shared with others. Together they created a magnificent goal at Villa Park in December 1998, the pair twice exchanging passes before Anelka, with a stunning turn on the byline, astutely pulled the ball back for Bergkamp to slide it home through the narrowest of gaps. And finally, after Anelka's departure for Real Madrid, there would be Thierry

Henry, with whose arrival the whole team's play moved into another gear as, in 2002, Wenger's Arsenal secured a second double.

The previous year had been Bergkamp's worst in London. Returning to a new domestic season from a defeat by Italy in the semi-final of the European Championships, he found it hard to refocus. Wenger told him that there would be no automatic place for him: he would have to win it on merit. In 2000–01 there would be only five goals, which made it look as though he was back to his Italian form. He started to think about another move; perhaps he had gone stale. After a long close-season break, however, he rededicated himself to Wenger's cause, and the results were spectacular. Arsenal's football, much of which flowed through him, rose to a new level of dynamic complexity. With speed, skill and an intuitive understanding of each other's movements, the team seemed to flow as one. At times they appeared unstoppable; tentatively at first, but with gathering conviction, people began to advance the view that this was the finest football ever seen in England, where the game had been invented a century and a half before.

And on 2 November 2002, at St James's Park, Newcastle, Bergkamp emphasized Arsenal's new standing as a creative force by doing something that no one had ever seen before. When Robert Pires made ground along the left wing and sent a low ball into the Newcastle United penalty area, Bergkamp waited for it to arrive. His back was to the goal and behind him, and slightly to his right, stood Nikos Dabizas, the Magpies' Greek defender. Bergkamp flicked out his right foot, allowing the ball to spin off it and around the right-hand side of Dabizas; as the defender's eyes followed the ball, Bergkamp spun in the opposite direction, anti-clockwise, around Dabizas's left-hand side. Making full use of his litheness and power, in a couple of strides Bergkamp had rounded the bemused defender and was reunited with the ball, which he promptly despatched past the goalkeeper from a distance of eight yards. It happened so quickly that no one in the stadium really understood what had happened; only when he saw the smiles on his teammates' faces did Bergkamp himself realize that he had done something extremely special. That night the goal was replayed over and over again; it took a dozen slow-motion viewings before the viewer's brain could piece together what the Dutchman had done by instinct. 'For me it was the quickest way to the goal,' he said. 'The whole move was inch-perfect, but of course it could have gone completely wrong ...'

The move might have been new, but the finish was utterly familiar. Once again Bergkamp had opened his body and used the side of his right foot to guide the ball across the goal and past the goalkeeper's left hand, striking at the earliest possible opportunity in order to reduce the time available for his opponent to calculate the angles and set himself for the shot. Although Bergkamp probably scores his goals in a greater variety of ways than any forward who has ever played the game in England, this particular element of technique is his standby. It did not figure, however, in the goal that most would consider, taking the context into account, to be his masterpiece.

The match-up was too good for a mere quarter-final. Holland versus Argentina promised to be one of the outstanding contests of the 1998 World Cup, not least because it offered a chance for the Dutch to make amends for their disappointing performance twenty years earlier, when the Cruyff-less Total Footballers had been overcome by the swarming hosts in a blizzard of confetti in Buenos Aires. For this rematch, Marseille's Stade Vélodrome offered a European equivalent to the Estadio Monumental: a cauldron of passion, thronged on all sides by solid blocks of orange.

After eleven minutes Bergkamp manufactured the opening goal for Patrick Kluivert, cushioning a header into the path of the man who had taken his place in the Ajax line-up. Four minutes later, however, Arthur Numan tripped Ariel Ortega,

Diego Simeone rolled the free kick to Gabriel Batistuta, and Juan Sebastian Verón and Ortega combined to play in Claudio López, whose cunning shot went between the legs of Edwin van der Sar. Five minutes before half-time Bergkamp was unlucky when his delicate chip went over the head of the goal-keeper, Carlos Roa, as intended, but bounced softly past the far post. After the break both sides gave as good as they got until Numan and Ortega were sent off in separate incidents. The match seemed certain to be heading for extra time, and probably penalties, when, with thirty-four seconds of normal time remaining, lightning struck.

Frank de Boer was deep in his own half, on the left flank, when he spotted Bergkamp advancing down the right. With the initiative and precision characteristic of the best of Dutch football, he launched a sixty-yard diagonal ball that seemed to hang in the air as Roberto Ayala, the experienced Argentinian defender, came across to cover the danger. Ayala was almost on his opponent's shoulder when Bergkamp brought the ball down with his right instep, touched it inside Ayala with the same foot and stroked a left-footed shot past the helpless Roa. It had happened in an instant, as if in a single movement; it was a moment of perfect balance, perfect grace, perfect econ-omy, perfect visualization, perfect execution, a whole ballet in a single man's turn and shot. And it gave Argentina no time to construct a reply. They were out, eliminated by a stroke of genius.

That goal broke Faas Wilkes's Dutch international record of thirty-five goals, but Bergkamp's failure to produce anything to match it three days later, when Holland met Brazil in the semi-final, is the reason some people place a question mark against his career. Two years after he left Ajax, they won the European Cup; that was one missed opportunity. And in the big international tournaments, he and his fellow Dutchmen failed to punch their weight with any consistency. Now, returning to the Vélodrome to face the defending champions, he put a shot over the bar in the second minute but thereafter failed to figure in the match until, with the score tied at 1–1 at the end of extra time, he converted his penalty attempt by shooting low past the left hand of Claudio Taffarel. The Brazilian goalkeeper's success in blocking the efforts of Philip Cocu and Ronald de Boer, however, meant that Holland were denied the chance to appear in their third World Cup final. Many neutrals felt that with a bit more assertiveness all round, the match would have been theirs for the taking.

Assertiveness of a less attractive kind was something that occasionally erupted in Bergkamp's performances for Arsenal, whose lamentable disciplinary record during Wenger's early years was reinforced by three red cards for the Dutchman. The first, in 1997, came against Sunderland. The second, five years later, came for stamping on Nils-Eric Johansson during a 2–1 defeat by Bolton. The third, in 2003, was for striking Lee Bowyer of Newcastle. From such an apparently placid foot-baller, outbreaks of violence seemed anomalous, as though someone else had temporarily taken possession of his body. Sir Alex Ferguson, however, did not take long to come to the con-clusion that Bergkamp was fond of getting his retaliation in first, choosing a moment when the referee's attention was else-where to leave an arm or a foot in. For his part, Bergkamp never denied a willingness to fight fire with fire, and those inclined to defend him could point to distinctly similar behav-iour patterns in Ruud van Nistelrooy, Ferguson's own Dutch striker. 'A lot of Dutch players have a brilliant ability and can win a match in one move,' Bergkamp himself observed, 'but we also have a nasty side. Van Basten had it; I've seen him elbow someone in European games. I could give you loads of examples. We like to play fair, and we like nice football, but we also have a darker side.'

The darker side of Bergkamp, however, was almost always obliterated by the brilliant rays of his creative talent. No one really minded that a dread of flying limited his appearances for Arsenal in the Champions League and probably lay behind the decision to bring his international career to a premature close. While finding more ways to score goals than anyone since Pelé, he brought to the game a sense of continuity that also stemmed from his Dutch background, providing the core of mature invention that transformed Arsenal and gave them, finally, the momentum to go through the 2003–04 season without defeat in the league, the first team ever to accomplish that feat in the English league's top division. It enabled him to play at the highest level into his thirty-seventh year; it made him the richest of all Dutch footballers, with a fortune estimated in his final season at around £40 million; and it allowed him and his wife to bring up their three children in the gated tranquillity of a north London suburb – nice and quiet, as he said all those years ago, and never in the gossip papers.

10 Zinédine Zidane

Those deep-set hazel eyes never leave the ball as it spins towards him through the Glasgow night. His body is already starting to make the necessary shape: arms spread wide but relaxed; his weight transferring to the right leg, hips rotating anti-clockwise, right shoulder dropping as the left shoulder pulls back like a trigger being cocked. The stadium, suddenly alert to what is about to happen, holds its breath. As the ball drops, his left foot is brought round in a flat arc; it is at the level of his waist when the shot is struck. The ball, its direction of travel changed by 90 degrees, flies the twenty-odd yards from his boot to the net before his opponents can grasp what he has done. For Hans-Jörg Butt, Bayer Leverkusen's goal-keeper, there is no chance of interfering with its progress. A few seconds before half-time, Zinédine Zidane has scored the unforgettable goal that will win a ninth European Cup for Real Madrid.

Among those watching are Alfredo di Stéfano and Ferenc Puskás, a pair of old men invited to share the celebration of a match taking place in the centenary season of the world's most famous football club. As a gesture to the past, the players' white shirts are devoid of a sponsor's logo. In the same ground, wearing similarly pristine white shirts in the pre-sponsorship era, Di Stéfano and Puskás scored the seven goals that defeated Eintracht of Frankfurt to win the 1960 competition in the best-remembered club match in football's history, in front of a crowd of 135,000. Also present tonight is Sir Alex Ferguson, the manager of Manchester United, who was among those spectators forty-two years ago at Hampden Park, a teenager starting to make his way in the game and transfixed by what he saw. He is no less transfixed now by the virtuosity of Zidane as the stadium erupts in recognition of the goal; once upon a time, he reflects, he had considered bringing the Frenchman to Old Trafford but had mused aloud about the difficulty of determining which was his best position. A season or two later, after Zidane had gone to Juventus, Manchester United met the Italian club in the Champions League; during the build-up Ferguson foolishly dismissed the Frenchman as 'a performing seal'.

The characteristics of this particular goal are grace and inevitability. Zidane is a big man, 1.85 metres tall and weighing 78 kg. He has a slightly ponderous gait and shoulders that tend to stoop, giving the illusion of ungainliness. He does not have lightning-fast feet or much of a sprint. But when the ball comes to him he suddenly reveals the lightness of a ballet dancer and the footwork of a fencer. Gracefulness falls upon him. Then he can do anything he wants with the ball, from the impossible delicacy of a running spin through 360°, his famous *roulette*, to the shattering violence of a waist-high volley fired from a range of more than twenty yards with his notionally weaker left foot. And when he does something like that, no one in the stadium envisages any other outcome.

I, too, was among the crowd in the stadium when Zidane hit that shot. His teammate Raúl González had opened the scoring for the Spanish side after seven minutes, capitalizing on an error by Lucio, Leverkusen's Brazilian centre back. Lucio himself made amends by scoring an equalizer. And then, in the final minute before the interval, Santiago Solari found Roberto Carlos with a precise pass up the left touchline. When Madrid's Brazilian left back immediately dinked it inside towards Zidane, he was inviting genius to express itself.

There were no television monitors in the press box that night. I saw the goal once, with my own eyes and in real time, and never again. By the time I finished work and got back to my hotel room it was after midnight; the reruns on TV were over. In that moment I took the decision to try not to see it in the future. For, I think, a very good reason.

It was Frank Leboeuf, Zidane's former France teammate, who said that he never watched replays of an important match in which he had been involved (including, in his case, the finals of the 1998 World Cup and the European Championships two years later). He wanted, he said, to preserve the integrity of his memories, which would be compromised if someone else's images – those from a television camera – were imposed on them. He had played in the match, he had seen it from his point of view, and he didn't want the memories to be blurred or corrupted. In an era when television makes everything available for inspection and analysis from high angles, low angles, reverse angles, close-up, long shot, slow-motion and super slo-mo, I sympathized with him.

Maybe people growing up now, in the age of digital technology and media saturation, will develop a different attitude. But one of the pleasures of being a football fan is the archive of individual images saved on the memory's hard drive. That's where I store a George Best jink, a Johnny Haynes pass, a Bobby Charlton shot, a Bobby Moore tackle, a Joe Baker bicycle kick, a Glenn Hoddle volley. Each of them is divorced from its immediate context: only with the greatest difficulty could I dredge up the details of the match in question, never mind its result. That doesn't matter. Each of the little memory sequences is like an animated cigarette card, and together they form a completely portable file of images of some of the finest footballers I've seen. It's like people of my grandparents' generation, who committed vast amounts of poetry to memory, creating a resource upon which they could draw at any time, without paying a fee or making a call.

So I wanted Zidane's goal to claim a place in that personal file, and the best way to do it seemed to be to borrow Leboeuf's idea and preserve its wholeness by protecting it from outside influences. If I watched it again on television, I would inevitably be replacing my own image of the moment with that of a television camera, if only partially. The television image might be more accurate than my own recollection, and would certainly be a lot sharper, but it would not contain within it the surge of exhilaration and admiration that I felt in that moment and that remain part of the emotional response to replaying the goal as it was experienced from my own point of view at around twenty-nine minutes past eight on the evening of 15 May 2002.

Certainly Zidane's own words later that night did little to embellish the memory. 'I had a pass from Roberto Carlos and I slammed it in,' he said. 'It was a very nice volley.' His manager, the wise and lugubrious Vicente del Bosque, did much better: 'It was a goal that was spectacular, difficult and aesthetic,' he said. But what I liked best was what Klaus Toppmöller said, because it expressed a fundamental truth about football. 'We can spend all our time on the training ground planning for Real Madrid's tactics,' the coach of Leverkusen remarked, 'but then something happens that you can't plan for. In this case it was Zidane's goal.'

'In football, spontaneous creativity doesn't do the job,' Aimé Jacquet once said. 'You need hard work, conviction and confidence.' He said it in 1995, after a 3–1 defeat of Romania in Bucharest, which is to say three years before he guided Zidane and the rest of the France squad to victory in the World Cup in their glorious new stadium in Saint-Denis. I thought it was such a striking statement that I wrote it down and kept it, possibly to use in evidence against him one day, although that is not the spirit in which I wipe the dust off it now. It simply seems worth pointing out the contrast between Jacquet's view and what happened at the Stade Félix-Bollaert in Lens on the night when France met Paraguay in the second round of the 1998 tournament.

If anyone had ever been inclined to underrate the contribution made by Zidane to the functioning of his national team, they should have seen the match in Lens on that night in late June, when France were attempting to reach the last eight of a competition they felt themselves destined to win, sixty-eight years after a group of French football administrators invented the World Cup.

They had not started the competition as favourites. That honour belonged to Brazil, the defending champions, but it was generally recognized that the return of the competition to France for the first time since 1938 was coinciding with the maturing of an unusually talented group of players, some of them the early flowering of the seeds planted in the network of *centres de formation* set up by the French football federation, with their headquarters at the carefully planned complex known as Clairefontaine, amid wooded hills to the south of Paris. The nation had mourned when the Platini–Giresse–Tigana generation failed to take the trophy in 1982 and 1986; now, however, Jacquet's squad appeared to have just as much talent and rather more depth. Their progress in the summer of 1998, however, turned out to be not quite as smooth as they might have wished.

In their opening match, they beat South Africa 3–0 in Marseille's Stade Vélodrome. In the ground where he had watched his idols as a boy, Zidane took a corner that was met by the head of his close friend and former Bordeaux teammate Christophe Dugarry for the first goal. Pierre Issa conceded an own goal for the second, and a chip by the young Thierry Henry completed the scoring. France were also dominating their second match, against Saudi Arabia, when the course of Zidane's World Cup changed. With twenty minutes to go his side were leading 2–0 thanks to Henry and the substitute striker, David Trezeguet, when the No. 10 lost his patience. All through the match he had been subjected to nudges and tugs and trips. Now he could restrain himself no longer. As he got up after another physical challenge from the Saudi captain,

Fuad Amin, he walked across the back of his opponent. The referee, Arturo Brizio Carter of Mexico, had no alternative: under the eyes of a full house at the Stade de France, Zidane, the poster-boy of the entire tournament, was shown a red card. A two-match suspension for violent conduct was the inevitable price. 'It's unpardonable,' his captain, Didier Deschamps, said. 'I know he's impulsive, but he's put us all at risk. He's been punished as an individual, but the rest of us have been punished, too.' The ten men, however, managed to score two more goals, through Henry, again, and the left back, Bixente Lizarazu. With maximum points from their first two games, they were already through to the next round; a relaxed 2–1 win in Lyon against Denmark, without Zidane, in the final group match put them among the top seeds in the last sixteen, which meant that they would be given opponents considered less testing.

Paraguay were those opponents, and it was assumed that Zidane's continued absence would impose no significant handicap. The South Americans, however, came to make a game of it, relying on a stout defence, marshalled by their captain and goalkeeper, José Luis Chilavert. They were clearly hoping, by the use of any means necessary, to keep the French at bay long enough to get their chance in a penalty shoot-out. In the event, they failed by a mere six minutes.

If Paraguay were unadventurous in attack, France presented a picture of barren incompetence. As the match wore on and the extent of their haplessness became evident, the crowd of 41,000 fell silent. Where were the bold musketeers they had come to cheer? Suddenly the bitter criticisms directed before the tournament at Jacquet's leadership by the writers and editors of *L'Équipe*, the powerful daily sports paper, appeared to have some foundation. It had been felt by many observers that France, splendidly equipped in defence and attack, were light in the goal-scoring department, with Henry and Trezeguet probably too inexperienced at this exalted level to make up for the known shortcomings of Dugarry, Bernard Diomède and Stéphane Guivarc'h. The teenaged Nicolas Anelka, omitted from the squad, was off on holiday somewhere instead of scoring goals for the team. Now *L'Équipe*'s fears were seen to have foundation. Facing resolute opponents without the set of keys provided by Zidane's artistry and imagination, France sank deeper and deeper into a kind of terrified paralysis. As extra time began, with the prospect of the match being settled by a 'golden goal', it could be seen that the forwards had even given up their laboured efforts to score; all they wanted to do, when someone gave them the ball, was to pass it on to someone else as quickly as possible. If this had been something of more consequence than a mere ball game, you would have called it an outbreak of collective moral cowardice, and their watching supporters were horrified by the gruesome spectacle.

Only one man could rise above it: Laurent Blanc, whose experience and intelligence had earned him the nickname *le Président*, and who, in the 114th minute of the match, stepped forward to save his nation's honour. When Robert Pires, on the pitch as a substitute for the injured Henry, centred from the right, Trezeguet headed the ball back across the area, and Blanc, charging in, found the presence of mind to place a right-footed shot past Chilavert, whose iron-clad defence had succumbed at the last. A great wave of relief crashed around the stadium, spilling over the rim of the grandstands to engulf the whole of France. Henry, his ankle heavily bandaged, limped across the pitch to congratulate *le Président*. But many minds were already saying prayers of thanks for the imminent return of the man whose influence had never been more noticeable than in its absence.

All France saw Zidane as the *homme-clé*, the key man, as much a symbol of the team as the beauteous figure of La Marianne was of the republic. In Marseille, his image became a mural on the side of a high-rise office block. 'Zidane, Zidane,

Zidane . . . France was in the grip of "zizoumania",' Marcel Desailly wrote in his autobiography. 'I never imagined it could grow to such proportions. Sometimes I asked myself if one human being could withstand such passion. And did he, in any case, quite resist it? At the start of the tournament we found him a little febrile, more stretched, more demanding than usual, at least on the pitch. That febrility culminated in his expulsion against Saudi Arabia. And after a moment of depression, he reacted like a champion and started to prepare himself for the quarter-final.'

With the return of Zidane for the match against Italy came the restoration of France's fluency. Cesare Maldini, Italy's coach, helped his opponents by preferring Alessandro Del Piero to Roberto Baggio in the playmaker's role and took more than an hour to recognize his error. By that time Italy were fortunate not to have given way to the constant pressure from the French, but France were the lucky ones in extra time when Baggio met Demetrio Albertini's diagonal cross to the near post with a beautifully executed volley that curled across the goal and just wide of the far post. It was the first real chance of the match, and a few minutes later France had one of their own when Youri Djorkaeff met Henry's pass with a chipped shot that Gianluca Pagliuca saved. At the end of such a tight match, the shoot-out was agonizing. Zidane and Baggio went first, and scored. Lizarazu and Albertini both saw their shots saved. Then came Trezeguet and Henry for France, Costacurta and Vieri for Italy: all scored, which meant that with one pair of spot kicks remaining, the sides were level. Up stepped Blanc to put his shot into the middle of the net, exactly where Pagliuca had been standing before he chose to dive. But poor Luigi Di Biagio, Roma's sturdy midfield player, sent his powerful shot crashing against Fabien Barthez's crossbar. France were through. *Merci encore, M. le Président.*

It was Blanc who found himself again at the centre of the drama in the semi-final, when the disgraceful play-acting of

Slaven Bilic, the Croatian defender, persuaded the referee, José Manuel García Aranda of Spain, to dismiss the Frenchman. Blanc left the field knowing that were France to reach the final, he would miss it. They were 2–1 up at the time, having just taken the lead through the second of the two goals with which Lilian Thuram, their vigorous right back, gave them victory. Once again, however, France had been short of ideas; at times such an anxious hush fell over the Stade de France that not only could you hear yourself think, you could almost hear the players think. And in the case of the French, what they were thinking was: how on earth are we going to score?

Zidane's doggedness was the first attempt at an answer. He shot on sight throughout the first half, but nothing was quite coming off. Among the Croatians, hope was growing. Big men with short strides and neat control, they had thrashed Germany in the quarter-final and looked like the only European team who still believed that football matches could be won if you strolled around, caressing the ball from one player to another in complex short-passing patterns, playing slow-slow-quick-quick-slow in the hope of catching the opposition napping. And with a finisher like Davor Šuker, who had the face of a concert pianist and the feet of Fred Astaire, they would always have a chance in a low-scoring game. Šuker gave them the lead less than half a minute into the second half; it was the first goal France had conceded in open play since the start of the tournament. Once Thuram had done his stuff, however, they knew they would be meeting Brazil in the final without the linchpin of their exceptional defence.

'This World Cup has shown a double elegance in the attitude of the protagonists and the game,' an editorial in *Libération* proclaimed as the tournament approached its climax. 'Fair play on the field, purity of action, sophistication of tactics. Football has achieved a choreographic dimension which has charmed a reticent public.' The spectating Diego Maradona begged to differ, expressing his disappointment with the quality of the footballers in the tournament as a whole. 'They're all suffering from crossed feet,' he said. 'They're a bunch of Robocops. They're more in need of an oil change than a massage.' The final would do little to change his opinion. First there was the extraordinary mix-up over Ronaldo's participation: an hour before the kick-off he was absent from the official team sheet, replaced by Edmundo; half an hour later he was back on it, at Edmundo's expense, apparently having recovered from an alleged fainting fit that afternoon. Then there was the strangely muted nature of Brazil's performance. In a startling variation from their habitual procedure, they had missed the pre-match warm-up, leaving France to exercise alone. And when the hosts began the match with a series of high-speed attacks, they seemed content to sit back and soak up the aggression without producing a response, as if waiting for the game to take shape before they committed themselves.

Zidane gave it shape in the twenty-sixth minute, when he leapt above the yellow-shirted defenders to get his head to Emmanuel Petit's inswinging corner kick from the right. 'I'm not usually very good with my head,' he said afterwards. But twenty minutes later, with the referee calculating the stoppage time before blowing for the interval, he headed a second goal, this time meeting Djorkaeff's corner from the left. Brazil were going in at half-time 2–0 down, having shown nothing to justify their reputation; even so, none of the 80,000 in the stadium would have bet against a revival.

But they had left it too late and paid the price for refusing to inject pace into their movements in the first half. When they needed acceleration and a flow of fresh ideas, they were unable to locate a higher gear. Barthez stood up bravely to save from Ronaldo, Desailly was sent off for bringing down Cafu after collecting an earlier booking for dissent, and in the second minute of injury time France inflicted a final blow to Brazil's pride when a flowing counter-attack involving Dugarry and Patrick Vieira, one of the substitutes, sent Petit away to make the final score 3–0. In the stands, Jacques Chirac waved his 'Allez les Bleus' scarf, while tears of joy blurred the small tri-colours painted on the famously pronounced cheekbones of Johnny Hallyday (who was born Belgian, but became France's very own rock-and-roll hero).

That night a million and a half people, it was said, danced in the streets of Paris, making the Champs-Elysées, from the Etoile to the Place de la Concorde, the venue for celebrations on a scale not seen since the Liberation. This was, everyone agreed, a triumph for the republic and for its historic claim to Liberty, Equality and Brotherhood. The ethnic composition of Jacquet's squad was much analyzed. The players could trace their origins, or those of their parents or grandparents, to Algeria (Zidane), Argentina (Trezeguet), Armenia (Djorkaeff), the Basque country (Lizarazu), Ghana (Desailly), Guadeloupe (Thuram), Martinique (Henry), New Caledonia (Christian Karembeu) and Senegal (Vieira), as well as Seine-Maritime (Petit), the Var (Leboeuf), the Ariège (Barthez), the Cevennes (Blanc), Aquitaine (Dugarry), Hérault (Vincent Candela), Basse-Pyrenées (Deschamps) and the Loire-Atlantique (Guivarc'h). In the France of 1998, with Jean-Marie Le Pen's ultra-rightist Front National threatening to take votes from the mainstream parties, *black-blanc-beur* seemed to send out a powerful message about the potential of the nation to rise above its fears and its divisions.

The art of the *roulette* and the technical skills had been devel-oped in the streets of La Castellane, the Marseille housing project where Smaïl and Malika Zidane brought up their chil-dren. Smaïl had arrived in France from the Kabylie region of Algeria in the late 1950s, settling first in Saint-Denis, a suburb to the north of Paris, and later heading south. Zinédine was known to the family and his friends as Yazid. It would be his other family, that of French football, who gave him a second nickname, Zizou, to go with Lolo (Blanc), Titi (Henry), Manu

(Petit), Liza (Lizarazu), Duga (Dugarry) and the rest. To his real family, however, he was always Yazid, and it seemed a better fit. Zizou was a toy name, a twee marketing name, a name better suited to the furry blue mascot of France '98. Yazid was the boy who grew up teaching himself to juggle with a football in the Place Tartane, an open space in La Castellane; at this stage he was taller than most of his contemporaries, but only by mastering his tricks through tireless repetition did he begin to stand out among his friends in their informal games. There were those who believed that judo might become his main sport: he had taken it up at the age of six and his promise was recognized by the award of a brown belt, only one step below the black. But on his way to and from school there was always a ball at his feet.

His father worked as a warehouseman, and the children were brought up in a warm and loving environment. La Castellane was an immigrant suburb with a high rate of unemployment, but Zinédine refused the obvious temptations. 'I saw plenty of poverty and crime in Marseille,' he said, 'but I managed to avoid it. I never stole and I never took drugs, and I'm proud of that.' At eight years old he became a member of La Castellane's football club; twenty years later they would make him their honorary president. At thirteen he – and his brother Noureddine – moved to another club, Septèmes, in the north of Marseille. It was there that he was spotted by a scout for AS Cannes, of the French first division. 'I've found a boy who has hands where his feet should be,' Jean Varraud told his employers. A three-day trial failed to convince them, but Varraud's advocacy was eventually persuasive. He also had to talk Zidane's parents into allowing their son to leave home and join the club's *centre de formation*, which would mean lodging with a local family. Varraud promised Smaïl and Malika Zidane that their son would continue to get an education good enough to give him a qualification should he not be chosen to pursue a career as a professional footballer.

In Cannes he and another young apprentice were billeted with the family of one of the club's directors. Zinédine took the room of a son who was away on military service, and put up a poster of his favourite player, Marseille's Enzo Francescoli. In training he worked on the parts of the game at which he was weakest, particularly his heading and the use of his left foot. It was also noted that although he never started trouble on the pitch, he knew how to take care of himself, and occasionally he would respond to provocation in a way that might have been expected from a boy formed in a tough quarter of a hard-nosed city, where an injury might be repaid with a headbutt. The club's manager, Luis Fernandez, had been the fourth member of the great midfield completed by Platini, Giresse and Tigana, and in May 1989 he added the sixteen-year-old Zidane to the first-team squad for a match against Nantes. A few minutes on the pitch as a late substitute held out a promise that would be fulfilled when Fernandez made him a regular member of the side the following season. When he scored the decisive goal in a 2–1 win over Nantes, the club's president made him a gift of a new Renault Clio, his first car. The following season, however, Cannes were relegated and an offer came in for Zidane. Roland Courbis, the new manager of Bordeaux, was a native of Marseille and had noted the gifts of his fellow citizen. For 3 million francs, or about £300,000, the twenty-year-old moved to the south-west, where he became reunited with Dugarry, an old friend from junior international days.

His first senior international appearance came in August 1994, in a 2–2 draw in a friendly against the Czech Republic; both of the goals were his and followed his arrival on the pitch in a sixty-third-minute substitution, after the visitors had taken a 2–0 lead. With a right-footed shot from outside the area and a header from a corner kick, Zidane brought France level; in the following morning's newspapers it was announced that a new Platini had arrived. After their last-minute failure to qualify for the World Cup finals that summer, France needed a saviour. Here was the candidate.

Zidane would remain with Bordeaux for four seasons, but his involvement in the town continued when he and Dugarry opened a restaurant, Nul Part Ailleurs (Nowhere Else), in the city. In football terms, the highlight of his stay came during his final season, when Bordeaux, having qualified for the UEFA Cup through the Intertoto Cup, reached the final, after beating AC Milan 3–2 over two legs in the quarter-final. Zidane missed the away leg of the final against Bayern Munich, a 2–0 defeat, through suspension; despite his return, they lost the home leg 3–1. It was Zidane's sixty-fifth game of a season that had started with the Intertoto matches the previous July; the whole squad was exhausted. But his quality had been noted in Italy, where Marcello Lippi, the coach of Juventus, urged his president, Gianni Agnelli, to make Bordeaux an offer. In the summer of 1996, for a sum of around £3 million, the deal was done.

Before he could make his début in Serie A, however, there was the matter of Euro '96, to be held in England. France's hopes, which had been raised by the arrival of a new generation of players, were dealt a severe blow on the eve of the tournament when Zidane crashed his car into a guard-rail at around sixty-five miles per hour, while trying to avoid another vehicle. His head hit the roof and his right buttock hit the gear lever, giving him cuts to the former and deep bruising to the latter. Coming at a time when he was still trying to recover his strength after a gruelling season, it was exactly what he did not need. His subdued form was one of the principal factors underlying France's unexpectedly poor performance in the tournament, causing Agnelli to remark, with a note of aristocratic disdain: 'Is the real Zidane the one I've heard so much about, or the one I've been watching?'

When he arrived in Turin to play his first matches for Juventus, there would be further comparisons with Platini; this time they were not so favourable. His predecessor, an outgoing and highly *médiatique* personality, had become part of the club's legend. After a handful of undistinguished perform-ances, greeted with mutters of disappointment from the fans in the new Stadio delle Alpi, Zidane felt constrained to explain himself. 'Platini is unique and inimitable,' he said. 'I'm Zinédine Zidane and it's important that the fans understand that I can never be Platini, on or off the pitch. I'm not the sort who stirs people up. It's not a part of my character.'

It took a change of formation, from 4–3–3 to 4–4–2, to enable Zidane to settle down and begin making his contribu-tion to Lippi's team. With Didier Deschamps and Antonio Conte winning the ball, Alessandro Del Piero floating and Christian Vieri and Alen Boksic up ahead, he began to do what was apparently alien to his character and stir up the support-ers. It began with a wonderful goal from long range against Internazionale and continued with a significant role in the 1–0 victory over River Plate in Tokyo that secured the Inter-continental Cup for Juventus in November 1996. This was the first senior trophy of Zidane's career, at the age of twenty-four; among the opposition was Francescoli, his boyhood idol. Zidane would win two Italian championships with Juventus, in 1996–97 and 1997–98, fuelled at least in part by a physical fitness regime that featured the use of creatine, the muscle-building drug. Juventus's medical team eventually came under investigation by the Italian authorities, but not before their techniques had helped Zidane to overcome a problem that had dogged his early years, when his size had never been matched by his stamina. His performances in his first two seasons in Italy and in the 1998 World Cup brought him *France Football*'s *Ballon d'Or* that year, together with FIFA's World Player of the Year award. Now, when people in Turin dis-cussed Platini and Zidane, they were talking about men of equal stature. (He would win the world governing body's award twice more, in 2000 and 2003; in 2002 he was voted Most Valuable Player by UEFA.)

Two years after the World Cup came Euro 2000, held in Holland and Belgium. Still glowing with confidence from that coronation in Saint-Denis, with Jacquet stepping down to be replaced by his former assistant, Roger Lemerre, and with young players such as Henry, Trezeguet and Pires benefiting from experience gained in the intervening seasons, France won a second consecutive trophy, beating Italy in a tense final in Rotterdam's De Kuip Stadium. Marco Delvecchio gave Italy the lead, Sylvain Wiltord equalized with practically the last kick of normal time, and France took the match and the title with another 'golden goal' in extra time, on this occasion scored by Trezeguet from Pires's centre. Zidane had played his part in their progress through the tournament, but no longer did it seem that his teammates were being carried on his shoulders.

In the summer of 2001 he made the move from Juventus to Real Madrid, whose president, Florentino Pérez, agreed a fee of £47 million with Juventus: a world record, still unequalled four years later. At twenty-nine, with a four-year contract in his pocket, he was joining Roberto Carlos, Luis Figo and Raúl in the president's select band of *galácticos*, a group that would be expanded in the coming seasons by the addition of Ronaldo, David Beckham and Robinho. As a French member of *los meringues*, he was following in the footsteps of the great forward Raymond Kopa, who played for Stade de Reims against Madrid in the 1955 European Cup before switching to the all-white strip and becoming a member of the winning sides of 1957, 1958 and 1959. 'I'm very proud,' the perennially reticent Zidane said, 'but it's a lot of pressure.'

For Bordeaux and France he had worn the No. 10. At Juventus he was given the No. 21, since Del Piero already had possession of the 10; he made no complaint. At the Estadio Santiago Bernabéu the 10 belonged to Figo; when the president suggested that he might like to take the No. 5, which had been worn for eighteen seasons by Manuel Sanchís, Zidane took it as a compliment. Pérez said he wanted him to wear a number between 1 and 11, since that was how he liked to see a football team turn out. 'I don't think I'll be here as long as Sanchís,' Zidane said. 'Maybe just four years . . .'

The European Cup final in Glasgow salvaged an otherwise disappointing centenary year for the club. They threw away a good lead in the Spanish championship and lost the final of the Copa del Rey, the Spanish cup, in their own stadium. But to win Europe's club championship for the ninth time was satisfaction enough, thus drawing further ahead of their nearest challengers, Milan (who, at the time, had five titles to their credit). And in 2003, with Zidane and Ronaldo – opponents on an historic evening in the Stade de France five years earlier – striking up a fruitful partnership, there was another Spanish league title to be added to the club's honours board.

When France attempted to defend their world championship crown under Lemerre in South Korea and Japan in 2002, however, another pre-tournament misfortune for Zidane contributed to the side's miserable collapse. Only days before the start of the tournament, during a warm-up match against South Korea in Sujon, he left the field clutching his thigh and retired to the bench, where an ice pack was applied. He missed the startling 1–0 defeat at the hands of Senegal, France's former colony. He also missed a highly physical goalless draw against Uruguay. And although he returned, his thigh heavily strapped, for the final group game against Denmark, when only a win would carry them through to the last sixteen, his movement was clearly restricted and he could seldom escape the close marking of the Danes. An utterly demoralized team went down to a 2–0 defeat and caught the next plane home, leaving their reputation somewhat tarnished.

Perhaps, after all, they did still need his shoulders to carry them. Two years later, when Jacques Santini took over from Lemerre and led them to the European Championships in Portugal, Zidane struck an extraordinary late double blow against England, scoring from a penalty and a free kick to wipe out the 1–0 lead that David Beckham and his teammates had taken into injury time in Lisbon's Estádio da Luz. The two hammer blows had the ring of inevitability, silencing the premature celebrations of England's fans, who outnumbered those of France by at least five to one. Zidane scored with a header in the 3–1 win over Switzerland and scored again with a deflected free kick in the 2–2 draw with Croatia; he was powerless, however, to influence the course of the quarter-final in which France went out by the only goal of the match to the eventual winners of the tournament. Greece, their conquerors, played a brand of football based firmly on non-stop running and close marking; it stood at the opposite extreme from the graceful artistry and constant variations of pace that characterized the French at their best. To some observers, the Greek victory looked like a harbinger of football's nuclear winter.

In August of that year Zidane announced his retirement from international football, after ninety-three caps and twenty-six goals over a period of ten years in which he had reached the peaks of the game. He had promised as much in 1999, when he said: 'I'll give it five more years, I think.' He was as good as his word. Until, that is, a year after his withdrawal. Then, with France in danger of missing qualification for the 2006 World Cup, he heeded the entreaties of Raymond Domenech, the new coach, and returned to the colours for one final campaign, along with two other retirees, Lilian Thuram and his former Madrid teammate, Claude Makelele. In the absence of the injured Patrick Vieira, Zidane accepted the captain's *brassard* and, to the mingled shame and relief of the younger members of the squad, the veterans did the trick. With wins over Cyprus, the Faroe Islands and the Republic of Ireland, and a draw against Switzerland, France emerged at the top of the group. The players and their fans could book their tickets for Germany.

So modest that in his early years of playing abroad he hid the trappings of success from his old friends on visits to his family's home in Marseille, Zidane was never the sort of playmaker who ordered others around. He would simply get hold of the ball, keep it for a while and either manufacture a scoring chance for himself or give it to someone better placed. His key techniques belonged to him alone: the astonishing ability to reach up with a foot to bring down a high ball in a single economical movement ('hands where his feet should be') and the way he ran with his head over the ball, keeping it close, making it almost impossible for opponents to dispossess him. And, of course, those amazing tricks, like the *roulette*, performed with such light-footedness by such an apparently heavy-set figure. Sublime artistry without wasted motion was what made him the perfect player for Real Madrid, an authentic heir to Puskás and Di Stéfano, a man whose silhouette became his signature and whose goals carried the mark of the *auteur*.

He was a marvellous symbol for France, too: the gifted son of hard-working Algerian immigrants who rose from an unfavoured suburb to bring glory to the republic. That whole *black-blanc-beur* thing, however, turned out to be wishful thinking at best, window dressing at worst. For a while the French could gaze upon their heroes and think comforting thoughts about themselves. But in the autumn of 2005, in just the kind of suburbs in which Zidane (and Henry and Anelka) grew up, suddenly factories and fast-food restaurants were being torched and riot police were dodging petrol bombs and, sometimes, bullets as the children of immigrants gave vent to their manifold dissatisfactions with life in the land of *liberté, egalité et fraternité*. Football's power had some limits, after all. In the end, Zinédine Zidane was just a footballer, albeit one of the greatest who ever lived.

Acknowledgements

As usual, I owe a debt of gratitude to a number of people: to Lee Brackstone at Faber and Faber, for his imagination and patience; to Kate Ward, also at Faber; to Ian Bahrami, for his copy-editing; to my agent, Clare Alexander; to my friend Simon O'Hagan, for his comments on the manuscript; to Ken Jones of the *Independent*, for a conversation that helped my thoughts; to Ben Clissitt, the *Guardian*'s sports editor, for his kindness; to Giancarlo Galavotti, the London correspondent of *La Gazzetta dello Sport*; and most of all to my late father, Ieuan Williams, whose conversation on many topics – including politics, theology, the natural world and humanity's foibles, as well as sport in all its forms – never failed to provoke and stimulate.

Sources

Ball, Phil: *Morbo* (When Saturday Comes, 2001).

Ball, Phil: *White Storm* (Mainstream, 2003).

Barbero, Sergio: *Tutti Gli Uomini della Signora* (Graphot Editrice, 1996).

Barend, Frits, and Van Dorp, Henk: *Ajax Barcelona Cruyff* (Bloomsbury, 1998).

Bellos, Alex: *Futebol* (Bloomsbury, 2002).

Borges, Jorge Luis (trans. Norman Thomas Di Giovanni): *Selected Poems 1923–1967* (Allen Lane, 1972).

Brooks, David: *The All Time World Cup* (The Parrs Woods Press, 2002).

Burns, Jimmy: *Barça* (Bloomsbury, 1999).

Burns, Jimmy: *Hand of God* (Bloomsbury, 1996).

Castro, Ruy: *Garrincha* (Yellow Jersey, 2004).

Charles, John: *King John* (Headline, 2003).

Crow, John A.: *The Epic of Latin America* (University of California Press, 1992).

Desailly, Marcel: *Capitaine* (Éditions Stock, 2002).

Dinenzon, Victor (dir.), with Osvaldo Bayer, Julio César Pasquato and Enrique Macaya Marquéz: *Futbol Argentino* (Channel 4, 1994).

Downing, David: *The Best of Enemies* (Bloomsbury, 2000).

Downing, David: *England v Argentina* (Portrait, 2003).

Duras, Marguerite: *What Kind of Game Is This – Demonic and Divine?* (from *Perfect Pitch* No. 4, Ed. Kuper, Simon).

Fox, Norman: *Profit or Traitor?* (The Parrs Wood Press, 2003).

Freddi, Cris: *The Complete Book of the World Cup* (Collins Willow, 1998).

Galeano, Eduardo: *Football in Sun and Shadow* (Fourth Estate, 1997).

Glanville, Brian: *Champions of Europe* (Guinness, 1991).

Glanville, Brian: *Football Memories* (Virgin, 1999).

Glanville, Brian: *The Story of the World Cup* (Faber and Faber, 2002).

Green, Geoffrey: *Pardon Me for Living* (George Allen and Unwin, 1985).

Hamilton, Adrian: *An Entirely Different Game* (Mainstream, 1998).

Hamilton, Ian (Ed.): *The Faber Book of Soccer* (Faber and Faber, 1992).

Harris, Nick: *England, Their England* (Pitch Publishing, 2003).

Hayes, Alex: Dennis Bergkamp interview (*Independent on Sunday*, 9 February 2003).

Hesse-Lichtenberger, Ulrich: *Tor!* (When Saturday Comes, 2002).

Hopcraft, Arthur: *The Football Man* (Simon & Schuster, 1988).

Jenkins, Garry: *The Beautiful Team* (Simon & Schuster, 1998).

Kuper, Simon: 'The Caring Face of Pure Genius' (*The Times*, 21 April 2003).

Kuper, Simon: *Football Against the Enemy* (Orion, 1994).

Lovejoy, Joe: 'Dennis the Menace' (*Sunday Times*, 14 November 2004).

Ludden, John: *Once Upon a Time in Naples* (The Parrs Wood Press, 2005).

Macnab, Geoffrey: Jean-Luc Godard interview (*Guardian*, 29 April 2005).

McIlvanney, Hugh: *McIlvanney on Football* (Mainstream, 1999).

Maradona, Diego: *El Diego* (Yellow Jersey, 2004).

Mason, Tony: *Passion of the People?* (Verso, 1995).

Melegari, Fabrizio, with La Rocca, Luigi, and Tosi, Enrico: *Almanacco Ilustrato del Milan* (Panini, 2005).

Moynihan, John: *The Soccer Syndrome* (McGibbon & Kee, 1966; Simon & Schuster, 1987).

Netzer, Günter: *Aus der Tiefe des Raumes* (Rowohlt, 2004).

Oliver, Guy: *The Guinness Record of World Soccer* (Guinness, 1992).

Radnedge, Keir: *50 Years of the European Cup and Champions League* (Carlton, 2005).

Rees, Jasper: *Wenger* (Short Books, 2003).

Taylor, Chris: *The Beautiful Game* (Victor Gollancz, 1998).

Taylor, Rogan, and Jamrich, Klara (Eds): *Puskás on Puskás* (Robson Books, 1998).

Winner, David: *Brilliant Orange* (Bloomsbury, 2000).

Index

(Photos are indicated in *italic* type)